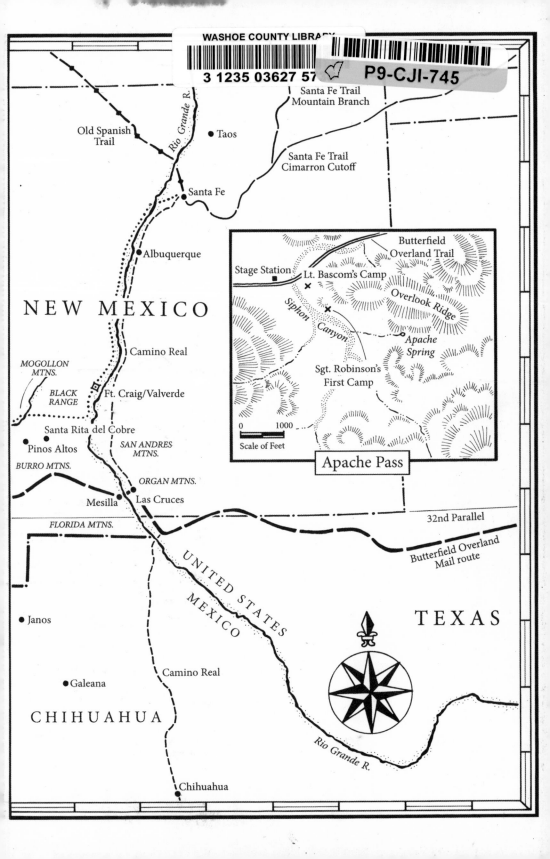

Old Spanish
Trail

Rio Grande R.

• Taos

Santa Fe Trail
Mountain Branch

Santa Fe Trail
Cimarron Cutoff

• Santa Fe

• Albuquerque

NEW MEXICO

MOGOLLON
MTNS.

Camino Real

BLACK
RANGE

Ft. Craig/Valverde

Santa Rita del Cobre

• Pinos Altos

SAN ANDRES
MTNS.

BURRO MTNS.

ORGAN MTNS.

Mesilla   Las Cruces

FLORIDA MTNS.

32nd Parallel

Butterfield Overland
Mail route

• Janos

UNITED STATES

MEXICO

TEXAS

Camino Real

• Galeana

CHIHUAHUA

Rio Grande R.

• Chihuahua

Apache Pass inset

Butterfield
Overland Trail

Stage Station

Lt. Bascom's Camp

Overlook Ridge

Siphon Canyon

Apache
Spring

Sgt. Robinson's
First Camp

0   1000

Scale of Feet

Apache Pass

The

WRATH
of
COCHISE

TERRY MORT

PEGASUS BOOKS
NEW YORK LONDON

THE WRATH OF COCHISE

Pegasus Books LLC
80 Broad Street, 5th Floor
New York, NY 10004

First Pegasus Books cloth edition April 2013

Interior design by Maria Fernandez

ISBN: 978-1-60598-422-3

10 9 8 7 6 5 4 3 2 1

Printed in the United States of America

Distributed by W. W. Norton & Company, Inc.

For Brooks Arthur Mort.
May your defining moments all turn out
just the way you would wish them to.

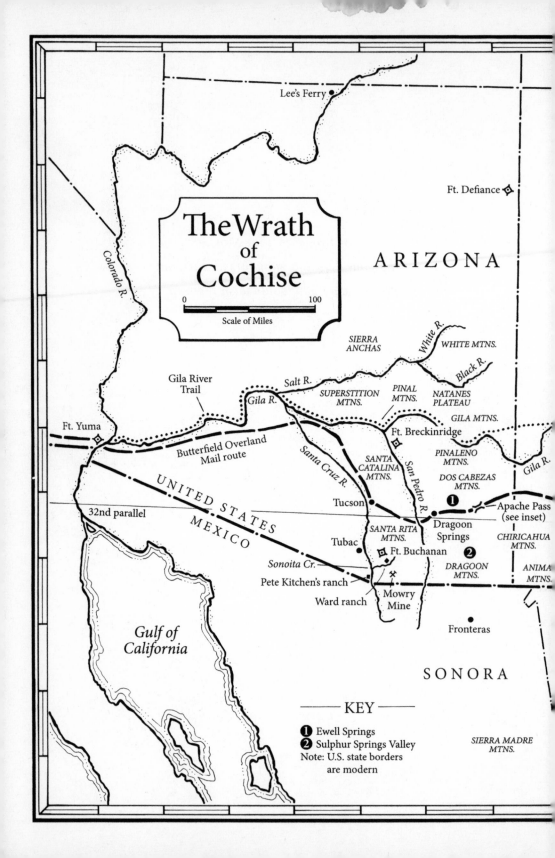

The Wrath of Cochise

0   100

Scale of Miles

Lee's Ferry

Colorado R.

Ft. Defiance

ARIZONA

SIERRA ANCHAS

WHITE MTNS.

White R.

Black R.

Gila River Trail

Salt R.

SUPERSTITION MTNS.

PINAL MTNS.

NATANES PLATEAU

Gila R.

GILA MTNS.

Ft. Yuma

Butterfield Overland Mail route

Ft. Breckinridge

PINALENO MTNS.

Gila R.

UNITED STATES

Santa Cruz R.

SANTA CATALINA MTNS.

San Pedro R.

DOS CABEZAS MTNS.

32nd parallel

MEXICO

Tucson

❶

Apache Pass (see inset)

Tubac

SANTA RITA MTNS.

Dragoon Springs

CHIRICAHUA MTNS.

Pete Kitchen's ranch

Sonoita Cr.

Ft. Buchanan

❷

DRAGOON MTNS.

ANIMA MTNS.

Ward ranch

Mowry Mine

Gulf of California

Fronteras

SONORA

KEY

❶ Ewell Springs
❷ Sulphur Springs Valley
Note: U.S. state borders are modern

SIERRA MADRE MTNS.

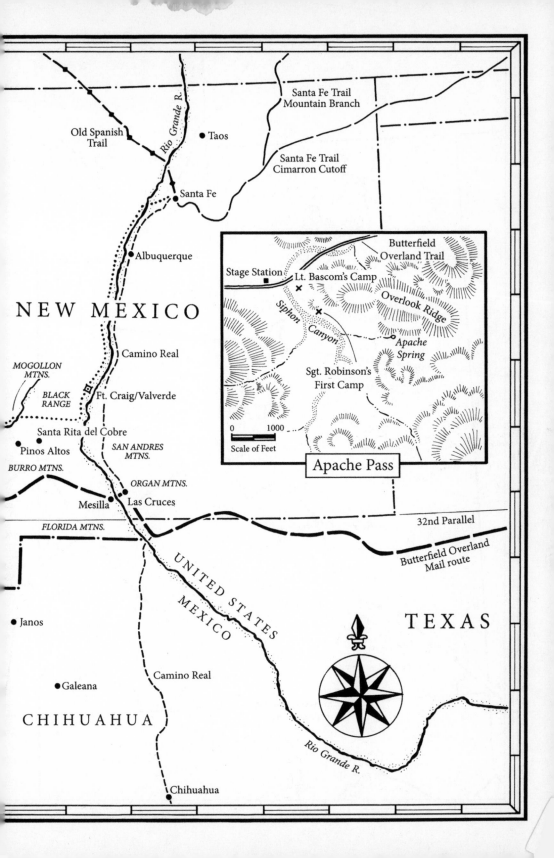

NEW MEXICO

Old Spanish Trail

Rio Grande R.

● Taos

Santa Fe Trail
Mountain Branch

Santa Fe Trail
Cimarron Cutoff

● Santa Fe

● Albuquerque

Camino Real

MOGOLLON MTNS.

BLACK RANGE

Ft. Craig/Valverde

Santa Rita del Cobre

● Pinos Altos

BURRO MTNS.

SAN ANDRES MTNS.

ORGAN MTNS.

● Mesilla   ● Las Cruces

FLORIDA MTNS.

32nd Parallel

Butterfield Overland
Mail route

UNITED STATES

MEXICO

● Janos

TEXAS

● Galeana

Camino Real

CHIHUAHUA

Rio Grande R.

● Chihuahua

Apache Pass inset

Stage Station

Butterfield
Overland Trail

Lt. Bascom's Camp

Overlook Ridge

Siphon Canyon

Apache Spring

Sgt. Robinson's
First Camp

0   1000

Scale of Feet

Apache Pass

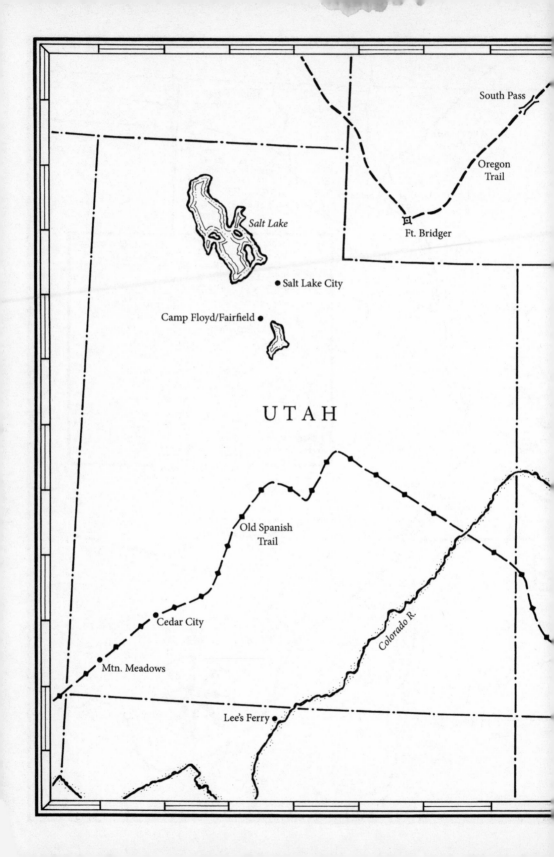

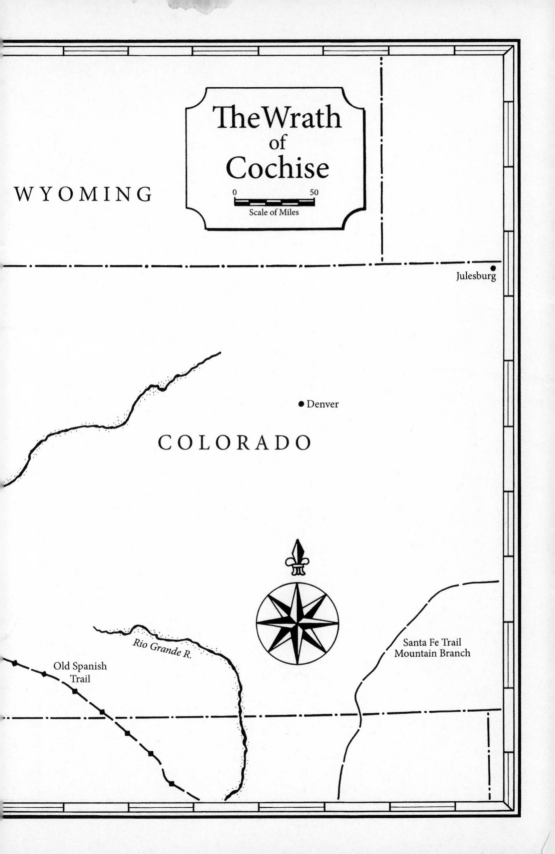

The Wrath
of
Cochise

0   50

Scale of Miles

WYOMING

Julesburg

● Denver

COLORADO

Rio Grande R.

Old Spanish
Trail

Santa Fe Trail
Mountain Branch

CONTENTS

INTRODUCTION

APACHE PASS LIES BETWEEN THE DOS CABEZAS AND CHIRICAHUA mountain ranges in southeastern Arizona. There, in February 1861, an incident occurred that started a war between the Chiricahua Apaches, on one side, and the U.S. Army and the white settlers of Arizona and New Mexico on the other. It was not war as the whites understood it. There were no major battles in which large numbers of troops and warriors were engaged. It was a guerrilla war. Attacks were often made against innocent noncombatants— on both sides. The Chiricahua effectively used their mobility and knowledge of the vast Southwest to frustrate the far less nimble U.S. Army, so that the army's greater manpower and firepower were nullified for much of the conflict. The first phase of this war lasted more than ten years—until 1872—with devastating costs in lives and property. There followed a two-year period of peace, but war broke out again and did not end until 1886 with the capitulation of the last remnants of the Chiricahua and their removal to a prisoner-of-war camp in Florida.

The broad outlines of this decades-long war are generally well known, as are the names of the principal Apache leaders: Mangas Coloradas, Geronimo, Juh, Nana, Victorio, and, perhaps most famous of all, Cochise. And it was Cochise who was there at the start of things in Apache Pass in 1861 when he was confronted by and, in turn confronted, a young army officer named George Bascom.

At the time of the incident, Cochise was in his forties, perhaps late forties, although no one knows precisely the year he was born. He was the leader of his immediate circle, called a "local group," but he was not yet the all-powerful war chief he would become. He had rivals among the Chiricahua, men who led their own respective local groups and who were sometimes at odds with him. He also had allies, such as his father-in-law, Mangas Coloradas, who cooperated with Cochise politically and militarily. The decentralized social and political structure of the Chiricahua—and indeed of all the Apache tribes—meant that alliances and enmities often shifted according to the success in war and raiding enjoyed by one leader or another. And the Apaches were not immune to jealousies and political rivalries. A leader's personality and rhetorical skills also affected his standing among his people and bolstered—or limited—his ability to rally other groups to his standard.

So in 1861, Cochise was one of many chiefs and did not have the kind of political power over the wider population of Chiricahuas that he would later achieve during the subsequent war against the whites. There are few contemporary accounts of him at this period, and those that exist are unflattering. Butterfield stage agent and subsequent Arizona Ranger James Tevis knew Cochise at this time and described him as treacherous, dangerous, and untrustworthy. But Cochise successfully led his people in guerrilla war for more than ten years, and when he finally agreed to make peace— primarily on his own terms—the army officers and civilians who met him were impressed by his gravitas, his honesty, and his dignified implacability, to say nothing of the iron-fisted command he exercised over his people—truly a unique situation among the independent-minded Apaches. His reputation today is largely based on later, more flattering accounts of him, due in part to the fact that he kept his word to restrain his warriors when he made peace in 1872. It was only after his death two years later that war broke out again. It's fair to suggest, therefore, that the man at the beginning of the war was somewhat different from the man who ended it. A decade or more of fighting will change anyone. That may help to explain the inconsistencies in his story, for the barbarities he committed during the war are in sharp contrast to his statesmanlike conduct and demeanor in the last two years of his life.

Whereas the reputation of Cochise has grown over the years, that of his antagonist, Lieutenant George Bascom, has gone in the opposite direction. Indeed, Bascom is generally blamed for shattering the delicate relationship between the Chiricahua and the U.S. government and army. In fact, Bascom is invariably portrayed as a stereotypical young army officer whose blunders and poor judgment led to a conflict that turned out to be disastrous to the white civilians in the territory and ultimately to the Apaches as well.

Thus the accepted history of the incident has given us the two main characters—Cochise, a leader admired for his tenacity, regal bearing, and command, and George Bascom, an inexperienced officer who, when given the chance, made all the wrong decisions. There is a grain of truth in these characterizations, but as usual with binary constructions, the whole truth is rather more complicated. One of the objects of this book is to examine as much as possible the reasons the two main characters acted the way they did.

Further, the Bascom Affair, as it has come to be known, is one of those footnotes of history that invites consideration of the larger issues surrounding the settlement of the West. Of course, the whole question of relations with the native tribes is front and center. But other large events and issues are also relevant to the story—the Mexican War, North-South politics and slavery, the impact of the Civil War, military training and strategy, the roles of mining, emigration, and transportation. In short, in the Bascom Affair we have a microcosm of, and in some ways a metaphor for, the development of the West.

Chapter One

SOME AWFUL MOMENT

. . . the most dangerous thing in the world is a second
lieutenant with a map and compass.
                          —Old service adage, quoted by
                          Philip Caputo, *A Rumor of War*

But who, if he be called upon to face
Some awful moment to which Heaven has join'd
Great issues, good or bad, for humankind,
Is happy as a Lover, and attired
With sudden brightness like a Man inspired;
                          —William Wordsworth,
                          "Character of the Happy Warrior"

WARRIORS WHO GO IN HARM'S WAY AND STAY THERE LONG ENOUGH
will almost inevitably be confronted with a defining moment, one
that can forever alter their view of themselves—for good or ill. In
rare cases, those moments also affect the course of history. The
tensions of these moments, along with the excitement, are intensified for someone in command, especially a young officer, not only

because he has to make a decision with little experience to guide him, but also because he has to make it in front of his troops—men whose good opinions he values, whose loyalty he depends on, and whose lives he is responsible for. Worse yet, there rarely is much time in these situations to think the matter through or to seek counsel, assuming any is available. One of the most difficult questions a young officer ever has to answer is "What should we do, Lieutenant?" It's the same question he is asking himself, and the more anxious the moment, the less sure he is of the answer.

To a romantic poet like Wordsworth, with no experience of war, the "happy warrior" greets these moments cheerfully and with confidence and inspiration. No doubt such heroes have existed. After all, Wordsworth was writing about Lord Nelson, who fit the image and made decisions that generally worked out well, for the British, at any rate. But Nelson and people like him are not necessarily the norm. Closer to the norm is Lieutenant George Nicolas Bascom, West Point, class of 1858. When faced with his own defining moment, Bascom made a decision that started a war with Cochise and his Chiricahua Apaches that would cost thousands of lives and end with the virtual eradication of a people and their culture. The incident certainly qualifies as "some awful moment to which Heaven has join'd great issues, good or bad," although Bascom did not know that at the time. Faced with a difficult situation, Bascom did what he thought was right. Unfortunately, events proved he made a tragic mistake, a mistake that let slip the proverbial dogs of war.

Why did Bascom do what he did? Why did Cochise, an older man, wise in councils and respected by his tribe, respond the way he did? What historical forces combined to bring them together in Apache Pass, a remote and rugged corner of southern Arizona?*

---

* "Arizona" did not exist as a separate entity during the time of this story; it was part of the New Mexico Territory. But in this narrative I will refer to "Arizona" to simplify geographical references and to avoid the awkward repetition of "the area that would become the state of Arizona."

And if what happened was a tragedy, does that mean it was inevitable?

❖

While eyewitnesses, both Apache and U.S. army troops, disagree on some of the details of the incident, all agree on the prevailing outline of the story:

In 1860, John Ward was living with his Mexican common-law wife and her twelve-year-old son, Felix, on a ranch in the foothills between Tucson and the Mexican border. Like many men living on the edges of civilization, Ward was forced to scramble to make ends meet. If his scrambling now and then included snatching some cattle from across the border, it did not bring him much in the way of prosperity. His ranch was nothing more than a ramshackle house, a few cattle, a patch of garden, and some chickens scratching in the yard. When and if he had anything to sell, his only markets were the army post, Fort Buchanan, a few working mines, and the sleepy adobe villages along the Santa Cruz River, Tubac and Tucson. But Tubac and Tucson were many miles away. To supplement his meager income, Ward could hunt, for the country was rich in game—deer, antelope, elk, javelina, and even bear. There were also quail and, in season, the occasional migrating duck. If desperate, he could hunt coyotes and wolves for their pelts. There were plenty of them. Mountain lions too. But it was a difficult life, and Ward was far from prosperous. Or comfortable.

Despite the presence of the fort a dozen miles away, Ward and his family, like all the scattered settlers in the area, were in more or less constant danger from marauding Apaches, as well as from Mexican desperadoes who came across the border to steal what little there was to be had in the tiny settlements and remote ranches of southern Arizona. Perhaps the settlers' poverty should have made them unappealing targets, but there was always the risk that a raider had even less than they did, or wanted to raid simply for the sake of raiding. There were

3

such people. So if Ward and the few others like him felt they were out on a limb, they had good cause. To get an inkling of a settler's emotions, you only need to sit quietly in this still remote corner of Arizona and imagine, especially in the darkness, that there is not a friend for miles; there's no one to call on for help in any emergency, no one to help in case that movement you hear in the tall grass is something more sinister than just a prowling coyote or javelina.

Despite the exposure and its risks, Ward did have some aesthetic compensations, assuming he was able to appreciate them. His ranch was in the beautiful Sonoita Valley, thirty miles or so from the Mexican border and fifty miles south of Tucson, on the eastern side of the tall Santa Rita mountain range. Sonoita Creek, a spring-fed stream that flowed all year long, was a reliable source of good water. "Sonoita" is a Papago word meaning "place where the corn grows."[1] With good water and abundant grass, it was possible to make a living, albeit precarious, as a farmer or rancher in this country. Were it not for the Apaches and bandits, one might do very well, in fact. The elevation of Ward's ranch was about four thousand feet above sea level, so the weather was generally moderate and grasslands and timber abundant. (Western weather and vegetation are as much a function of elevation as of latitude, if not more so.) Daily temperature swings of forty degrees or more were common all year, and winter temperatures could reach single digits, while summers were comparatively mild and seldom got much above ninety degrees. Technically, the area was part of the Sonoran Desert, but it was not desert as most people think of it. Rainfall averaged eighteen to twenty inches a year, and the rolling land and foothills were dotted with mesquites and cottonwoods and live oaks that were green the year-round, except in spring when the leaves turned yellow and dropped off to make way for new ones. It was the opposite of autumn, and an easterner might be excused for being disoriented. The land was covered with grama grass, a particularly nutritious forage for grazing animals, and from a distance the stirrup-high blades made the rolling hills and canyons look soft and welcoming. Until you entered them. Then you understood that the grass was growing on hard and rocky soil. Loose stones made the footing difficult for men and animals. Still, it was beautiful country. The air was generally clear and dry. It was always sunny, except during the summer monsoons—a vital rainy season that replenished the grass that Ward's cattle and most of the game animals depended on. Then vast clouds would gather above the mountains, and Wagnerian lightning bolts and rolling thunder would light up the night, and the rain would come, necessary and wished for and yet dangerous when it gathered in flash floods and swept through the canyons and arroyos. And then the grass, which most months was the tawny color of a mountain lion, turned green, and the valleys and canyons changed character and the air smelled from the perfume the grasses and the sage let loose. Washed by the rain, the oaks and junipers, the cottonwoods and sycamores, and the mesquites shone forth in various shades of green that said this land was renewing itself and undergoing a cleansing and necessary cycle.

Northwest of Ward's ranch, the Santa Rita Mountains rose to almost ten thousand feet, their summits above the timberline. Many a winter morning the mountains would be dusted with snow. Now and then a foot or so of snow would fall in the lower elevations, though the sun would melt most of it by early afternoon. It was welcome moisture, because there was no runoff, and nothing was lost from erosion.

The Santa Cruz River Valley lay to the west of Ward's ranch. The Santa Cruz flowed north from Mexico along the west side of the Santa Ritas, dropping down through Tubac and Tucson, and on to its juncture with the Gila River just south of what is now Phoenix. Then it was nothing but desert except where the Pima Indians and their friends and allies the Maricopas had dug irrigation canals for their crops. Land that looked utterly barren could and did become bountiful when irrigated. To the north and east of the Santa Cruz and Gila River Valleys lay rugged mountain ranges, well forested and watered. These mountains were the home of the western Apache tribes.

The Santa Cruz Valley was a major highway for Apache raiders on their way into and out of Sonora, and for Mexican bandits coming north on their forays. The Apaches, some of whom lived in the mountains north of Tucson, kept the tiny outposts of Tucson and Tubac under virtual house arrest. Other bands lived in the mountains to the east. The Apaches lived primarily by raiding, and they terrorized not only the Mexicans in the valley and in Mexico, but also the peaceful Arizonan Indian tribes—the Pimas, Papagos, and Maricopas. These tribes were farmers, and the Apaches regularly extorted harvests from them, leaving enough to keep their vassals alive to bring in future harvests. Now and then these tribes would strike back, for although they were peacefully inclined, they were not docile. But as a rule, the Apaches held them in a kind of thralldom, because the Apaches were manifestly not peacefully inclined and not only lived by raiding but defined themselves by it. They were warriors. And warriors obviously need someone to fight with.

Aside from Tucson and Tubac, there were some scattered ranches in the Santa Cruz Valley. The redoubtable Pete Kitchen lived in a veritable fortress near the borderline, where he and his Mexican wife and in-laws and their Indian and Mexican vaqueros did their ranch work, always alert to the possibility of Apache ambush. They had good reason—Apache raiders had killed Kitchen's twelve-year-old adopted son—and they periodically attacked the ranch, killing animals or running off stock.

The Apaches had no fear of the recently arrived U.S. Army. Fort Buchanan, established near Sonoita Creek in 1856, was a pitiful excuse for a post, exposed and undermanned. In fact, the Apaches probably welcomed the presence of the fort, because it meant another potential supply of horses, mules, and the occasional rifle and ammunition of a careless soldier who wandered too far from the fort.

The Apaches' primary raiding territory, though, was Mexico. And they did not raid merely to acquire livestock for their own consumption; they were also in the business of trade. There were active illegal markets on both sides of the border—Bent's Fort, Taos, Santa Fe, Chihuahua City, Janos, as well as a number of smaller, even ad hoc markets—where Apache raiders could meet Mexican and American traders who were interested in acquiring stolen stock. Apaches could and did steal cattle and horses in Sonora and sell them in the neighboring state of Chihuahua—and vice versa. Buyers were not hard to find. These traders had what the Apaches needed more than anything—arms and ammunition. But the markets were not just for cattle. Apaches also sold captives into slavery, or for ransom. Kidnapping was therefore an element in the Apache economy. Sometimes, though, they would adopt captives, especially small boys, into the tribe. And now and then they would keep Mexican women as slaves. Having no proscriptions against polygamy, an Apache man might add an attractive captive woman to his household, although she would most likely suffer the displeasure of the warrior's other wives. But Apaches invariably killed Mexican adult males. If lucky, the Mexicans were killed during the raid. If unlucky, they were taken back to the Apaches' camp and killed there, slowly, or turned over to the women for execution in their own particular style.

The Mexicans reciprocated in the slave trade by attacking Apache (as well as Navajo) rancherias and capturing women and children, whom they would sell to wealthy landholders in Mexico and along the Rio Grande Valley. The 1850 census of the Territory of New Mexico, which included what became Arizona, showed sixty-one thousand people living mostly in the settlements along the Rio Grande.[2] In other words, there were plenty of potential buyers of Indian children to be baptized and then raised as peons. (Baptism might seem a rather thin fig leaf to cover trade in human chattel, but it's worth remembering that Catholics were told by their priests that baptism meant saving the immortal soul of a savage who would otherwise be damned.) This two-way trafficking in captives is at least a partial explanation of the inveterate hatred

Apaches felt for Mexicans. Mexicans returned that hatred with interest. This enmity was the result of centuries of fearsome warfare and cruelty, including not only slavery but scalp bounties and uncountable raids and murders, both suffered and committed.*

Needless to say, the borderland between Mexico and Arizona was a dangerous place.

In January of 1861, Apaches raided John Ward's ranch. They stole a few cattle and captured Ward's twelve-year-old stepson, Felix. Ward was away at the time, but when he discovered what happened, he rode to Fort Buchanan, a dozen miles from his ranch, and reported the incident to the commanding officer, Lieutenant Colonel Pitcairn Morrison. Ward accused Cochise's band of Chiricahua Apaches. He had no real evidence for naming Cochise. In fact, the Chiricahuas' homeland was seventy miles to the east—in and around the mountain range of the same name. But the Chiricahuas ranged far and wide in Arizona, New Mexico, and Mexico, so the accusation was not entirely far-fetched. And the trail of the raiders led east. What's more, two years before, Cochise's band had been guilty of a similar raid near Sonoita Creek, when the raiders stole a few horses. That problem was solved by the diplomatic efforts of Captain Richard S. Ewell. He led a contingent of soldiers from Fort Buchanan into Cochise's territory and, through a show of force combined with an offer of trade goods, resolved the possible crisis. Cochise returned the captured stock and as a bonus released a captive Mexican boy.[3] So although in the Ward case, Cochise and his band were innocent, Ward's suspicion was not unreasonable. By this time too, along with Mangas Coloradas, Cochise was the most famous, or notorious,

---

* The practice of slavery was not the sole province of the Mexicans and Apaches. The Utes, for example, were notorious slave traders. Also, adopting captured children (and sometimes adults) was widespread among the tribes of North America.

Apache chief, and so was often accused of depredations he had no part in—though he was far from an innocent bystander. Like Jesse James later, who was accused of every train robbery, Cochise's name naturally came up whenever there was an Apache raid. And as with James, sometimes the accusations were legitimate.

(Ewell, by the way, went on to become a Confederate general; he commanded Lee's left wing at Gettysburg. In Arizona, though, he was still a captain after nearly twenty years of service. Promotion came slowly in the peacetime regular army.)

There was little, if any, civilian law in the area, so the army acted as the frontier constabulary as well as a military force. Some of Morrison's troops were out on patrol, and he was not able to organize enough men to go in search of the raiders for several weeks. Also, he had only infantry at his immediate disposal and therefore needed to assemble enough mules to provide transport. Finally, in February, he sent Lieutenant George N. Bascom along with fifty-four soldiers toward Apache Pass in search of Cochise's camp. Ward went along as interpreter. He didn't speak Apache, but he knew some Spanish, and many Apaches were Spanish speakers, as a result of their long years of raiding, warfare, and trading in Mexico.

In modern histories that touch on this incident, Bascom is portrayed as the stereotypical "shavetail" lieutenant, fresh from West Point and eager to make a name for himself. (The term shavetail comes from the army's practice of shaving the tails of young and untrained mules to distinguish them from the older, more reliable animals.) Charles D. Poston, a Kentuckian, who was in southern Arizona at the time of these events, remembered the young lieutenant: "Bascom was a fine-looking fellow, a Kentuckian, a West Pointer, and, of course, a gentleman; but he was unfortunately a fool. . . ." Historians also regularly note that Bascom finished twenty-sixth out of twenty-seven in his class at West Point.

Bascom led his troops roughly seventy miles eastward into Apache Pass, a notch in the rugged Dos Cabezas Mountains that lie at the northern edge of the Chiricahua mountain range. Apache

Pass was a favorite camping spot for Cochise's band, because there was a spring that provided reliable flows of water all year long. From a practical point of view, he also liked it because the pass was close to the border and was therefore a convenient jumping-off point for going into Mexico for plunder, captives, and random murders. Because of that spring, Apache Pass had also become the east-west corridor for all military and civilian traffic, including the Butterfield stage line, which had recently built a stage stop there.

The pass overlooks a grass-covered stretch of desert to the north, east, and west—a stretch that would have been (and is now) a relatively flat and easy road. But there was no water in those lower elevations. And at this time in Arizona, there could be no transportation without water. Everything relied on animals to pull the wagons—mules, horses, oxen in some places. And they in turn needed food, water, and people to care for them. Life was reduced to the simplest of verities in the West—water and grass, wood for warmth and cooking, game to hunt, edible vegetation to gather. But these same verities would make life difficult for the white migration that was gathering. The stark simplicity of the environment's resources and demands created enormous problems of supply for many of the whites, army and civilian, who came there, most just passing through, others meaning to stay. Having lived in that country for centuries, the Apaches were not dismayed by these verities. They embraced them as integral to their lives, their culture, and cosmology. And to them, water was more than just essential. It was symbolic. The Apache culture hero who taught members of the tribes how they should conduct their lives was called Child of the Water.

Cochise must have thought long and hard about allowing the Butterfield stage stop to be built in Apache Pass. Prior to the establishment of the Butterfield line, a regular mail coach running east and west—the Jackass Mail—used the pass, but the operators hadn't built stage stops of any consequence. This new Butterfield stop featured a stone-and-adobe building and a corral. It would have seemed a kind of escalation to Cochise, but he did nothing to prevent it. The fact that he allowed this isolated outpost to exist indicates he was at least ambivalent about current and future relationships with the whites. Of course, Cochise understood that he could overwhelm this feeble station at any time. But he also knew that there might be something to be gained from the occasional east-west traffic, both stagecoach and freight wagons. There was even more to be gained, perhaps, from maintaining peace on this side of the border. There was a good reason for this line of thought. The Americans had appointed an Indian agent, Dr. Michael Steck, whose primary interest was maintaining peace with both the Navajos and Apaches in the territory. Steck visited Cochise for the first time in December of 1858. He distributed some cattle, cornmeal, blankets, and kettles in return for promises of amity. Steck and Cochise may also have reached an understanding, probably tacit, that Cochise was welcome to live his usual life in Arizona, without fear of the army, as long as he kept his people from raiding north of the border. Mexico, on the other hand, was another story. What Cochise and his warriors did there was their business. The Chiricahua and Dos Cabezas Mountains would therefore remain a refuge from which Cochise could travel into Mexico to go raiding and to which he could return to safety.*

Cochise realized that this could be a very good arrangement—sanctuary in a favorite place, raids into Mexico whenever he chose to go, and periodic presents from the U.S. government. In return for this understanding, letting a small stage stop operate was a minor concession to the whites. In fact, there were other nearby stage stops that went through Chiricahua country, roughly twenty

---

* There's no proof that there was an agreement, but logic suggests it was understood, in the same way it was understood fourteen years later when Cochise made a similar arrangement with General O. O. Howard. This was realpolitik. Mexico could look after itself. Besides, Steck was no fool; he realized that, whether he wanted to stop incursions into Mexico or not, he was powerless to do so.

miles apart between El Paso and Tucson, but Apache Pass was the most important symbol of the arrangements, because of its favored location near the mountains and the water.

The Butterfield manager in 1860, a man named Charles Culver, believed he was on reasonably friendly terms with Cochise, whose band occasionally supplied wood to the stage stop. Yet there had been disquieting incidents now and then that made the Butterfield hostlers and stage drivers a little nervous. (The next westerly Butterfield station had been raided for stock in April; Cochise was suspected of the raid. And Cochise had an acrimonious relationship with Culver's predecessor, James Tevis.) But while Cochise no doubt regarded the whites with a certain amount of wariness, it was nothing like the hatred he and his people felt for Mexicans. Not yet, anyway. There had never been and still weren't enough white people in the area to cause much trouble for the Chiricahuas. There had been isolated and troubling incidents in the last fifteen years or so. But these had nothing to do with the U.S. government and were the result of renegade white men, some of whom operated from Mexico.

Most likely, Cochise's primary emotion when considering the whites he had encountered was contempt: Captain John Cremony knew the Apaches well, and his assessment of them is echoed in other accounts: ". . . the proud savage does consider himself not only the equal, but the superior of his white brother."[4] (Obviously, "brother" is used facetiously.) The more the Apaches understood the white man's way of life, the greater the scorn they felt for it, and the more they thought their own way of life was preferable. The Apaches felt the whites were inferior to them in almost every important category (except, as they would ultimately learn, numbers and firepower.) When remembering a particular atrocity committed by whites against whites, Apache warrior Daklugie said, "No Apache would have done that, but these White Eyes—savages."[5] His use of the word "savages" conveys more than a little irony.

The Apaches would come to understand that the whites were not prepared or even able to live in this country as it was. To survive there, they would have to change it. Change was the white man's specialty. There was an unchallenged assumption that change, which went hand in hand with progress, was not only inevitable but virtuous and necessary. Apaches, on the other hand, believed that things should stay as they always had been. To keep things that way was the Apaches' mission. In moments of reflection, the wiser Apaches must have suspected that their mission would ultimately fail. But there were and would be enough victories in the immediate future to give them some hope that they could withstand the gathering flood of whites. For how long was another question.

When Bascom's troops arrived at Apache Pass, they pitched camp near the Butterfield stage stop. To avoid alarming Cochise, Bascom sent word, through the Butterfield stage driver James Wallace, who was on cordial terms with Cochise, that the patrol was just passing through on their way eastward. The message also invited Cochise to come into camp for a friendly parley. A day or so later Cochise arrived. A few years after the incident a young army officer described Cochise: "He was a remarkably fine looking man, fully six feet tall, as straight as an arrow, and well proportioned, the typical Indian face, rather long, high cheekbones, clear keen eyes, and a Roman nose. His cheeks were slightly painted with vermillion. A yellow silk handkerchief bound his hair which was straight and black. . . ."[6]

While the precise details of his appearance may differ slightly, account by account, all the descriptions of Cochise by people who met him agree that he was an imposing and dignified figure.

With Cochise were his brother, Coyuntura; two nephews; another warrior; one of Cochise's wives; and two children.* Cochise was obviously not expecting anything more than a chat. Bascom

---

* Most accounts state that two of the warriors were Cochise's nephews, but that is not certain.

invited Cochise into his tent, where he gave him a cup of coffee and then summarily accused Cochise, through the interpreter Ward, of stealing the cattle and kidnapping the boy. Surprised, Cochise denied involvement and suggested that another band of Apaches, who lived in the mountains north of Tucson, was probably responsible. He offered to find out, but Bascom refused, saying that he did not believe Cochise and that he would hold him and his relatives hostage until the boy and the stock were returned. Incensed, Cochise drew his knife and, as the legend goes, cut his way out of the tent and escaped up the hillside, while bullets from the soldiers' rifles spattered around him. The third warrior also made a run for it but was shot and killed. Meanwhile Bascom's troops secured the other hostages, including Coyuntura, who also tried unsuccessfully to escape. The troopers retreated to the stage stop, where the stone-and-adobe building and corral offered a better defensive position than the exposed campsite. Bascom was alert enough to suspect what might be coming next.

He did not have to wait long. The next morning, the hills were filled with Apaches. Cochise had assembled his own warriors as well as those of his father-in-law, Mangas Coloradas. There was no firing at first. In fact, the Apaches showed a flag of truce and offered to parley. Bascom, Ward, and two soldiers came out, also carrying a flag of truce. Cochise and three of his warriors met the soldiers about one hundred and fifty yards from the stage stop. Cochise asked Bascom to release his family, but Bascom refused, saying they would be free when the Ward boy was returned. At this point, Wallace and two Butterfield employees, Welch and Culver, emerged from the stage stop. They apparently thought they could help in the negotiations. It was bad judgment. They were seized by Apaches who had been hiding in a ravine. Cochise and his men then ran for cover, while his concealed warriors opened fire on Bascom and his party, wounding one of the soldiers. Welch and Culver managed to escape and ran toward the stage stop, but Culver was shot in the back and Welch was killed in the crossfire between the

Apaches and the soldiers. Wallace was still a captive. Bascom and his men made it back to the stage stop without further injury even though the firing was now intense.

Gradually the firing slackened and then stopped. On a hill overlooking the stage stop Cochise appeared, leading Wallace by a rope around his neck. Wallace's hands were tied behind his back. Cochise offered to exchange Wallace for his family. Bascom refused, saying once again that the hostages would be released when the Ward boy was safely delivered. After shouting imprecations and vowing revenge, Cochise led Wallace away and disappeared into the hills.

Some hours later, the westbound Butterfield stage was approaching the eastern entrance to the pass. It would have been easy pickings for Cochise, except that the Apaches were now watching the western entrance. They were following the progress of a wagon train heading east for Las Cruces, New Mexico. The wagon train was carrying flour and was operated by three Americans and nine Mexicans, none of whom had any specific reason to anticipate trouble, although they would have felt understandable wariness while traveling through Chiricahua country.

As the wagon train ascended toward the summit of the pass, Cochise and his warriors sprang from their hiding places and surrounded the teamsters, who surrendered without a fight, no doubt thinking, or hoping, that the usual offer of presents and provisions would buy their way out of the predicament. Cochise had other plans. He and his warriors cut loose the mules and loaded them with the sacks of flour. They then tied the nine Mexicans to the wheels of the wagons and burned them alive, while the horrified Americans watched. All the Mexicans died, their heads down over the fires—a vivid symbol of the unrelenting hatred Cochise and all the Apaches felt for Mexicans.

Cochise now had four American hostages to exchange. He instructed Wallace to write a note to Bascom, offering to trade. The note was tied to some brush near the stage stop, but Bascom did not receive it until it was much too late. Meanwhile, Cochise made plans to attack the eastbound Butterfield stage that was just then entering the pass. Just before the stage reached the burned-out freight wagons and the charred remains of the Mexicans, the Apaches opened fire, killing one mule, wounding another, and wounding the driver. His partner jumped down and cut the dead mule loose and started the remaining mules forward toward the stage stop. The Apaches had broken down a small stone bridge near the station thinking that when the coach tried to cross, it would capsize. But the driver whipped the mules into a frenzied gallop and managed to get across the ravine where the bridge had been. He made it to the stage stop, even though the Apaches were firing sporadically from the hills. (One of the passengers on the stage was Lieutenant John Rogers Cooke, the son of General Philip St. George Cooke, commander of the Mormon Battalion in the Mexican War.)

The next morning, the Apaches were gone. When Cochise did not receive an answer to his note, he decided to remove his people, especially the women and children, from the area. He planned to return and fight again. Before leaving, he gathered the four white hostages and tortured them to death, mutilating the bodies and leaving them in a place the soldiers were sure to find. Wallace could later be identified only by the gold in his teeth.

When he realized that the Apaches were gone, at least temporarily, Bascom sent messengers to Tucson and Fort Buchanan, asking for reinforcement. The detail from Fort Buchanan started immediately, and on their way to Apache Pass they encountered three Apache warriors driving stolen cattle. These Apaches were not from Cochise's band and probably did not know anything about the hostilities. Had they known, they would have scattered when they saw the army. The soldiers took them prisoner and continued to Apache Pass.

Bascom now had six warriors as hostages as well as Cochise's wife and two children. And when he discovered the mutilated bodies of the four Americans as well as the blackened remains of the nine Mexicans, he conferred with his colleagues about what to do next. Jointly, they decided to execute the six warriors, and after burying the four Americans, they hanged the six Apaches from the oak trees that stood above the Americans' graves. There was some discussion about what to do with the woman and two children. They decided to take them back to Fort Buchanan and release them there. Bascom assigned a squad of soldiers to protect the stage station and then, leaving the six Apaches dangling from the oak trees, he returned to the fort, not knowing, of course, that he had just started a war.

Chapter Two

THE MEXICAN WAR AND ITS AFTERMATH

The Apaches and Navajos come down from the mountains and carry off your sheep and your women whenever they please. My government will correct all this. They will keep off the Indians, protect you in your persons and property.

—General Stephen Watts Kearny in Santa Fe

THE SEQUENCE OF EVENTS THAT LED TO THE MEETING BETWEEN Bascom and Cochise in Apache Pass had begun more than a decade before, with the war between the United States and Mexico. Some of these events were major international and national incidents; others were minor ironic coincidences. They all ultimately had an impact on what happened in Apache Pass.

The war with Mexico began in the spring of 1846 over a border dispute. The Mexicans claimed that the border of Texas, which had become an American state in December of 1845, extended only to the Nueces River, not to the Rio Grande. American troops were sent into the disputed area, shots were exchanged, men were killed, and the war was on.

As is often the case, the war was popular at first, but then doubts began to creep into the public discourse. Political agendas also came into play. Opponents began to suspect that President James K. Polk's war aims went significantly beyond establishing the Rio Grande as the Texas border. As usual in antebellum politics, the question of slavery complicated the debate. Northern abolitionists began accusing Polk of fighting a war of conquest in order to add new territories and thereby strengthen and expand the institution of slavery. Texas had been admitted as a slave state. What would be next? Indeed, the question arose early in the war, when President Polk asked Congress for an appropriation of two million dollars to be used as a cash down payment to Mexico for the new territories Polk expected to acquire one way or the other from that country, once the war was concluded. Polk thereby inadvertently reinforced abolitionists' suspicions that his war aim was not merely to expel the Mexican army from the disputed border of Texas.[1]

Polk denied the charge and in his State of the Union address of 1846 said: "The war has not been waged with a view to conquest, but, having been commenced by Mexico, it has been carried into the enemy's country and will be vigorously prosecuted there with a view to obtain an honorable peace and thereby secure ample indemnity. . . ."[2]

Regardless of the aims and claims, the war did ultimately result in the acquisition by the United States of vast new territories—what is now Utah, Nevada, most of New Mexico and Arizona, all of California, and parts of Colorado and Wyoming. It was not as easy a conquest as some might have expected, but this was no different from most wars that are begun with the belief that they will be short and costly to the enemy primarily, if not exclusively.

There were three major American military campaigns during the nearly two years of conflict. General Stephen Kearny led a contingent of regular army dragoons (essentially cavalry equipped with heavy infantry weapons) and a larger contingent of volunteers—1,350 men in all—from Fort Leavenworth southwest along the old trail to Santa Fe, where he brushed aside Mexican resistance and declared New Mexico now to be the property of the United States. He issued proclamations guaranteeing religious freedom for the new U.S. citizens, who were primarily Catholic, and promising to protect them against Indian raiding. He then followed the old Camino Real south until he turned west and crossed the mountains to the headwaters of the Gila River. The goal was California. Continuing west, he passed by the Santa Rita del Cobre copper mines, mines that had been worked for years by Mexicans but had been abandoned because of Apache attacks. In fact, Kearny met with Apache chief Mangas Coloradas and some of his warriors, who, when they heard what he was doing, swore friendship to the whites because of their eternal hatred of their common enemy, the Mexicans, following the principle "the enemy of my enemy is my friend." Kearny—and his guide, Kit Carson—were skeptical of their declarations but thought it best to appear to believe them. They had other business at hand anyway. Later they met another small group of Apaches from whom they bought some stolen Mexican mules.

Dropping down from the headwaters of the Gila, Kearny's "army of the west" traveled through the most brutal desert in southern Arizona. His route took him along the Gila River and therefore well north of Apache Pass. Worn-out, with many of his pack animals and horses dead along the trail from exhaustion and lack of food and water, Kearny finally made it to Southern California, where, in December 1846, he fought a battle at San Pasqual. By this time, his force had been reduced to a hundred dragoons, because he had left some of his men in New Mexico to garrison the area and sent another contingent south into Chihuahua.* As a result, the battle

---

* Along his march south, Kearny met Kit Carson, who was returning from California with dispatches announcing the U.S. victories there won by Commander Robert F. Stockton and John C. Fremont. Kearny therefore felt the extra troops were not necessary. He ordered Carson to join him and guide him back to San Diego.

at San Pasqual was close-run. Kearny was wounded there, and his besieged troops had to be rescued by a contingent of marines and sailors who had earlier landed in San Diego. Afterward there was some political squabbling between Kearny and Commodore Stockton, the naval commander.* There was also a minor skirmish at Los Angeles. But the major objectives of the campaign were achieved—New Mexico (which at the time included Arizona) and California were now in the hands of the United States.

One offshoot of Kearny's campaign was Lieutenant William H. Emory's survey of the trail between the Rio Grande and Southern California. Emory was a member of the army's topographical engineers. His job was not only to map the trail but also to take careful notes on the quantity and quality of grass and the location and accessibility of water—two elements without which no army or civilian expedition could survive. He also took note of the fauna and flora, especially of trees and edible plants as well as the geology of the trail, on the lookout, no doubt, for indications of precious metals. But as he said in his report, "There may be mineral wealth in these mountains, but its discovery must be left to some explorer not attached to the staff of an army making forced marches into an enemy's country."[3] Emory published his notes and a map based on two thousand astronomical observations and 357 barometric readings.[4] The map became the chief guide to thousands of gold seekers starting in 1849.

The other two campaigns in the war were commanded by General Zachary Taylor and General Winfield Scott. Taylor had

---

* The argument was about who should be governor of California. John C. Fremont, acting as a freelance, had organized a group of civilians as the "California Battalion" in the north and had been active in the declaration of the Bear Flag Republic and in the early battles with loyal Californios. With Stockton's support he claimed the governorship. Kearny had orders from the War Department to assume the governorship. The dispute ultimately led to Fremont's court-martial and conviction on charges of mutiny. But like many nineteenth century adventurers, he bobbed up again during the Civil War, only to suffer further disgrace.

been in command on the Rio Grande when hostilities erupted, and he crossed the river with his troops and fought a series of battles culminating in the difficult fights at Monterey and Buena Vista, in which his subordinate, Jefferson Davis (West Point, 1828), played a conspicuous and heroic role. Davis had earlier resigned from the regular army to become a cotton planter, but when war broke out he volunteered to become colonel of a Mississippi volunteer regiment, and he would use the prestige gained from his action to strengthen his position in Mississippi politics. Another famous name to be, Ulysses S. Grant, wondered if he had chosen the right career the first time he heard shots fired in anger: "For myself a young second lieutenant who had never heard a hostile gun before, I felt sorry that I had enlisted."[5] But Grant went on into the thick of the fighting and soon came to the conclusion that anticipation of combat was worse than the actual experience.[6] Others might have disagreed, but it was a lesson Grant would carry with him into the Civil War.

Taylor halted after the battle of Buena Vista, perhaps because Polk's war aims were in fact directed toward arranging a negotiated peace. But the Mexicans were not interested in talks, and so the final stage of the war—Winfield Scott's campaign—was put into operation.

In the end, Scott applied the coup de grâce to Mexico. He led an amphibious attack at Veracruz and then marched to Mexico City and captured it. Captain Robert E. Lee distinguished himself in this campaign especially as a leader of reconnaissance patrols designed to find the best routes for Taylor's objectives on the march from Veracruz to Mexico City. A member of the prestigious engineer corps, Lee was an excellent judge of terrain, the geography of war.

In all of these battles, the Americans were outnumbered and often surprised by the tenacity and bravery of the Mexican opponents. Those who went into these fights feeling contempt for the enemy emerged with different ideas. But in the end it was the U.S. firepower, especially the artillery, that made the difference.

Mexican artillery was generally restricted to solid shot, while Americans employed a variety of ordnance including grapeshot and canister—essentially large shotgun charges that devastated opposing infantry.[7] American mortars that fired high-angle explosive shells were crucial in reducing a besieged position. The Americans' skill at siege warfare was especially important in Veracruz. The combination of combat engineering and artillery was decisive, although frontal attacks with the bayonet gave the infantry a major share of the credit too. These were military ideas that survived even into World War I—massive artillery bombardment followed by infantry assault. While they were disastrous in subsequent wars, they worked in Mexico.

The war ended in 1848 with the signing of the Treaty of Guadalupe Hidalgo. Under its terms, Mexico ceded to the United States a vast territory—essentially the entire Southwest plus California. And Mexico agreed to the Rio Grande as the border of Texas. The United States would pay Mexico $15 million for these new territories. At first glance, this seems to be a bargain on the scale of the purchase price for Manhattan. On the other hand, prosecuting the war cost the United States some $100 million and the lives of 13,780 of its men, most of whom died from disease rather than enemy action. (Only one in eight was killed in combat.) These figures do not include the losses from disabling wounds.[8] The cost to Mexico in treasure and lives was even higher, though precise figures are not available. Most likely, the number is somewhere around twenty-five thousand killed and countless more wounded and maimed. So perhaps the new lands were not such a bargain after all. Still, it was a conquest of immense size and ultimate importance. Although many, including U. S. Grant, criticized the war and its results, the idea of conquest as a legitimate function of nation-states was more acceptable in the nineteenth century than it is in most quarters today.

But what exactly was there, there? With the exception of the old Spanish settlements along the Rio Grande Valley in New Mexico and the coastal communities of California, this new territory was essentially empty, except, of course, for the various Indian tribes. There were no surveys or maps until Emory published the results of his work. There weren't any roads to speak of. John C. Fremont had explored and surveyed some of the land in the northern edges of what had been Mexican territory. But places like Arizona were terra incognita, except to the handful of Mexicans living in tiny villages like Tucson or Tubac. There were mountain men and trappers operating out of Taos who worked in the beaver-rich headwaters of the Gila in western New Mexico; some of these became important guides for future emigrants. (One such, Kit Carson, was with Kearny at the Battle of San Pasqual and was one of the men Kearny sent to San Diego with a request for help. Carson had also been with John C. Fremont during Fremont's early expeditions to California.) And there were traders who were familiar with the old Santa Fe Trail that ran between Missouri and New Mexico, and even the Camino Real that led south from Santa Fe along the Rio Grande to El Paso and old Mexico. But aside from these people, few knew much, if anything, about this new territory. And, of course, no one in Washington had any idea.

Nor did they know much about the current inhabitants. The cultures among the various western tribes are and were truly diverse, something that the white settlers and policy makers never did seem to understand. The agriculturist Pueblos, whose interlocking adobe houses emphasized their preference for living in established communities, were utterly different in their culture, religion, and economy from, for example, the Chiricahua Apaches, who never stayed long in any one place, built no permanent houses, and lived solely by hunting, gathering, and raiding. While there was some trade among the various tribes and occasional cultural cross-fertilization (such as in crafts), the disparities of languages, geography, and economies meant that the various tribes staunchly maintained their individual characteristics. Cochise's Chiricahuas were different even from other Apache tribes. Although they all spoke basically the same language, many aspects of the Chiricahua economy and culture were unique. They were, for example, the only Apaches who never planted any crops, even in a modest way. They ate what they gathered in the wild. Or hunted. Or stole. They were the very definition of "otherness" to the whites who encountered them as the emigrants flooded into and through the territory.

Ironically, it was a handful of regular army officers who took the time to study the cultures of the Indians they encountered. A few even published scholarly papers and books on the tribes they met and sometimes fought against. But culture is conveyed at least in part through language, and the difficulty and variety of Indian languages meant that even the most well-intentioned and interested army officers remained ignorant of the complexities and nuances of Indian cultures. And the vast majority of people in the United States, including the politicians, knew nothing whatever of these new territories or their inhabitants. To them it was the Great American Desert, as foreign as the steppes of Russia. As for the Indians, they were stereotyped as "savages."

The Treaty of Guadalupe Hidalgo contained a provision called Article Eleven that enjoined the United States to protect Mexican borders against marauding Indians, which meant, mainly, Apaches, although the Navajos and Utes were also troublesome; so too the Comanches and Kiowas, who came to raid from Texas. Additionally, the article required the United States to repatriate any captured Mexicans whom U.S. troops or officials might recapture, and to make it illegal for an American citizen to buy from the Indians any stolen Mexican property of any kind, including captives held as slaves. The fact that this article was included in a treaty to end a war indicates the severity of the Apache problem in Mexico.

It's difficult to say whether U.S. politicians agreed to Article Eleven out of naïveté, ignorance, or cynicism. It was unenforceable for any number of reasons. First, after the war, Congress was in a penny-pinching mood and was never going to authorize the amount of funds necessary to maintain an army large enough to police the border. Second, there was a long-standing aversion to the idea of maintaining a professional army of any size. Third, the very people who were likely to enter these new territories were in many cases precisely the sort who would, and did, ignore any law that interfered with their opportunities. Army officers who wrote about their experiences frequently described the character of the white civilians who drifted into the new territories. Captain John Cremony wrote about this in 1860, the year before Bascom's encounter in Apache Pass: ". . . Arizona and New Mexico were cursed by the presence of two or three hundred of the most infamous scoundrels it is possible to conceive. . . . In the graveyard in Tucson there were forty-seven graves of white men . . . and of that number only two had died natural deaths, all the rest being murdered in broils and barroom quarrels."[9]

These were not the kind of people who paid attention to international treaties or the laws derived from them. But they were the kind who would trade whiskey and weapons to the Apaches, Navajos, or anyone else, in return for stolen Mexican horses, cattle, and captives.

As might have been predicted, the United States failed miserably to live up to Article Eleven, whether through indifference or parsimony. In the several years after the war, the Mexican state of Sonora alone recorded Apache raids that killed 840 citizens, wounded 97, and kidnapped 89—to say nothing of the countless cattle, horses, and mules that were stolen.[10] And Sonora was not even half of the Apaches' raiding ground. The neighboring state of Chihuahua received attacks of equal severity and frequency. The U.S. Army, such as it was, did try to live up to the terms of the treaty. But the troops were far too few in number. They did harbor the occasional Mexican woman who had escaped from her captors, and they tried when possible to recover kidnap victims. But their resources were too scanty to do very much of this work. The exasperated Mexican government tried to counter these attacks by establishing a line of forts, or "presidios," along the border, but they were too widespread and too poorly garrisoned to cause any annoyance to the Apache raiders. The only value these outposts had was in response—they could send a party of soldiers to chase the Apaches, once a raid was over. But this was cold comfort to the victims. What's more, the Mexican government, always shifting and always worried about revolts, both actual and potential, had outlawed firearms for civilians, so that the people on the frontier could not (legally, at least) defend themselves against Apache incursions, except with primitive weapons.*

The Treaty of Guadalupe Hidalgo set the Arizona border at roughly the line of the Gila River, which runs east to west below present-day Phoenix. The Chiricahua Mountains, Cochise's homeland, were south of this line and therefore remained in old Mexico, at least for the time being.

In addition to territory, the Mexican War provided the regular army with important new experiences from which they drew far-reaching conclusions. Or perhaps it's more accurate to say that the experiences reinforced existing assumptions and practices.

The regular army had performed very well, and their morale and espirit de corps were bolstered. Most of the regular army officers were graduates of West Point. They therefore had a sense of themselves as a tightly knit fraternity of professionals who knew their business, and proved it in Mexico. At West Point they had learned the art of set-piece battles from French military manuals. These tactics were essentially unchanged from the time of Napoleon, but they seemed to work well against the Mexicans—the

---

* The central government had good reason to worry. The northern states of Mexico had an especially independent attitude. And, in fact, a ferocious civil war broke out in 1858 and lasted until 1861, which meant at the time of the Bascom incident, the Mexicans were fighting two wars—against each other and against the Indians from across the border.

combination of artillery preparation followed by infantry attacks with the bayonet. (Infantry muskets on both sides in Mexico were so inaccurate except at close range that U. S. Grant once said, "A man might fire at you all day without your finding it out.")[11] The Mexican army obliged the Americans by employing the same sort of tactics. Both sides played by the same rules, although the Mexicans were dismayed by the Americans' apparent willingness to take casualties. Anyone puzzling over the tactics of the Civil War—the incredible carnage of massed frontal attacks, such as Pickett's Charge—should consider where men like Lee and Grant got their first experience. But at the time of the Mexican War these tactics seemed to have proved themselves. In fact, at a dinner given by Winfield Scott near the end of the war, Scott said that if not for the "science of the Military Academy . . . this army multiplied by four could not have entered the capital of Mexico."[12]

The regular army also could compare itself favorably with the volunteers who flooded to the colors at the outbreak of the war. (Of the total numbers in service there were 31,024 regular troops versus 73,532 volunteers.)[13] The volunteers were civilian soldiers, enlisted state by state from three to twelve months or the duration of the war. They knew little if anything about discipline and campaigning. Their camps were often disorderly and unhealthy in comparison to those of the regulars, who kept themselves and their units separate from the volunteers. Their officers were often politicians who were eager for the fame but not so well versed in the less glorious but essential aspects of campaigning, such as questions of supply, water, and forage for draft animals, food for the men, and camp hygiene. This pattern would also be repeated during the Civil War. Volunteers suffered disproportionately from disease, for they knew nothing about the connection between camp hygiene and health. The regulars did not know much more about the causes of malaria and dysentery, but they did understand how to maintain an orderly camp, and that the coffee tasted better when the water was drawn upstream of where men were watering and washing themselves and their horses. Their common sense and field experience helped keep the regulars healthier than the amateurs next door.[14] The regulars held the volunteer contingent in contempt: "They are useless, useless, useless," said brand-new West Point graduate George B. McClellan, "expensive, wasteful, and good for nothing."[15]

But the volunteers were necessary to augment that regular army that had traditionally been maintained at very low numbers. There was at least one regiment of volunteers that Zachary Taylor was especially glad to have—mounted volunteers from West Texas, the Texas Rangers. They were old hands at fighting Mexicans; they'd been doing it since the battle for Texas independence. Not surprisingly, they were unruly, but they knew their business and were superb irregular troops.

Kearny too had an unlikely regiment of irregulars—the Mormon Battalion. At the outbreak of the war, Brigham Young and his people were still living in Nauvoo, Illinois, although they had started to move across the Mississippi to escape the violence of the "Gentiles," that is, the non-Mormons. (A mob had murdered Joseph Smith, the founder of the church, and his brother Hyrum in June of 1844.) Young had heard (apparently through the published reports of John C. Fremont) of the land around the Great Salt Lake. To Young, this looked like a remote enough place to move his people and thereby escape the persecution they had been suffering for years. But he was short of the cash needed to buy wagons and draft animals. He therefore offered to raise a regiment of Latter-day Saints, roughly five hundred men, for the war. Each of the volunteers would receive forty-two dollars from the U.S. government for uniform allowance, but since they were not required to wear uniforms, the money became a windfall for the church. The men were not especially enthusiastic about volunteering (essentially serving a government that seemed hostile to their beliefs). But they were obedient to the dictates of the church and dutifully turned over the money and began a trek that went from Fort Leavenworth to San Diego, roughly following Kearny's line of march. In Santa Fe, Philip St. George Cooke, of the regular army, took command and led them to California. They arrived in California in January 1847, too late to help Taylor at San Pasqual but in time to support his efforts to pacify the population and solve his political problems with Stockton and the ubiquitous Fremont. Brigham Young, meanwhile, used the Mormon Battalion's cash from uniform allowances to begin his migration to "Zion." No doubt he also believed he had gained some political capital with the powers that be in Washington.

Perhaps. But there would be trouble for these Mormons in the years to come, troubles that would send 2nd Lieutenant George N. Bascom, west—and ultimately to his appointment in Apache Pass.

In sum, the Mexican War proved to the regular army professionals that their tactical doctrines and their method of training new officers to execute those doctrines were just what they should be.

Not surprisingly, the Apaches looked at the business of war differently. Their tactical ideas were precisely the opposite of those of the professional white soldiers. Small groups traveling fast, unburdened by supply wagons or heavy armament, attacked only after careful scouting and observation of the enemy. And they attacked only when they were virtually certain of victory. Stealth and concealment were essential elements in their thinking, ambush the preferred method of attack. Taking casualties was to be avoided at all costs, for they did not have the population to replace significant losses, and in many cases the warriors were bound by family ties, unlike the white officers, who drew from an inexhaustible pool of anonymous manpower. And the Apaches took no adult male prisoners. They understood that the object of war was to kill the enemy, and they were trained in the business from childhood.

"The Apache was a hard foe to subdue," said Captain John Gregory Bourke, "not because he was full of wiles and tricks and experienced in all that pertains to the art of war, but because he had so few artificial wants and depended almost absolutely on what his great mother—Nature—stood ready to supply."[16]

Where the western militaries dragged wagon trains loaded with supplies, or at the very least led pack-mule trains, the Apache warrior grabbed his rifle and ammunition belt, a wicker jug for water and some jerked meat, and set off. Unencumbered and in superb physical condition, Apaches generally had little trouble in outdistancing their pursuers. An army officer who knew the Apaches well from fighting and studying them, Captain Bourke said, "Seventy-five miles a day was nothing at all unusual for them when pursued, their tactics being to make three or four such marches in the certainty of being able to wear out or throw off the track the most energetic and intelligent opponents."[17] (As a cavalryman, Bourke used the word "march" to include mounted travel. A normal cavalry march was twenty miles a day.)

The Apaches were mystified by the white soldiers' tactics and apparent willingness to suffer casualties, and even by the army's process of appointing leaders: "They are officers because they served their sentences in this thing called a school, not because of either ability to fight or ability to get others to fight. Don't their warriors desert in flocks? Don't their men hate them? Don't they send their men into battle instead of leading them? And don't they use stupid tactics that cost many lives instead of using strategy in the selection and management of their fights?"[18] So said Daklugie, Apache warrior and son of Juh, a Chiricahua chief and inveterate enemy of the white man.

This difference in attitudes about what war was, or should be, and how it was fought, was just one of the many dichotomies between the whites and the Chiricahuas. Indeed, it is hard to conceive of two peoples who were more different.

Chapter Three

HATRED

If a person asks, Who are you? To what people do you belong? You give the name of your band. But if someone asks you where you live, you say that you are one of a certain local group.[1]

—Anonymous Apache

ALTHOUGH THE APACHES BELIEVED THEY HAD ALWAYS LIVED IN the mountains of Arizona, New Mexico, and the Sierra Madres of old Mexico, anthropologists trace their origin to the shores of Lake Athabasca in northwest Saskatchewan and northeast Alberta. It's impossible to say precisely when the people who would become known as Apaches and Navajos started migrating south. Most likely it was in the fifteenth century. Though they spoke the same language, somewhere along the line they split into different areas of the Southwest, with the Apaches concentrating in the mountains of southern Arizona and the west of New Mexico and the Sierra Madres of old Mexico.

The taxonomy of the many Apache tribes is sometimes a little confusing. Different people, Apaches and white anthropologists, tell different stories about their organization and give the various sub-groups different names. But the most commonly used organization chart shows that the Indians who migrated from Canada fell into three major categories—Navajos, eastern Apaches (Lipan and Jica-rilla), and western Apaches. Of these last, there were six separate tribes: White Mountain, Pinal, Coyotero, Arivaipa, Mescalero, and Chiricahua. The first four were scattered in the mountains north and west of Tucson and present-day Phoenix, while the Mescaleros lived in New Mexico, in the mountains bordering the Rio Grande. The Chiricahuas settled in southeastern Arizona, western New Mexico, and in the Sierra Madres.*

To make matters even more complicated, the Chiricahuas had four separate "bands"—Chihenne (or Warm Springs, from their homes in New Mexico), Bedonkohe, Nednhi, and Chokonen. These bands might number a hundred or so warriors, although a precise census is impossible. (Rough estimates suggest the Chiricahuas of all bands numbered between one and two thousand.)[2] The Bedonkohe were a smaller band and sometimes intermingled with the Chokonen. (Geronimo was said to be a Bedonkohe.) Cochise was chief of the Chokonen band, which had its homeland in the southeastern corner of Arizona in the Chiricahua, Dos Cabezas, and Dragoon Mountains. The Dos Cabezas were on the northern end of the Chiricahua Mountains, while the Dragoons were thirty or so miles to the southwest. Both ranges ran roughly north and south and were separated by a wide, flat valley called Sulphur Springs. The other bands tended to live in the nearby mountains of New Mexico or sometimes over the border in the Sierra Madres.

These bands were too large to allow them to live as a unit. The strain on resources was too great for so many people to live

---

* Adding to the confusion, the White Mountain Apaches are often called Western Apaches.

together. So each of the bands divided itself further into "local groups." Writes anthropologist Morris Opler:

> The local group is a cluster of encampments in one general locality. It is a division of a larger group, the band. The people in it all camp around some well-known spot from which the local group gets its name. Those who camp around Mora Mountain are called "People of Mora Mountain." This refers to all the people living together in this region. But within this local group there would be other divisions. All would not live at one place. Some would camp on one side of the mountain, some would camp on the other. Others might camp at any favorable spot near water. These smaller groups or camps are decided along relationship lines. That is, all the relatives and those who marry into a certain family live together. These smaller groups, the extended families, are referred to by means of the leading men in them. . . . The local group consists of a number of extended families living near some prominent family who has a good leader. This leader would be expected to lead the men of the local group when they go on a raid or engage in war.[3]

The Chiricahuas—all the Apaches, for that matter—never stayed in one place very long, although they moved in regular orbits within their territory. They moved according to the seasons when gathering mescal or acorns or piñons. They also moved for security, going from place to place in the mountains to keep Mexican soldiers and later the U.S. Army from locating and surprising them. And they moved because a campsite after a while needs a rest from both human and animal occupation.

Their organization underscores the vital role of kinship in the Chiricahuas' "life-way." Families were the basic building blocks of their society. The loss of a warrior or a wife or child was not only a

personal catastrophe but also a social one. The extended family—
and indeed the entire local band—suffered and grieved when one
of theirs was lost.

Every account of Apache life written by soldiers who got to
know them (albeit not very well) emphasizes their sociability
and especially their kindness to and affection for their children:
"Around his own campfire the Apache is talkative, witty, fond of
telling stories, and indulging in much harmless raillery," wrote
John Gregory Bourke. "He is kind to children, and I have yet to
see the first Indian child struck for any cause by either parent or
relative."[4]

In these small groups of people, related by blood or marriage,
everyone knew everyone else intimately, so that peer pressure
was a powerful force within the group. Storytellers related the
myths and legends and the history of the people, so that everyone,
including the children, would understand who they were and
what was expected of them, how the universe worked, and how
they should worship their deities. The Chiricahua had no laws, but
they had customs that, combined with peer pressure, were much
stronger in controlling behavior than any legal system could possibly have been.

Each local group was responsible for its own economy. (And
within that group, extended families often operated as independent
economic units) One group might find itself running short of meat
and decide to go into Mexico—or Sonoita—to steal cattle. Another
local group living nearby might not need to be involved. The second
group might not, and probably would not, know of the raid until
after it was over and socializing between the two groups led to
storytelling. (The Chiricahuas distinguished between raiding and
war. The object of a raid was plunder; the object of war was to attack
and kill the enemy. War parties were therefore larger and would be
combinations of several local groups, and sometimes other bands.
Raids would involve one local group, as a general rule. Raids were
motivated by economics, war parties usually by revenge.)

Cochise was unusual because he was ultimately the leader not only of his extended family and his local group but also of his entire band, the Chokonen. This was strictly the result of his force of character and his success as a warrior; it was power that he acquired over time.* But in most cases, the basic social and military structure was the local group, each of which had its own leader. And even when he was the acknowledged chief of his band, Cochise did have subordinate "captains" who looked after their individual local groups.

To an outsider trying to make sense of Apache behavior, trying to make agreements or treaties, trying to assign responsibility for a raid, trying to decide who was in charge, this social organization would be a bewildering maze. For a white person, especially a soldier, who was used to hierarchical organizations, the Chiricahua society would seem strangely inverted. There was little command and control. True, there were chiefs, but they served at the local group level, by and large. And their authority was moral rather than official. So instead of a vertical organization, the Chiricahuas were mostly structured horizontally; decentralized rather than centralized.

Ironically, this organization—or, to the white man's eyes, disorganization—helped lead to the incident in Apache Pass, for a soldier like Bascom would not have understood or, more likely, not have believed that such an arrangement was possible. All his instincts would have told him that someone must be at the top of the pyramid, that someone must have ordered the raid on Ward's ranch. Cochise was a well-known name among all Apaches at this time, known to be a chief, and therefore Bascom must have thought he was behind the Ward raid, regardless of what he said. In Bascom's world, junior officers did not take it upon themselves

---

* At the time of the Bascom incident, Cochise was only one of several leaders within the band; his broader political power developed as a result of the subsequent war with the whites.

to initiate much of anything; they needed orders from a senior. To the white man and the Mexican, Apaches were members of a consolidated, homogeneous group, regardless of their geographical dispersion, which was regarded, rightly, as a necessary concession to scarce resources. And such a group, a tribe, must have had an organization in which some people were in charge, which by definition implied a hierarchy. But the various tribes called Apache didn't even refer to themselves that way. "Apache" was based on a Zuni word meaning "enemy."[5] To themselves they were *inde*, the people. It was a generic word, as in "human beings." But they thought of themselves, identified themselves, as members of a particular band and from the geography of the local group, as in "People of the Mora Mountain." To them, there was no such thing as the Apache tribe. (Indeed, there was enduring enmity between and among several of the tribes within the Apache language family.) This decentralization was a reasonable response to their environment, a response that they had evolved over the centuries. And it also made sense from a military point of view. Small groups that were highly mobile were more difficult to find and attack.

The tendency to lump all Apaches together was responsible for a number of tragedies, because the Mexican army and later the U.S. Army would attack local groups that might have been innocent of a particular raid (though it was unlikely that they had clean hands in general). And the Apaches treated the Mexicans and later the whites in exactly the same way. Guilt was assigned by tribe or nationality, not by fact. Sometimes the adversaries got it right, of course, and guilty parties on both sides of the border were attacked and punished. But more often, generic enemies were substituted for the actual guilty parties. When revenge was the object, anyone at all would do.

When a brave warrior is killed, the men go out for about three Mexicans. They bring them back for the

women to kill in revenge. The women ride at them on
horseback, armed with spears.[6]

—Anonymous Apache warrior
quoted by Morris Opler

The Chiricahuas and their related Apache tribes abhorred Mexicans. They had been at war with them for as long as people could remember, and it was pitiless war to the knife. Why was it so?

It seems fair to say that their hatred had nothing to do with race, since the villages the Apaches attacked and the ranchos they destroyed were inhabited mostly by Indians like themselves—different tribes, but similar racial characteristics. (In the middle of the nineteenth century, the population of Mexico was seven million, of whom four million were Indians, two million mestizos, or mixed blood, and only one million pure Spanish.)[7] It seems unlikely that the Apaches thought of anyone in racial terms as we understand them—until the coming of the white man, that is. To the Chiricahua, Mexicans of any color were legitimate targets. They hated them for their political allegiance, for the fact that they were there, and for their shared history.

Especially their history. Relations between Apaches and Mexicans involved not only attack and counterattack but capture and slavery. And it seems reasonable to think that when it came to slavery, the Spanish started it.

From the earliest times, the Spanish introduced the *encomienda* system throughout their colonies in the New World. It was basically a form of feudalism in which a Spanish settler was granted the use of all the Indians within a certain area. The settler or Patron was responsible for the education and, with the help of Spanish priests in the missions, the spiritual conversion of these Indians. In return, the Indians were to provide labor for the ranches, farms, and mines. This seems rather a one-sided bargain, but the combination of the Bible and the sword made it work. "As in the times of Abraham, the peons and workers born on the haciendas belong to them and are bartered or claimed or exchanged or sold and inherited as are herds, tools and land," according to Mexican historian Enrique Krauze.[8]

There was a parallel system called *repartimiento* under which Indian villages in Mexico were required to provide a certain number of weeks of labor—in return for essentially nothing. While these systems worked reasonably well with the docile tribes, the northern tribes living in the mountains would have none of it. As more and more silver was discovered in the mountains to the north, more and more labor was needed. At first the Spanish tried importing Indians from the south but gradually the supply dwindled, and the Spanish army started looking at the intractable tribes along what is today's border. The Spanish knew or quickly learned that these Indians could not be converted to Catholicism and thereby kept in line, so they decided that attacking them and forcing them into slavery was the next best idea. It would solve not only the labor problem but also, by definition, reduce the Indians' ability to wage war. The Spanish allied themselves with some tribes who would act as their agents in the capture of hostile tribesmen. In this way, a system of slave trading gradually grew up, with some tribes attacking others for trade, while the Spanish continued raiding for their own accounts. The system thereby pitted one tribe against another and distracted at least some of them from attacking Mexico.[9]

The Apaches were not excluded from these attacks. Consequently, the Apaches retaliated, and a vicious cycle of raiding and warfare began. Captain John Gregory Bourke says: ". . . the Apaches resolved upon a war of extermination upon the Spaniards when they learned that all their people taken captive by the king's forces had been driven off, to die a lingering death upon the sugar plantations of Cuba or in the mines of Guanaxuato."[10] (Guanaxuato is a state located in central Mexico that was rich in gold, silver, and copper mines.)

Not surprisingly, Indian reprisals led to escalating military attacks against the Apaches and their sometime allies, the Navajos. There were periods of uneasy peace during which the Mexican government switched strategies and tried to buy off the Indians with rations. But this sort of peace never lasted. Even if one local group wanted to live peacefully and draw rations from the Mexicans, another might be in a fighting mood. No one was empowered to make peace for all the Chiricahuas.

During periods of strife, the Mexican government (meaning the governor of a state) would call for volunteer companies to conduct expeditions and, rather than paying the men, offer to let them keep any plunder they captured—cattle, sheep, horses, captives. That resulted in gangs of mercenary or freelance raiders.

The Apaches were not the only tribe hit by organized slavers. The Navajos were also repeatedly attacked. The stolen children of both tribes were baptized and raised as Mexicans, and it is their baptismal records that give some indication of the scope of the trade: "The decade of the 1820s witnessed numerous sanctioned and clandestine slaving expeditions against the Navajo; and there are over two hundred and fifty recorded baptisms of Navajo captives for this period. If entries in ecclesiastical documents identified those captives listed only as 'Indians,' this total would undoubtedly be doubled."[11]

Most of those other captives would have been Apaches. (In 1865 a U.S. government survey of Indian slavery in New Mexico concluded that there were twelve hundred Indian slaves: "They were held by all classes of citizens; however, the most were possessed by people of ease and influence who have in some instances upwards of a dozen.")[12]

In summarizing his findings, this same government official wrote: "The Indian is endowed with the same attributes of justice, love, and affection that pertains [sic] to the civilized world—and when robbed of his children, he cannot but experience the deepest sorrow—added to this loss, the reflection that those children are beyond his reach, and guided by his untutored sense of wrong, the Indian is speedily nerved to brave his life against the enemy; and then his deeds are characterized by the most brutal atrocities that man can describe or the mind conceive."[13]

It was the most vicious of cycles, and it lasted well past the American acquisition of the Southwest. In 1864, the newly appointed governor of the New Mexico Territory, Henry Connelly, issued a proclamation outlawing civilian expeditions aimed at capturing Indians. The proclamation concluded with: "It is proper in this connection to warn the people against further traffic in captive Indians. The laws of the country as well as those of justice and humanity positively forbid such traffic. Measures are now being taken by the Department of the Interior to have all Indians surrendered who have been sold into slavery, and the people have this timely warning to refrain at once from any such traffic in Indian captives as has heretofore been practiced among them."[14]

No one paid attention to this. Besides, it was next to impossible to identify Indian children who had been baptized, given Christian names, and raised by Mexican families.

Given this history—which began in the sixteenth century in Mexico—it seems reasonable to assume that the bitter enmity between the Apaches and Mexico was at least the indirect result—if not the direct result—of Spanish slave trading. There is a grim irony in the fact that the Apaches would come to benefit from these same markets, selling captured Mexican women and children to New Mexican residents and American traders who would come into New Mexico to buy captives for distribution into regions beyond the Southwest.

After a while, though, slavery became so widespread and the animosity so deep-seated that no excuse was needed for either side to engage in hostilities. The antagonism was intensified by two incidents involving both Mexicans and Americans—incidents that became part of tribal history and initiated the suspicions the Chiricahuas were beginning to feel about the whites.

In 1837, a group of Chiricahuas raided deep into Mexico. They attacked a ranch thirty miles north of Moctezuma (which is roughly two hundred air miles south of today's border), killed several men, captured some women and children and a herd of mules, and then retreated north to their camping grounds in the mountains of southwestern New Mexico. (The raid amply demonstrates how far into Mexico the Chiricahuas and other Apache tribes would penetrate, the distances they were willing and able to travel.) Soon after the raid, a party of American traders arrived from Missouri looking to buy mules, but there were none available because of the numerous Apache raids in the area. The Missouri men met with John Johnson, an American who lived in Sonora, and together they got permission from the governor to follow the raiders and retrieve the mules. Their compensation would be half the recovered stock. Johnson's party consisted of seventeen Missouri men and five Mexicans. They traveled north to Fronteras and conferred with the local military commander, who advised them not to continue, since their party was so small. But Johnson was determined, so the commander shrugged and perhaps salved his conscience by lending Johnson a swivel gun—a small cannon.

Johnson's party made contact with the Chiricahua in the Animas Mountains of New Mexico. Johnson bought a Mexican woman captive and then offered to exchange some trade goods in return for the stolen mules. Two days of amicable trading passed, but on the third day, when the Apaches came into camp and while they were still mounted and getting ready to trade, Johnson fired the swivel gun, which was loaded with primitive grapeshot—scraps of metal and chain. The Missouri men also opened fire with their rifles (the five Mexicans had left before this incident), and twenty Apaches were killed.

The way the story is traditionally told, the swivel gun did most of the damage, but this is impossible. A swivel gun generally has a caliber of one inch to perhaps one and a half inches. It could not possibly contain enough shot to hit twenty men who were reported to be still mounted. And even if it could, the pattern of shot would not be wide enough to encompass twenty Apaches. Further, scraps of metal when fired will fly erratically because of their uneven shapes. What's more, the Apaches' horses would have absorbed much of the shot. But there were undoubtedly twenty bodies when it was over, which suggests that the Missouri men and Johnson did not merely "finish off" the wounded but actually opened fire at the same time. That means they would have been arranged in a loose semicircle to avoid hitting each other in the melee. They would have known that black powder smoke would obscure the field immediately, that horses would be rearing. So the initial firing had to be simultaneous—cannon and rifles together—in order to make sure of targets. The operation had to be planned carefully. It's odd that the Apaches did not suspect something or notice the formation, if there was one. It's possible that the Apaches were shot from ambush as they arrived at the trading site. Anyone planning such a thing would probably think of that as the first option. In any case, after two days of friendly trading, perhaps the Apaches' guard was down—unusual, but possible. Whiskey had been involved in the trading, so that may have accounted for their inattention.

All of this was, of course, academic to the survivors who escaped to tell the tale. The Americans left the bodies on the field and returned to Mexico, so that when the survivors came back to the scene they could see that the three principal chiefs involved in the trading had been scalped. The story goes that one of those who did escape the carnage was Mangas Coloradas, Cochise's future father-in-law.[15] (This was reported by Lieutenant William Emory, who met Mangas when the army of the west traveled through Mangas's territory and heard the story from Mangas himself.)

Not surprisingly, there are many different versions of the Johnson story. In one, the captive woman Johnson bought warned him that the Apaches intended to attack him. In another, she said she knew nothing about it, having been a captive for such a short time; she did not understand their language and had no way of learning their plans. In still another, Johnson said he detected signs of impending trouble and struck before being struck. We can safely assume that Johnson's instincts about such things were at least somewhat reliable. He could not have lived where and how he lived without developing some nose for danger. Finally, there is the Chiricahua version in which the peaceful, unsuspecting warriors were killed by stealth while standing (not mounted) around a barrel of flour or pinole. And while the Apaches had no legitimate grievance when their favorite tactics—surprise and ambush—were used against them, that irony was irrelevant to them.

What actually happened is unknowable and, in a very real sense, insignificant. The only story that mattered was the story the Apaches told themselves. Only the lore that was passed from band to band, local group to local group, extended family to its members, mattered. And the underlying message of that story was that the white man, like his Mexican patron, was treacherous. It's important to remember that the Chiricahua warriors who were killed had just returned from a raid into Mexico in which they killed several men, kidnapped women and children, and stole the mules they were trading with Johnson. The warriors were hardly innocent victims. That, of course, meant nothing to the outraged survivors.

Twenty-two trappers on the upper Gila paid the immediate price for Johnson's work. Trappers tended to be solitary characters, so the Chiricahua probably killed them one by one. Then they attacked a wagon train on the Camino Real and killed the twelve teamsters and traders.[16] Afterward the Chiricahuas turned their attention to Mexico.

During periods of particular strife between the Mexican government and the Apaches, mercenary gangs could make a living by bringing in Apache scalps in return for government bounties— one hundred pesos for a warrior, fifty for a woman, twenty-five for a child.[17] Of course, there never was a government official who could tell the difference between an Apache scalp and that of any other Indian or any Mexican. Or the difference between those of a man and a woman and a child, for that matter. So scalp hunters could attack even peaceful tribes or Mexican peons. It was much safer, and no one knew the difference. Anyone loathsome enough to engage in the business of scalp bounties was unconcerned about where or how he got his one hundred pesos' worth of human hair. And killing peons or peaceful Indians was far less dangerous than going after the real thing.

James Kirker was an immigrant Irishman and a scalp hunter to whom the Mexican government in Chihuahua turned to help deal with Apache raiders. Following the Johnson massacre, the Chirica-huas had stepped up their attacks in Mexico. The size and severity of the attacks looked more like war parties, rather than simple raids for plunder. Villages along the border were terrorized. People were afraid to go to their fields, and harvests suffered. Geronimo told the story of an attack on a village in which the Chiricahua waited until Sunday morning, when all the villagers were in church, and then barricaded the doors and dropped a flaming chili bomb through a hole in the ceiling (a chili bomb was a mixture of ground peppers and soft wood that gave off noxious vapors when ignited). All the Mexicans died from suffocation or from the fire started when the chili bomb exploded. The Chiricahua then went through all the houses, took what they wanted, rounded up all the horses and cattle, and returned home. This attack was in retaliation, because the Mexicans had captured some Chiricahua women, whom the raiders were able to free from prison.[18]

This raid was typical of the attacks and counterattacks along the border. In exasperation, the governor of Chihuahua hired Kirker to hunt down and kill Apaches. Kirker was familiar with the Chirica-huas, because he had been trading with them at the Santa Rita del Cobre site—one of the illicit markets to which Apaches brought Mexican plunder to trade for weapons, food, and whiskey. It was even reported that Kirker once went on a raid with the Chirica-huas. The governor canceled his contract in 1840 during one of those on-again, off-again peaceful interludes. But he hired Kirker again five years later, and in one of the most infamous incidents in Apache history, Kirker lured nearly one hundred and thirty Chiricahuas—men, women, and children—to a trading session in the Mexican town of Galeana. Once again, whiskey was involved and the Chiricahuas—the adults, at any rate—got drunk. When they had all passed out, Kirker and the citizens of Galeana beat their brains out with clubs. They then scalped them all and sent the scalps to Chihuahua City, where they were put on display. It is possible that Cochise's father was one of the victims.[19]

All things considered, it's little wonder then that the Apaches hated Mexicans. Or that they were developing a deepening distrust of white men. Kirker reminds one of Captain John Cremony's remark that "Arizona and New Mexico were cursed by the presence of two or three hundred of the most infamous scoundrels it is possible to conceive."* There were other peaceful settlers coming into the territory too. But the Chiricahuas were not inclined to draw nice distinctions. A white man was a white man, just as a Mexican was a Mexican.

---

* Lieutenant Emory, who traveled with General Kearny, was later assigned to survey the border after the Treaty of Guadalupe Hidalgo. The survey at the juncture of the Gila and Colorado was hampered by the presence of the Glanton gang, notorious scalp hunters and bandits. Glanton's depredations became the basis of Cormac McCarthy's novel, *Blood Meridian*.

Chapter Four

MINERS AT THE TIP OF THE SPEAR

We were stark mad with excitement—drunk with happiness—smothered under mountains of prospective wealth—arrogantly compassionate toward the plodding millions who knew naught of our marvelous canyon—but our credit was not good at the grocer's.
—Mark Twain, *Roughing It*

IN THE POPULAR IMAGINATION, THE WEST WAS SETTLED MOSTLY BY ranchers and homesteaders who fought the Indians with the help of the cavalry, who, depending on one's particular orthodoxy, were underpaid but gallant cavaliers or homicidal Indian haters, while the Indians were either mostly harmless, wandering philosophers or bloodthirsty savages. Somehow the real story—the less glamorous story of mining—gets overlooked. Consider the legends and stories surrounding Tombstone, Arizona—the Earps versus the Clantons at the O.K. Corral; John Clum and his newspaper, the *Tombstone Epitaph*; prostitutes in the Bird Cage Theatre; gamblers in the Crystal Palace Saloon. All of it is true, of course. But there never would have been a Tombstone if not for a lone prospector who discovered silver in the surrounding hills. No one would have otherwise settled in that inhospitable desert. (Indeed, the prospector, Ed Schieffelin, named the area Tombstone because an army officer had told him all he would find in the area was his grave, courtesy of the Apaches.) As was often the case in the West, the discovery of precious metals started the process of development.

Of course, the most dramatic case was California.

In an epic example of unlucky timing, Mexico agreed to the terms of the Treaty of Guadalupe Hidalgo a week after gold was discovered at Sutter's Mill, California. The treaty was a formal recognition of reality, because California was already occupied by the U.S. forces. Still, Santa Anna, Mexico's once and future president, must have reflected ruefully on the sequence of events.

Gold in California started a mass migration. Many hopeful gold seekers went by ship around Cape Horn; some went by ship to Panama, by canoe across the Isthmus and down a jungle river, to a further stretch of jungle paths on mule back, and finally to another ship heading north to California. But just as many went overland; it was faster. They would take a steamboat to Fort Leavenworth. From there, some would take the most direct route, across the Rockies. But others chose the southern route where the winter weather was not a problem. They would follow the Santa Fe Trail to southern New Mexico, turn west, and go through the Chiricahua country, following the Gila River trail, essentially the same trail blazed by Kearny first and then by the Mormon Battalion. (The Mormon Battalion, however, followed a more southerly route in Arizona, because they were burdened with wagons, unlike Kearny's dragoons. They would therefore have followed the desert floors between mountain ranges. It's unlikely that any of them went through Apache Pass, but certainly they passed close by. Similarly, gold-seeking Argonauts traveling in wagon trains would follow the Mormon Battalion's route.)

The Chiricahua and related Apache tribes must have initially regarded this migration as their own kind of bonanza, for here were hundreds and thousands of gold seekers plodding along with their wagons and animals, all bent on passing through, few wishing to stay, but all offering rich opportunities for plunder. An estimated thirty thousand Argonauts used the Gila River and southern trails during the Gold Rush. Some never made it. They either succumbed to the rigors of the journey or to the marksmanship of the Apaches.

Many, if not most, of the Argonauts who did make it to California found only disappointment. Much of the gold in California was discovered through placer mining. Finding the small grains that had washed down into alluvial deposits in and alongside streams could be as simple as panning or as difficult as washing the dirt in sluice boxes, so that the heavier gold particles would become separated from the soil. This seemed an easy enough matter; anyone with energy and a shovel could get rich. So it was believed. As a result, most of the Argonauts were not sophisticated mining engineers but rather a diverse cast of amateur dreamers and adventurers. Nor were they all Americans. People came from as far away as Australia and China to try their luck. Ultimately some three hundred thousand miners— and camp followers—came to California.

This horde of hopefuls strained the delicate resources of the territory to the limit and beyond. William Emory, now stationed in Southern California with the commission assigned to draw the new border between Mexico and the U.S., wrote: "Most of the resources of the country have been drawn to the gold miners; inferior horses sell here, at this distance from the miners, at 150 and 200 dollars, and there is not a mule to be had. . . . The cultivation of the rancherias has been totally neglected in the last year, and there is no grain to be had in this vicinity, so that the animals must depend for subsistence on grass and cannot, on that food, be put in condition to move over a large extent of barren country like that along the line of our operations."[1]

Everyone, it seemed, was headed for the gold fields. In the army, desertions were commonplace. Who wanted to be a low-paid soldier living in wretched conditions when there was gold waiting to be picked up off the ground? "The lure of the mines made it impossible to keep the companies at more than skeleton strength," writes historian Robert Utley, "indeed they were laden with men who had enlisted with the intention of deserting as soon as the government transported them to the gold fields. Captain Erasmus D. Keyes had a typical experience. Assigned a company of 86 newly arrived men at San Francisco, he lost two thirds within a few weeks."[2]

Some Argonauts did hit pay dirt, of course, but many quickly realized that the best way to take advantage of the situation was to throw away the shovel and turn to providing services to the miners who were too stubborn to quit, and to the fresh optimists who were arriving daily. Where there is need in a free enterprise system, there is usually a quick response from agile entrepreneurs. Stage lines and roads rapidly developed to get the miners to the gold fields. Steamboats were built to carry miners up the Sacramento River. Express companies (such as Wells Fargo) took charge of the miners' gold and carried it to the newly established banks. Merchants came too (Levi Strauss, for one), and there quickly followed all the blessings and curses of civilization—newspapers, saloons, doctors, lawyers to straighten out claims and titles, gamblers and harlots, hardware and feed stores, grocers, lawmen and bandits, and soldiers to protect the exploding population from the threat of Indian attack—although the grotesque savagery of the white emigrants toward the local Indians suggests that the army was protecting the wrong people. On the other hand, the army's limited (and dwindling) manpower resources made either job difficult, if not impossible.

Throughout the West, the spread of white American culture often began this way—with the miners. The process was just compressed and accelerated in California because of the nature and richness of the gold find. Even that most iconic of western American events—the cattle drive—owes something to the miners; in 1866 Nelson Story drove three thousand longhorns from Texas to Montana. It was the first long-range cattle drive, and Story's intended markets were the booming mining towns.*

That quintessential American, Mark Twain, personifies this process. After a brief and inglorious two-week stint with the Confederate army, Twain and his brother took a stagecoach west to Nevada, where Twain soon got the gold fever and tried his hand in the mines near Virginia City. An amateur at this and any other business he ever tried, he soon learned that silver and gold nuggets were not to be picked up off the ground; finding the stuff involved backbreaking labor with a shovel. He then decided that it might be easier to become rich quick by trading leases and mining claims in the local stock market. And when those speculations failed, he gratefully accepted a job as city editor at the local newspaper, the Virginia City, Nevada, *Territorial Enterprise* for twenty-five dollars a week. His day sometimes started with a visit to the local saloon (Bret Harte once remarked upon Twain's "bright smile greeting the morning bartender"), after which he would wander around town collecting news and, when there wasn't much going on, making it up.

It might seem odd that these fledgling towns, some mere mining camps, would want or support a newspaper. But the economics of the business were pretty simple—an itinerant printer would arrive in a wagon with his press, which generally cost no more than $200, set up shop, and begin issuing his paper. (During the Gold Rush in California, San Francisco became the banking and commercial center and as such supported as many as twelve daily newspapers.)[3] He would survive on printing legal notices, which were required to perfect the many mining claims, and as the town grew, advertisements from the merchants as well as subscriptions. If the town did not grow (because the mines became exhausted), he would pack up his press and head for the next boomtown and start again.

---

* Readers of *Lonesome Dove* will recognize some similarities in the stories.

Admirers of Mark Twain who wonder how he developed his pitch-perfect voice and ironic style might have a look at these frontier newspapers. "The Celebrated Jumping Frog of Calaveras County," though published later in 1865, is a good example of the frontier style. No one believed it, but most appreciated it.

The papers were also highly opinionated, especially when reviewing rival papers. Politics were as contentious then as they are now—more so, really, though that seems hard to believe—and men then were better armed. As Ambrose Bierce wrote, "There is no recorded instance of punishment for shooting a newspaper man. The restrictions of the game laws do not apply to this class of game. The newspaperman is a bird that is always in season."[4]

But these newspapers were part of the process of development—perhaps of empire—for it was in their interest, and in the interest of the town promoters, to sing the praises of the towns and the richness of the nearby mines. In this way, new immigrants could be enticed, and new real estate and town lots could be sold. "Booming"—that is, aggressive promotion of a particular town—became one of the newspapers' main functions.

There was also a hunger for the news among the miners. The local papers subscribed to fledgling news services from back East and therefore helped to reassure the miners' sense that they were not really on the edges of civilization, appearances notwithstanding. At the end of a day of shoveling dirt into a sluice box, not every miner wanted to go into a canvas-walled saloon complete with gamblers and "soiled doves." Some had left families to make their fortunes, and after twelve hours of backbreaking labor, they needed something to assuage their loneliness, perhaps some news from home.

There was a corresponding hunger for the mail from the East. Getting the mail to the West was a major logistical problem. Aside from news from home, there was an obvious need for regular business correspondence between the newly developing commercial interests in California and the centers of law and capital in the East.

Such things moved by paper then. (The transcontinental telegraph was not completed until October 1861.) As with the Argonauts, some mail moved by ship—a slow and hazardous process whether around Cape Horn or over the Panama Isthmus.* A faster overland route was needed. The question became, what was the best route?

The mail problem amplified the arguments in Congress about how best to tie the two sections of the country together. (California was admitted as a free state in 1850—quick work by Congress primarily because of the Gold Rush and the subsequent population explosion.) The plan was ultimately to build the transcontinental railroad, although in the meantime, mail and passenger service would have to rely on stagecoaches. But the discussion over the best route was freighted with toxic politics. Southern sympathizers pointed out the unmistakable difficulty of winter weather through the Rockies. Northerners, who understood that the Southerners were trying to expand the economy of the South and extend slavery into the new territories, argued that the southern route was too long, since its proposed terminus was San Diego—far from the gold fields and developing cities of the North.

By 1853, Jefferson Davis was secretary of war. As a Mississippian, he naturally favored a southern route, but the old Gila Trail was too rugged for wagons, let alone railroad construction. He therefore lobbied President Franklin Pierce to acquire more territory from Mexico, this time by purchase. Pierce was sympathetic and commissioned James Gadsden, a South Carolinian, to negotiate with Mexico to buy a section of land below the Gila River border. This land, although veined by mountain ranges, also had wide, flat valleys that could accommodate wagons and ultimately a railroad.

---

* In 1850 then Lieutenant William Tecumseh Sherman traveled from his post in California by a steam-driven warship to Panama, across the Isthmus, where he caught another steamer for New York. The trip took thirty days and was considerably faster than sailing ships could manage. Even fast clipper ships could take one hundred days going around Cape Horn.[5]

The proposed route was virtually the same the Mormon Battalion had followed. Mexico, chronically short of cash, agreed to sell the land for ten million dollars. And, as part of that agreement, Mexico released the United States from its commitments under Article Eleven—not because they wanted to, especially, but because that was one of the terms of the deal. Mexico also no doubt understood by now that the United States was not living up to the original article anyway.

The Gadsden Purchase established the final borders of today's Arizona and New Mexico.

Captain John Gregory Bourke described this latest acquisition of territory as: ". . . a region in which not only purgatory and hell, but likewise heaven, had combined to produce a bewildering kaleidoscope of all that was wonderful, weird, terrible, and awe-inspiring, with not a little that was beautiful and romantic."[6]

And in the midst of this "bewildering kaleidoscope" was the homeland of the Chiricahua Apaches, a people whom the whites would find even more "weird, terrible, and awe-inspiring" than the land itself.

The same process of Anglo development was occurring in Arizona as it had in California, but it moved more slowly, for two reasons—the nature of mining there and the Apaches. Southern Arizona, western New Mexico, and northern Sonora were well known to be rich in silver and copper and, to a lesser extent, gold. Arizona was nothing like California in richness, but it was very definitely worth developing. The Spanish had been mining precious metals since the eighteenth century. But this was hard rock mining, which meant the precious metals were encased in other rock well below the surface. Mines had to be dug, vertical and horizontal shafts carved out and supported, the ore drilled or dug out and brought to the surface, where it was crushed and then treated with a mixture of intense heat from smelters and chemicals to separate the metals from the rock. Unlike placer mining, this sort of mining required engineering know-how, capital for heavy equipment, and a large labor force. It also required easy access to wood for charcoal and building materials, water, and decent roads to haul the silver or copper to a port where it could be shipped, either for further refinement or to market. Transportation meant wagons and mules or horses. Mules and horses needed land for grazing and good water; they also needed blacksmiths and harness makers and teamsters and herdsmen. And large labor forces required housing and food, which meant that when the outbound wagons off-loaded their cargos, they would return loaded with supplies, including grain for the mules and horses, who could not subsist on grass alone and remain healthy. (The Mexican port of Guaymas was the destination for southern Arizona mines—a five-hundred-sixty-mile round-trip.)

All such rich possibilities attracted Apaches, who were less interested in precious metals than in the animals that hauled them and the supplies they carried. The Apaches were not indifferent to material wealth; they just defined it differently. But they were not at all enthusiastic about seeing the land around them being developed by these mines. It was one thing when the Forty-Niners were passing through; it was something else when these miners came and stayed.

Nor did the miners' behavior have much to recommend them. As Maj. John Sedgwick wrote in 1860: "There never was a viler set of men in the world than is congregated about these mines."[7] Sedgwick was probably talking not only about the miners but also about the inevitable collection of people—gamblers, prostitutes, thieves, and drunkards—who came to the mining camps and boomtowns immediately after the mining began.

Captain John Gregory Bourke agreed: "Not very long previous to this Arizona had received a most liberal contingent of the toughs and scalawags banished from San Francisco by the efforts of the

Vigilance Committee, and until these last had shot each other to death, or until they had been poisoned by Tucson whisky or been killed by the Apaches, Arizona's chalice was filled to the brim, and the most mendacious real estate boomer would have been unable to recommend her for an investment of capital."*[8]

But despite Bourke's analysis, capital did come.

When Child of the Waters, son of Ussen, came to the Earthland, he gave the Apaches things good for them: herbs, plants for food, and weapons. To the Indians he gave the bow and arrow, the shield, the spear, and the sling. To the White Eyes he gave the pick and shovel. It was what he gave to them that caused all the trouble. With the pick and shovel the prospectors grubbed in the body of Mother Earth for the forbidden gold and caused the mountains to dance and shake their shoulders. Mother Earth opened up and swallowed whole villages.

—Eugene Chihuahua, Apache warrior[9]

To the Apaches, the most loathsome and degraded of all occupations was mining, especially for gold. There were several facets to their uniform aversion. The first was purely practical, according to Captain John C. Cremony:

The Apaches entertain the greatest possible dread of our discoveries of mineral wealth in their country. They have experience enough to assure them that the possession

---

* Historian Dan Thrapp quotes sources that said John Ward was one of these— "a castoff from the Vigilance Committee in San Francisco, and . . . in all respects a worthless character."[10] Vigilance Committees, of course, were citizen posses, also known as vigilantes.

of lucre is the great incentive among us to stimulate what is termed "enterprise." They know and feel that wherever mineral wealth exists to such an extent as to render it available, the white man fastens upon it with ineradicable tenacity. The massacre of the pioneer set does not deter another company from experimenting in the same engaging field. These localities are always rendered more valuable by the proximity of wood and water, two scarce articles in Arizona. To occupy a water privilege in Arizona and New Mexico is tantamount to driving the Indians from their most cherished possessions and infuriates them to the utmost extent. If one deprives them of their ill-gotten plunder, he is regarded as an outrageous robber; but should he seize upon one of their few water springs, he is rated a common and dangerous enemy, whose destruction it is the duty of all the tribe to compass.[11]

Obviously, competition for scarce resources has always been a cause of conflict. When the Apaches saw white miners co-opting and endangering their water sources, cutting down trees to turn into charcoal for their smelters, making roads through the mountains in order to ship ore for refinement, they were initially appalled, then outraged, and, finally, driven to attack these interlopers.

There was also an aesthetic and religious component to the Apaches' detestation of mining and miners. Apaches were a mountain-dwelling people. Many of their guiding spirits came in the form of Mountain People, or "gan." These were supernatural beings who lived nearby and regularly interacted with the Apaches' daily life. Their main role was to protect the people and the tribal lands, and they were associated with specific mountains, not just a generalized concept. (The parallel to the Olympic gods and goddesses, especially in Homer's epics, is hard to overlook; it is, in fact, just one of many parallels.) These gan were real beings to the Apaches and to see their homeland being despoiled by grubbing miners was not only outrageous but dangerous, for no one could say how these spirits would react. (Apaches attributed earthquakes to gan who were displeased.) By and large, the Mountain People were benign and helpful, but they could turn against the people if their proscriptions were violated. It was always difficult for some whites to understand the Apaches' devotion to a specific locality; after all, they had no concept of private property, at least not private real estate. But the mountains were the homes of their spirits. To be forced to leave would be a religious catastrophe. Indeed, banishment of an individual warrior who transgressed badly was considered the worst possible punishment: "To us the worst crime of which a man can be guilty is betraying his people," said Daklugie. "For that he could be banished, and to Apaches that is worse punishment than death. To be driven from one's family, tribe and country is terrible."[12] Though they had no permanent homes and wandered from camp to camp, Apaches wandered within a well-understood region, always near their mountains and their guardian spirits.[*]

There was a spiritual objection especially to the mining of gold. The Apaches considered gold to be sacred to Ussen, their primary god, life giver. Digging for it was forbidden. "At first there were few white people, and they were all going west; then, as wise old Nana knew, the lure of gold discovered far to our west . . . brought them in hordes," Daklugie said. "Though most of them went on, some stayed to burrow in Mother Earth for the ore sacred to Ussen. Nana was right in thinking that gold was to bring our extermination."[13]

Apache men would never have been miners even if there had been no environmental or religious objections to it. Said Apache Eugene Chihuahua "It was not intended by Ussen that Apache warriors

---

[*]   In this context, the final removal of the Chiricahuas to Florida in 1886 is even sadder.

work."[14] Since the Chiricahuas did not farm, there was very little manual labor to be done, and what was done was done by the women and children—building shelters, cutting and collecting wood for the camp, gathering piñon nuts and acorns, chopping mescal for baking. An adult man was a fighter and a hunter; those were the only proper occupations. He would no more have thought of doing manual labor than an English duke would have considered sweeping his own stables. Some whites mistook this for laziness. On the contrary, it was pride. And it was one more reason the Apaches looked down upon the ragged, dirty miners who spent their days not only despoiling the mountains but also besmirching themselves. And many of these miners were worthy of contempt. "People with all that hair were repulsive to us—they looked too much like bears," said Daklugie.[15] They were particularly repulsed by bald miners with beards. Such men represented an inversion of the natural order, both in appearance and behavior.

And when the lord thy God shall deliver them before thee, thou shalt smite them and utterly destroy them; thou shalt make no covenant with them, nor show mercy unto them.

—Deuteronomy 7:2

White Americans, of course, had no such prejudices against digging for precious metals. Entrepreneurship and enterprise were twin virtues.

One such entrepreneur was Sylvester Mowry. Mowry graduated from West Point in 1852 and served in California, the Northwest (surveying the Columbia River for railroad routes), and later in Salt Lake City during troubles with the Mormons. Then he was sent to Fort Yuma, a particularly desolate post in the desert along the Colorado River. (An old army joke tells the story of a sinful soldier who died and went to hell, whereupon he sent back for his blankets, because after his experience at Fort Yuma, the infernal regions were too chilly for him.) After Yuma, Mowry was posted to Fort Buchanan, where he served until he resigned his commission in July 1858. He moved to Tubac, which was growing as a result of an influx of Anglo mining interests. There he got into a dispute over mining issues with Edward Cross, the editor of Arizona's first newspaper, the *Daily Arizonian*. Heated letters were exchanged and reprinted as far away as the eastern press. Finally, Mowry lost all patience and challenged Cross to a duel. They faced each other with rifles at forty yards in the dusty plaza of Tubac. Neither man was injured, though, because after each had fired two (some say three) shots, Cross dropped his rifle and Mowry ceased firing, as one would expect from a gentleman and graduate of the Military Academy. (This is just one more incident that demonstrates how frontier editors needed to be prepared to back up their sometimes slanderous editorials with something more than additional words.) It's hard to believe the men could miss with rifles at forty yards, let alone miss twice each. This suggests that the code duello in this case did not preclude dodging and taking cover. But when it was all over, both men, no doubt relieved to be intact, shook hands and opened a barrel of whiskey to share with the crowd of onlookers.[16]

Mowry was an original "boomer" for Arizona and as such he was a firm supporter of the proposed southern route for the railroad. This route essentially followed the thirty-second parallel through the heart of the Gadsden Purchase. Other proposed routes followed the thirty-fifth, thirty-eighth, forty-first, and forty-seventh parallels. By 1859, all of these routes had been surveyed by the army engineers, and it's worth noting that the two officers who did the surveys of the thirty-second and thirty-fifth routes were a lieutenant and a captain—in other words, junior officers. That is an indication of the quality of the engineering education they received (like Emory, earlier) and the kind of responsibilities a junior officer was expected to handle. In his 1859 address to the Senate, Jefferson Davis (by then a senator) staunchly defended the most southerly route as the least expensive to build and most practical to operate through all seasons. As proof, he could point to the Butterfield Overland Mail stagecoach line that had been up and running since the year before, along the same route.

Mowry saw the prospects of wealth from the region's mining potential. In fact, there had been mines in the area for decades, operated by the Mexicans. One such was the Patagonia Mine in the mountains a few miles south of John Ward's ranch. Mowry bought the mine in 1860 and renamed it after himself.

A few years later, a famous traveler, J. Ross Browne, described the Mowry Mine in an article in *Harper's*:

> Approaching these mines we found indications of life and industry. Cords of wood lay piled up on the wayside; the sound of the axe reverberated from hill to hill; the smoke of many charcoal pits filled the air; the teamsters with heavily loaded wagons were working their way over the rugged trails and by-paths. . . . A more picturesque or cheering view I had rarely seen. Down in the valley of several hundred acres almost embosomed in the trees, stand the reduction works, storehouses and peon quarters. Smoke rose in curling clouds from the main chimney, which stands like an obelisk in the center of the mill, and sulphurous vapors whirled up from the long row of smelting furnaces in the rear. The busy hum of the steam engine and fly wheels fell with a lively effect on the ear; the broad smooth plaza in front of the works was dotted with wagons discharging their freight of wood and ore. . . .[17]

From today's more environmentally sensitive perspective, one would almost suspect that Browne was being ironic. Hardly. His rhapsodic description perfectly reflected the nineteenth-century view of progress. Change. Development. The white American view, that is. The Apaches looking at the same scene would have had different opinions. Although they would have appreciated the opportunities presented by those wagons and mules, this sort of change was precisely what they did not want—and in fact considered impious.

Mowry and his mine represented the commonly accepted nineteenth-century American, and indeed European, view that development, industry, and productivity were unmistakable signs of an advanced civilization. It was thought that all societies went through clearly defined stages. General Nelson Miles spoke for the majority of white opinion when he said, "[The] history of nearly every race that has advanced from barbarism to civilization has been through the stages of the hunter, the herdsman, the agriculturalist—and [has] finally reached those of commerce, mechanics and the higher arts."[18] Others theorized that the stages of development were from primitive to savage and ultimately to civilized. Regardless of minor differences in terminology, most theorists believed that these progressive steps were inevitable, like evolution, although some societies moved more slowly than others. Thus, the word "savage" (and the French *sauvage*), which had long been attached to all North American Indians, referred not so much to the Indian's behavior as to his state of development. Of course, there was no small element of condescension in the term, because someone in a savage state was by definition a step behind, a step removed from civilization.

But the word was also used to describe violent behaviors. Cremony refers to one Apache as "a savage savage."[19] Both adjective and noun. Two meanings of the same word. Perhaps this is splitting hairs, since someone mired in a savage state would be expected to act savagely. On the other hand, there were many Indian tribes, such as the Pimas and Papagos, who were peacefully disposed (toward the whites) and yet would have been regarded as continuing to live in a savage state of development. And the most docile, peace-loving of tribes would still be described as "savages."

Then, too, there was the school of thought surrounding the "noble savage," which again illustrates multiple meanings for the word. John Dryden first used the line in the seventeenth century. The idea was essentially that man in the state of nature would be free of the moral and physical corruption associated with civilization and would therefore conduct himself as a kind of natural gentleman. John Pope echoed these sentiments in *An Essay on Man*:

> *Lo, the poor Indian! whose untutor'd mind*
> Sees God in clouds, or hears him in the wind;
> His soul proud Science never taught to stray
> Far as the solar walk or milky way;
> Yet simple Nature to his hope has giv'n,
> Behind the cloud-topp'd hill, a humbler heav'n;
> Some safer world in depth of woods embrac'd,
> Some happier island in the wat'ry waste,
> Where slaves once more their native land behold,
> *No fiends torment, no Christians thirst for gold!*

The concept had some adherents in the United States, such as James Fenimore Cooper, as reflected in his sympathetic portrayals of his Indian characters—some of them. But the main feature of this sentimental idea is that it was formulated by people who had no experience of actually meeting an Indian. Not many army officers who had had real contact would have trivialized and caricatured the Indians they'd met in such a way, and the more intelligent would have understood that the Apaches were living precisely as they wanted. But "Lo, the poor Indian" became a phrase of wide-spread derision among the army, and when referring to Indians in general, many officers would use the generic "Lo." Their contempt was aimed more at the sentimental eastern scribblers than at the Indians.

"Stripped of the beautiful romance with which we have been so long willing to envelope him, transferred from the inviting pages of the novelist to the localities where we are compelled to meet with him, in his native village, on the warpath and when raiding upon our frontier settlements and lines of travel, the Indian forfeits his claim to the appellation of the 'noble red man.'"[20] This was the opinion of George Custer, and many, if not most, of the regular army men would have agreed with him.

Nor were the officers alone in their contempt for the concept. Charles Dickens said this: "To come to the point at once, I beg to say that I have not the least belief in the Noble Savage. I consider him a prodigious nuisance and an enormous superstition. . . . I don't care what he calls me. I call him a savage, and I call a savage a something highly desirable to be civilized off the face of the earth. . . . All the noble savage's wars with his fellow-savages (and he takes no pleasure in anything else) are wars of extermination—which is the best thing I know of him, and the most comfortable to my mind when I look at him. He has no moral feelings of any kind, sort, or description; and his 'mission' may be summed up as simply diabolical."[21]

Aside from the Noble Savage concept, another well-intentioned view of the Apaches, also generally from afar, was that their religion was all wrong, since it was not Christianity. Converting them to the true faith would solve all the problems. Cremony notes with a smile how earnest Christians "[urge us to] . . . take the red man by the hand as [we] have done to his negro brother, and guide him gently, kindly toward a better state in this world and the hope of salvation hereafter. I admit that these are very persuasive and forcible arguments; but, reverend sir, the red man absolutely refuses to come. He disdains to take my hand; he flouts my offered sympathy, and feels indignant at my presumption in proffering him my aid to improve his condition. He conceives himself not only my equal, but decidedly my superior. He desires only to be let alone. His forefathers lived well enough without our officious services, and he intends to do likewise."[22]

None other than William T. Sherman added his perspective on the subject: "There are two classes of people, one demanding the utter extinction of the Indians and the other full of love for their conversion to civilization and Christianity. Unfortunately, the army stands between and gets cuffs from both sides."[23]

Two cultures with two very different views of each other. The whites believed that the Apaches had somehow gotten sidetracked and stuck in a state of savagery—whether noble or ignoble. The Apaches were equally sure that they had evolved a way of living that precisely met their needs; they had no use for movement or change or industry and were contemptuous of the whites who came into their territory, contemptuous of their values and their incomprehensible work ethic and appetites. The white culture thought in linear terms. Indeed, the proposed transcontinental railroad was a metaphor for the white way of thinking—movement, straight ahead, by technology and industry. So, too, was Mowry's mine— an exploitation of natural resources accomplished through hard work, capital, and entrepreneurship. The Apaches, on the other hand, viewed the mine and mining as symbols of the white man's greed and irreverence. They had no "Christian[s'] thirst for gold." The Apaches' favorite game—a game reserved for men only and for which they would gamble anything they had—was the hoop and pole, in which a player would roll a hoop and then slide a long pole after it. Where the hoop fell onto the pole determined the score. That seems to be a useful metaphor for the contact between the whites and the Apaches—for one a straight line; for the other, a circle, self-contained. In the end it was the rolling hoop that inevitably had to topple.

Despite his enthusiasm for Arizona and its prospects for development, Sylvester Mowry never got the chance to reap much in the way of profits. During the Civil War, his southern sympathies (selling lead to the Confederate militia in Arizona) resulted in his being arrested and sent to prison at Fort Yuma. Released after six months, he returned to find his mine had been confiscated by the U.S. government. It took several years for him to get control again, and by that time the mine and its equipment had been ruined by neglect and Apache raids. Mowry died in London trying to raise capital to reopen his mine. (His erstwhile adversary Cross was killed at Gettysburg, fighting for the Union.)

Mowry embodies several historical forces that led either directly or indirectly to the Bascom affair—West Point and the regular army, economic development in the Gadsden Purchase (led by mining), Fort Buchanan, and local attitudes toward the Apaches. Of these last, Mowry wrote:

> Governor Pesqueira of Sonora has offered a bounty of $100 per scalp for Apaches and a proportionate sum for animals retaken from them. This should be imitated by the authorities in Arizona. The Pima and the Papago Indians would be most valuable auxiliaries in the pursuit and massacre of these "human wolves." . . . The children of Apaches, when taken young, make good servants and are sold by the Pimas in the Territory [Arizona] and in Sonora.
>
> There is only one way to wage war against the Apaches. A steady, persistent campaign must be made, following them to their haunts—hunting them to the "fastnesses of the mountains." They must be surrounded, starved into coming in, surprised or inveigled—by white flags, or any other method, human or divine—and then put to death. If these ideas shock any weak-minded individual who thinks himself a philanthropist, I can only say that I pity without respecting his mistaken sympathy. A man might as well have sympathy for a rattlesnake or a tiger.[24]

Mowry would have been a regular visitor to see his old comrades at Fort Buchanan. The Civil War that would split up the army and destroy the fort was still more than a year away. The fort was only twenty miles or so from Mowry's mine, and he would naturally have sought out the company of like-minded men now and then. And just as likely he would have met and gotten to know the new arrivals at the post—officers like George Bascom.

Chapter Five

THE EDUCATION
OF A SOLDIER

War reflects culture. Weaponry, tactics, notions of discipline, command, logistics—all such elements of battle arise not just from the constraints of terrain, climate, and geography but also from the nature of a society's economy, politics, and sociology.

—Victor Davis Hanson[1]

IN 1858, THE YEAR GEORGE BASCOM GRADUATED FROM WEST POINT, the regular army consisted of 16,367 officers and men. It was organized into three branches: the scientific corps, the general staff, and the line. The scientific corps included the engineers, topographical engineers, and ordnance. ("Engineers" were typically civil and military engineers concerned with the construction of forts and civilian projects. "Topographical engineers" were mapmakers and surveyors.) The general staff housed the administrative functions, such as those of the adjutant general and quartermaster, and the line consisted of artillery, cavalry/dragoons, and infantry.

There was a very clear hierarchy of prestige associated with the branches of the army. The engineers and topographical engineers (the scientific corps) were considered the elite, because the engineers especially were assigned to do public projects, such as improving harbors and building roads, canals, and fortifications. These assignments obviously required the kind of intellectual ability and professional, technical skills that were in contrast to the qualities required of, for instance, an infantry officer. Officers of the scientific corps were still expected to fight in case of war (for example, Robert E. Lee in Mexico). But in peacetime their assignments tended to be in comfortable, civilized places. The line officers, on the other hand, were most likely to be sent to forts on the frontier. New officers could not always expect their assignment to the scientific corps to be permanent. Robert E. Lee was assigned to a Texas cavalry regiment after he left his job as superintendent of West Point. The ubiquitous William Emory was assigned to a regiment of cavalry in the Indian Territory after he finished surveying the Mexican border. Often these assignments were at the officer's request, based on the desire to do something different and to see some active service.* But assignment to the scientific corps was the goal of many, if not most, of the cadets. According to Lieutenant John Tidball, West Point graduate, class of 1848:

> We were taught with every breath we drew at West Point the utmost reverence for this [hierarchy]; consequently it [became] a kind of fixture in our minds that the engineers were a species of gods, next to which

---

* Emory's friend Captain John Pope wrote to him, "I can hardly congratulate you on your appointment as major in one of the cavalry regiments. Your rank in the Corps will exempt you from any of the persecutions and annoyances to which younger officers are exposed [but] your high reputation as a scientific man in the U.S. will not be increased by any such barren advancement. The service is not to your taste and you have too high a standing in the country to bury yourself in the woods."[2] Pope went on to become a general during the Civil War and the loser at Second Manassas.

came the "topogs" only a grade below but still a grade—
they were but demi-gods. The line was simply the line,
whether of horse or infantry or dragoons. For the latter
a good square seat in the saddle was deemed of more
importance than brains. These ideas were ground into
our heads with such Jesuitical persistency, I do not
believe anyone of the old regime ever entirely overcame
the influence of it.[3]

Assignments were based on a cadet's class ranking at the end
of his four years at West Point. Testifying before a government
commission looking into West Point's curriculum and procedures
in 1860, Cadet Adelbart Ames, class of 1848, said, "The effort to
stand high is prompted almost wholly by the prospect it holds out
of selecting one's own corps, and being able to enter one of the
scientific corps."[4]

There were exceptions to this widespread preference for the
scientific branch. The ever-turbulent William T. Sherman graduated sixth in his class of forty-three and yet intended to choose
the artillery in the hopes that the tensions with England over the
Maine boundaries might erupt into war: "Every person seems
anxious for it and none more so than the very persons who would
most suffer by it, the officers of the army and the corps of cadets.
But ours, I fear, arises more from selfishness than from true patriotism, for should war break out we would be commissioned and sent
into the field—at all times preferable to studying mathematics and
philosophy, and it would undoubtedly prove a better school for the
soldier than this [that is, West Point]."[5]

West Point did not provide all the officers for these various
branches of the regular army. The infantry had the highest percentage of non-West Point graduates. (For example, John Rogers
Cooke, who met Bascom in Apache Pass, was educated at Harvard,
and there were other state military schools, such as Virginia Military Institute, that produced officers.) But officers of the scientific

corps—engineers and topographical engineers—were almost entirely West Point graduates.

That is no coincidence, because from the 1830s on, the Academy's mission was explicitly to turn out engineers who could also function as soldiers when required. Not the other way around. Consequently, the curriculum was heavily weighted toward mathematics, science (chemistry, geology, and mineralogy), and engineering—civil and military. Over 70 percent of the cadet's classroom time was devoted to those subjects. What's more, these subjects had a correspondingly greater impact on a cadet's class ranking. To put it in modern terms, if two cadets had the same grade point average, with one excelling in French but doing poorly in mathematics while the other had just the opposite record, the latter would rank significantly higher. All cadets took the same course of study.

Though some might argue (and critics of the Academy did) that this heavy emphasis on mathematics and civil engineering would be entirely useless to an infantry officer facing hostile Apaches in Arizona, the Academy believed that the mental discipline a cadet gained from these courses was as important as the content of the course: ". . . if the course has been carefully taught, the reasoning power will have been strongly exercised and disciplined, and a system or habit of thought acquired, which are invaluable in the pursuit of any profession, and as desirable for the infantry or dragoon officer as for any other officer in service."[6] (This was the official written policy of the Academy's academic board.)

The unanswered question, however, was would this kind of mathematical, mental discipline in fact lead to mechanical thinking; would it retard the flexibility or adaptability of mind that an officer needed when confronting alien surroundings and unusual situations? Would an ingrained habit of reliance on formulas interfere with an officer's ability to adjust his thoughts and actions to conditions in which standard formulas and solutions did not and could not work? Professionals of the day and of more recent vintages criticized West Point's rigid adherence not only to a scientific curriculum but also to a harsh system of regimentation in which minor infractions of behavior led to demerits, which in turn affected class ranking. Historian James L. Morrison Jr. wrote, ". . . taken in totality the institution must have encouraged a mechanistic outlook. . . . Success at the military academy depended primarily on the exactitude with which a student met requirements imposed by an instructor, a textbook, or a set of regulations; initiative and imagination, if not actively penalized, were not rewarded."[7]

The underlying theme of these criticisms is that the Academy taught conformity of thought and behavior and enforced this conformity with a rigid hierarchy, not only of officers, which is expected in any army, but of customs and values. As British soldier and military historian Sir Basil Henry Liddell Hart says in his biography of William T. Sherman (who, as a cadet, performed well academically but chafed at both the course of study and the behavior expected of all cadets): ". . . [Sherman's] Grail was real soldiering, stripped of the shams and conventions which mask its face, and enable connoisseurs of buttons to pass as soldiers."[8]

Whether West Point's curriculum was the best preparation for a soldier's career may be debatable, but it certainly seems true that the idea of disciplined thinking and a scientific orientation were in line with the prevailing attitudes and accepted verities of the larger society. To place civil engineering at the top of the hierarchy at West Point reflected nothing less than the American culture's agreed-upon virtues—development, growth, expansion. After their obligatory first term as soldiers, many officers resigned their commissions to go into private industry, especially in the railroads. George McClellan was one, although he rejoined the army when the Civil War broke out.

And in answer to critics then and now, there is Winfield Scott's toast to the Academy just after the Mexican War: If not for the "science of the Military Academy . . . this army multiplied by four could not have entered the capital of Mexico."[9] At another time, he went on to say, "I give it as fixed opinion that but for our graduated cadets the war between the United States and Mexico might, and probably would, have lasted some four or five years, with, in its first half, more defeats than victories falling to our share; whereas in less than two campaigns we conquered a great country and a peace without the loss of a single battle or skirmish."[10] (Scott apparently did not consider Kearny's march to California a campaign.)

Critics aside, there is no questioning the quality of the engineering curriculum per se. Secretary of War Jefferson Davis assigned two junior officers—a lieutenant and a captain of engineers—to survey potential routes for the proposed transcontinental railroad. It was an immense responsibility, but both officers performed exceedingly well. Other officers were sent west to survey and map the vast new territories. Lieutenant William H. Emory, again, was assigned to the committee to survey the new border with Mexico after the war. He was the chief astronomer, which meant doing celestial navigation on land.

The rest of the West Point curriculum consisted of French (necessary for reading French tactical manuals), drawing (for practical usage such as mapping and terrain sketches), natural and experimental philosophy (physics, astronomy), ordnance (weapons and munitions), gunnery, and an assortment of what today would be called liberal arts—English grammar, geography, political philosophy and law (military and civilian), ethics, rhetoric. These liberal arts courses were scattered throughout the cadets' four-year term. (Readers of Grant's memoirs and letters will be impressed by his exceptionally clear writing style—and occasional spelling lapses. But this clarity of language, and thought, must have been a natural gift, for at the Academy he excelled primarily in horsemanship.) In 1857, a course in Spanish was introduced, and so it is possible that Bascom acquired some familiarity with the language. One curious omission seems to be history, civil and military. Late in the decade, a survey of world history was added, but the absence of any emphasis on American history indicates an institutional lack of concern about promoting feelings of patriotism or a sense of nationalism.[11] The administration assumed that the atmosphere of the Academy was sufficient to convey and inculcate a sense of patriotism, in the event that a new cadet had not already formed his own strong feelings on the matter. In fact, there was very little, if anything, in the course of study or the practices of the Academy that was designed to appeal to the emotions of the cadets.

Religious life at West Point generally fell under the rubric "yet another duty." Bascom's uncle was an Episcopal bishop, but if Bascom was like most of the cadets, he was not particularly fervent. Pious cadets would have joined Lieutenant O. O. Howard's Bible study group.* Regardless of the cadets' religious enthusiasm or lack of it, there was a decided Episcopalian tone to the Academy. Chapel was required under penalty of demerits, and most cadets seemed to echo Sherman's observation that chapel was ". . . a service in which few take an interest, much less join in heartfelt devotion."[12]

Courses in practical military education were naturally part of the curriculum. During Bascom's time at West Point, the tactics instructor was Maj. William J. Hardee. Hardee was a cavalryman, but when Jefferson Davis was secretary of war, he asked Hardee to revise the current manual of infantry tactics, written in 1830 by Winfield Scott. Part of the motivation for this revision was undoubtedly changes in weaponry, specifically the minié ball and the rifled musket. Whereas the old smoothbore musket used in the Mexican War was inaccurate and had very limited range, the newly designed rifled musket fired a .58 caliber minié ball (the ball was actually a conically shaped bullet). When fired, the hollow base of the minié ball expanded and engaged the grooves of the rifle, spinning the projectile, so that its range and accuracy were increased dramatically. The bullet could travel with lethal effect

---

* Howard was the officer who, in 1872, would seek out Cochise and arrange for a peace treaty between the army and the Chiricahuas—this after ten years of war. By that time, Howard was a major general and a veteran of many Civil War battles.

as far as one thousand yards. There were, of course, weapons with rifled barrels before, but they were impractical for massed troops because they took a long time to load; the bullet was precisely the same caliber as the barrel and had to be pushed with a rammer slowly down the barrel to engage the grooves. The minié bullet's soft metal expanding base eliminated the problem. It could be dropped into the barrel, rammed against the powder charge, and fired. A competent soldier would be able to get off three rounds a minute, whereas an old-fashioned rifle might take a minute or more to load and fire.

The British and French were using the rifled musket and minié ball with great effect in the Crimean War, a war that a number of American officers went to observe, among them Philip St. George Cooke and George McClellan, who was impressed by the British and French use of the telegraph. Richard Delafield, the former and future superintendent of the Academy, led a committee of U.S. officers to Crimea, and though they arrived too late to see much action, they interviewed a number of officers on both sides of the conflict.

Maj. Hardee began his tactical revision by experimenting with the cadets to design new formations and movements. Over the next two years, he wrote his new manual, called "Rifle and Light Infantry Tactics for the Exercise and Maneuver of Troops When Acting as Light Infantry or Riflemen." Like its title, the manual is very comprehensive and covers everything from how troops should stand to how to maneuver a battalion. Infantry tactics, in other words, were still understood to be a matter of men in precise formation, officers issuing orders, and troops following them. As a result, "Hardee's Tactics," as it was popularly called, does not differ much in general concept from the earlier tactical manual written by Winfield Scott. In fact, both owed a great debt to the French tactical theories on loan since the Napoleonic era. The only apparent difference between Hardee's work and Scott's is an increased "emphasis on celerity of movement and looser formations," says historian James L. Morrison Jr.[13] Perhaps this emphasis on speed and more open formations was in recognition of the rifled bullet. But as the Civil War demonstrated, commanders still thought in terms of massed formations and frontal attacks, with disastrous results again and again.*

It hardly needs to be said that "Hardee's Tactics" did not address the question of fighting Apaches. Or any Indians, for that matter. The lack of interest shown by the West Point faculty and the army in the subject of Indian fighting seems strange, since some, like Hardee, had fought in the Second Seminole War, a grueling seven-year conflict waged on difficult terrain and against an implacable and competent enemy. Indeed, Winfield Scott had fought in the Black Hawk War as well as the Second Seminole War, along with Zachary Taylor. It would seem that their influence and experience might have raised at least the question of what this sort of warfare entailed. The reason for this oversight may well be that the Academy's curriculum and intellectual traditions were maintained by longtime professors who had not served in combat and who were wedded to the idea that West Point was primarily an engineering school. From their perspective, an officer with a well-trained and logical mind could be expected to work out practical military matters later, on the job. They also felt, understandably, that the army's primary combat mission would be to fight wars against nation-states, as they had in Mexico—that is, against people whose understanding of tactics and the art of war was essentially the same. In the 1840s, tensions over borders in Maine and the Pacific Northwest led many to believe that war with England was inevitable. And, of course, the British army's tactical theories would have been much the same as the Americans'. In the 1850s, the professors at West

---

* Hardee joined the Confederate army and rose to the rank of lieutenant general. He revised his "Tactics" in 1862. Both sides used the manual during the war. Hardee fought in a number of campaigns and was with General Joseph Johnson at the battle of Bentonville, North Carolina, the last major battle of the war.

Point would have viewed the Indians as bands of primitive raiders, little more than bandits and not worth using up valuable course time discussing. Indians could be troublesome, of course, but they were mostly a sideshow. It was, in short, a matter of priorities. The Academy could do only so much, and it would therefore concentrate on the subjects that mattered most.

(Most of the engagements against the Indians were at the company level. Captain Richard S. Ewell, the officer who preceded Lieutenant Colonel Morrison at Fort Buchanan, said he learned everything about commanding a company of dragoons while on assignment in the West, and "nothing about anything else"[14]— further proof that Indian fighting was a business officers were not trained for and had to learn on the job.)

Another reason for this lack of attention to Indian warfare was the design of the Academy. It was originally based on the idea of military academies in Europe, especially the French academies L'Ecole Polytechnique and Saint-Cyr and the British academies at Sandhurst and Woolwich. But both the French and the British divided the disciplines, so that cadets entering their version of the "scientific corps" were taught separately at L'Ecole Polytechnique and Woolwich, whereas the line officers—infantry and cavalry— were taught at Saint-Cyr and Sandhurst, respectively. West Point was the only federal military academy in the United States (and as such, resented by politicians, who were suspicious of a professional, standing army) and therefore had to train officers for all the branches of the service.* And because of the growing needs of the country for skilled engineers to build and develop infrastructure as well as to survey new territories, the Academy emphasized engineering and thereby created the hierarchy in which the scientific corps stood at the top. There was, therefore, no real tradition of

---

* The Naval Academy at Annapolis was established in 1845 to educate sailors and marines; the word "military" specifically refers to the army, even though today it is used to describe all armed forces. Purists disapprove of this modern usage.

the beau sabreur at West Point except in the minds of those few exuberant cadets who had scant interest in mathematics or science. (Custer comes to mind. His panache was the exception, not the rule. He also finished last in his class.) In comparison to the French and British line officer schools, it was more difficult for American line officers to develop an intense espirit de corps, when their branch was regarded as inferior to the scientific corps.

Further, the cadets who attended the English academies, such as Sandhurst, were from upper-class families and had in almost all cases attended prestigious public schools; they therefore had in general a better educational base.* In any event, the British cadets could spend time at the academy studying purely military matters. West Point believed that its mission was to educate its students in a wide variety of subjects, technical as well as "liberal," in order to make up for any deficiencies in the cadets' preparation.

The most influential faculty at West Point consisted of professors who spent decades at the school. The three department heads of the three most important subjects (mathematics, science, and engineering) were appointed in the 1830s and were still teaching and administering after the Civil War. They were the protectors of the traditions. One of the most stalwart was Dennis Hart Mahan, who taught civil and military engineering and also the "science of war," which consisted of "the composition and organization of armies, order of battle, castrametation [the art of laying out a camp], reconnaissance, outpost duties, attack and defense, together with the elements of grand tactics and strategy."[15] Mahan's text for his course was essentially a review of Napoleonic theories, for he believed that "the task of the present . . . has been to systematize,

---

* This is a very great generalization, since most English public schools in the first half of the nineteenth century specialized in Latin, Greek, and little else. The celebrated Dr. Thomas Arnold, father of Matthew Arnold, initiated reforms at Rugby School in the 1830s—reforms aimed at broadening the curriculum. But most public schools maintained their emphasis on the classics—and sports.

and embody in the form of doctrine, what was then largely traced out" (that is, by Napoleon.)[16]

Mahan balanced out this rather rigid view of the profession by emphasizing common sense. Unfortunately, while you can teach cadets what Napoleon did at Austerlitz, you cannot teach them common sense.

There were active-duty officers who cycled through as instructors for a year or two. The cadets would therefore have some contact with the real world of soldiering. One professor of chemistry, Henry Kendrick, had served in the 1851 surveying expedition of the Zuni, Little Colorado, and Colorado Rivers. Captain Lorenzo Sitgreaves of the Topographical Engineers was in command of this survey, and Kendrick was in command of the infantry escort. They had a fight with some Mojaves, a brief scuffle in which one soldier and four Mojaves were killed. But Kendrick had at least heard and fired shots in anger against Indians in the Southwest, so his experience helped balance the theoretical nature of most of the professors. On the other hand, Kendrick's brush with the Mojaves would reinforce the prevailing idea that Indian fighting, while potentially dangerous to individuals and small units, was not a matter for scientists or tactical theorists to spend valuable class time worrying about.

The other active-duty officers who came through added their own experiences, but in terms of Indian fighting there hadn't been much up until this point to talk about, not in the Southwest, for the obvious reason that the United States had only recently acquired the territory and was still in the process of sending army scientific expeditions out to learn what was there. True, these expeditions had been bothered by occasional Indian attacks that were primarily designed to steal army horses and mules. And gold seekers and emigrants had been attacked here and there. There were also raids against settlers and peaceful tribes in Indian Territory and Texas, and these were serious enough to motivate Jefferson Davis to raise two new cavalry regiments in 1855 for service in Texas and what is now Oklahoma. But to the powers at West Point, this was a long way away and a mere bagatelle in the grand scheme of things.

The superintendents of the Academy were regular army officers who served for only a few years. They were nominally in charge but did not argue with the faculty about the curriculum. In fact, some like Richard Delafield (who was superintendent during Bascom's last two years) wholeheartedly concurred with the faculty about the primacy of the scientific curriculum. Others, like Robert E. Lee, who was superintendent when Bascom matriculated, were not inclined to engage the faculty on radical or even minor curriculum changes. Having himself graduated second in his class and been assigned to the corps of engineers, Lee would have been in harmony with the overall approach, although his combat experience must have made him wonder now and then whether the cadets were getting as complete an education in soldiering as they would need. His main contributions were his popularity and probity, so that he was able to instill a sense of comradeship among the cadets, a loyalty to each other and the institution, if nothing else. The proverbial band of brothers. Of course, this loyalty and affection would be strained and in some cases broken in the Civil War, but not without many bitter tears and regrets.

In the summer of 1854, George Bascom arrived at West Point from Owingsville, a small village in northeast Kentucky. Owingsville was also the hometown of John Bell Hood who preceded Bascom at West Point by five years and went on to be a Confederate general. Hood's father was the local doctor so it's inconceivable that the families did not know each other. Perhaps Hood's appointment to the Academy inspired Bascom's ambitions.

Admission to the Academy was by congressional appointment, although there was an entrance exam administered once the would-be cadet arrived at West Point. The exam was not terribly rigorous and failure was not too common, although the new cadets approached the ordeal with not a little trepidation. But the majority of failures and dismissals would come later, once the cadet was well and truly into the curriculum. One minor source of sectional tensions was that the cadets from the North seemed to be better prepared academically when they arrived than were their southern colleagues. As a result, they tended to perform better in class, and that, of course, affected their class rankings, which in turn affected their ultimate assignments. This is a broad generalization, but it was felt among the cadets.[17] Given Bascom's origins in a northeastern village in Kentucky, it's possible that his academic performance was limited by comparatively poor preparation.

Bascom's background was fairly typical—most of the cadets were from rural or small-town America. They were generally from the middle class, although they had the necessary political contacts to secure appointment. But West Point was not especially a school for the privileged. With the exception of boys from the South, where there was a cavalier tradition and respect for the military as a career, few of the cadets came from wealthy or prominent families. Surveys taken in the 1850s and 1860s show only 4 percent of the cadets listed their families as "affluent," while 83 percent described their families' financial condition as "moderate." Another 11 percent described them as "reduced," and 2 percent as "indigent."[18] Personal wealth was not something that could distinguish the cadets, because as soon as they arrived at West Point they turned over all their cash. And although they were paid a salary of twenty-eight dollars a month, they never saw the money. It was placed in a treasurer's account for each cadet.[19] They had to apply to the commandant of cadets (a regular officer who was subordinate to the superintendent) for the necessities and meager luxuries of life. The money would be drawn from the cadet's account. This was part of the discipline process, for the administration felt that cadets with ready money were susceptible to temptations such as tobacco and strong drink. Which of course they were. And despite

the administration's best efforts, they succeeded in finding suppliers and the cash to pay them, even though being caught with
alcohol was a dismissible offense. Most likely, more than a few
didn't care. The Academy's attrition rate was in the neighborhood
of 50 percent. Some classes had even worse records. One hundred
cadets in Sherman's class matriculated, and only forty-three
graduated. Roughly half of the dropouts were academic casualties; the rest were sent off for disciplinary or personal reasons.
In academics, mathematics was the principal culprit in ending a
cadet's career.[20]

When he got off the steamboat at West Point's Hudson River
landing and climbed the hill to the plains above, Bascom would have
felt, as any new cadet would, a sinking sensation. It is one thing to
aspire to the Academy and another to realize suddenly that you have
turned your life over to a military organization so ably symbolized
by the austere-looking buildings on the cliffs above the Hudson. Any
young officer or enlisted man who has walked around Washington,
D.C., knows the feeling of powerlessness, the feeling that his fate is
in the hands of an impersonal institution as represented by the massive, faceless bureaucracy ensconced in public buildings. Trudging up
the hill, Bascom might have been wondering, What on earth have I
done? And he might have been correspondingly nervous about his
fitness for the academic and physical trials ahead. Could he actually
do this? Could he compete with cadets from all parts of the country,
boys who were probably better prepared than he was? All in all,
Bascom probably walked up the hill toward that imposing installation
with very mixed emotions; he might have dreaded the possibility
of failure and its attendant disgrace at the same time he was having
second thoughts about his decision to come there in the first place.
He might have had a hollow feeling in his stomach intensified by
the sense of being utterly alone and very far away from home and
family. After all, he was only eighteen.

Contemporary commentators had a range of views of West Point
at that time. Charles Dickens said the Academy "could not stand on

more appropriate ground, and any ground more beautiful could not possibly be." Timothy Dwight described the place as having "a melancholy sadness" and a "funereal aspect."[21] No doubt it depended on your status as a cadet which description seemed more appropriate. Certainly the place was isolated and remote and as such mirrored the feelings of most, if not all, of the new cadets who climbed the hill for the first time, hopeful and yet apprehensive, determined but unsure.

But on one thing everyone agreed—West Point's very position on the cliffs looking down on the Hudson was a perfect representation of its self-contained and self-assured attitude toward the curriculum and its understanding of the educational requirements of the professional soldier.

The first weeks of summer were devoted to summer encampment, when the new arrivals were turned over to cadet officers who began what would be a four-year process of marching in formation and military drills. The new boys also spent time learning the regulations and preparing for the entrance examinations. The new class would take the exams—along with a physical—and then, if passed, would receive their uniforms and begin the summer program in earnest. "Drills began at 530 AM and continued until 500 PM," wrote James L. Morrison. "During the day cadets took instruction in riding, dismounted drill, infantry tactics, musketry, artillery drill and firing, and fencing. In addition the boys walked guard, served on fatigue details, and, of course, paraded."[22]

Then, at the end of August, the academic year began. The cadets moved from their tents into austere, poorly heated, ill-lighted, and crowded quarters. There were no creature comforts, but at least by this time they would have formed friendships with their fellow sufferers and perhaps alliances against the occasional tyrannies of the upperclassmen. From here on, they would have their noses to the grindstone. They marched to meals that were ordinary and predictable—virtually unchewable beef and potatoes were the standard fare at dinner. In a letter to his mother, Cadet George

H. Derby, class of 1846, wrote: "India rubber boiled in aqua forte could give no idea of the toughness of our roast beef, and we are so accustomed to stale bread that the sight of a hot biscuit might occasion hysterics."[23] (Aqua forte is a cleaning solution used on machinery.)

Social life would have been minimal, and contact with women a dreamed-about improbability. Thomas "Stonewall" Jackson could not remember even speaking to a woman during his four years there.[24] (No doubt he was not counting occasional contacts with the wives of the professors and administrators. When Robert E. Lee was superintendent, he and his wife entertained cadets periodically. Lee apparently could remember his own time at the Academy, but perhaps the administration during Jackson's time—class of 1846—was less sensitive to the cadets' need for an occasional glimpse of a woman.)

The more adventuresome, and thirsty, cadets would now and then slip out of their barracks at night and travel a mile and a half downriver to Benny Havens tavern. It seems at least possible that they were able to enjoy feminine society there, along with Benny's famous "flip" (a mixture of liquors usually served hot) and fragrant hotcakes. Benny's was off limits, of course, but that did not stop a certain segment of cadets. The image of the austere Jefferson Davis is tarnished (or burnished) slightly by the story that he almost killed himself while escaping from officers raiding Benny's one night; Davis fell off a cliff while hustling back to the Academy. Whether it was the flip or the slippery path that caused his fall remains an open question.

Bascom's time at West Point was from the summer of 1854 until his graduation, July 1, 1858. It was a turbulent period of American history, a gradual building up of regional tensions and hatreds that would soon erupt into war.

In the context of the overall political situation in the country during Bascom's four years at the Academy, it's amazing that the country's poisonous sectionalism and political violence did not have a greater impact on the cadets or the Academy. After all, cadets were drawn from all parts of the country, and one would assume that they would have brought with them the prejudices and politics of their home states. While there was some political rancor among the cadets (which grew gradually throughout the decade), it was nothing like what was happening in the country at large. These were the years in which Preston Brooks, a congressman from South Carolina, beat Massachusetts Senator Charles Sumner with a cane on the floor of the Senate after Sumner denounced the attack on abolitionist Lawrence, Kansas, by eight hundred Missouri pro-slavery "border ruffians." The Missourians plundered the town, destroyed the two newspapers, and burned the hotel. In a speech to the Senate that lasted two days, Sumner denounced the attackers as "Murderous robbers from Missouri . . . hirelings picked from the drunken spew and vomit of an uneasy civilization [who committed] rape of a virgin territory, compelling it to the hateful embrace of slavery."[25] Brooks beat Sumner over the head some thirty times with his cane, leaving him bloodied and dazed beneath his desk in the Senate—all to the cheers from the southern press. Sumner's injuries sent him into semi-retirement for the next four years. Outraged by the Sumner incident, Kansas settler and abolitionist John Brown, who would later lead the raid on Harpers Ferry (and be captured by troops commanded by Robert E. Lee), attacked the home of some pro-slavery settlers and killed five with broadsword slashes through their heads. A vicious cycle of attack and retaliation, both actual and political, was well and truly under way. That series of events, known as "Bleeding Kansas," was occurring as Bascom and his fellow cadets sweated over their mathematics and tactical manuals.

Compared to what was happening in the wider world, the atmosphere at West Point was remarkably collegial during Bascom's term. It would get worse as the Civil War approached, but by then

Bascom had graduated and gone west. Part of the reason for this comparative calm was West Point's isolation and the strict control the Academy had over the schedules of the cadets. They were only granted one extended furlough between the second and third year. Other than that, the years were taken up by academics in the school year and summer encampment when classes were over. They had little contact with their families, much less the outside world. Letters from home were slow in coming and visits from families were hard to arrange simply because of the distance and difficulty of travel. The cadets were also so closely supervised that disputes rarely escalated into something serious—a few fights here and there, but those would have happened regardless of the political atmosphere in the wider world. Several hundred young men sequestered for essentially four years will now and then find reasons for a scuffle.

There was also the feeling of comradeship that Lee had emphasized during his tenure but that had been part of the fabric of the Academy from its earliest days. As J. E. B. Stuart (class of 1854) said: "There seems to be a sentiment of mutual forbearance . . . as a general thing we know no North, no South."[26]

Bascom graduated twenty-sixth out of a class of twenty-seven—a performance that placed him among the class's "immortals." But that does not necessarily indicate ineptitude. Given the Academy's high attrition rate, simply graduating was something of an accomplishment. (His fellow townsman John Bell Hood graduated forty-forth out of fifty-two.) "It is not thought a disgrace to be dismissed from here," George Derby wrote in another letter to his mother, "for the studies and discipline are very hard, and a man who succeeds should be thought uncommonly talented, and one found deficient should not be blamed, for I verily believe that not one half of those appointed can possibly graduate."*[27]

---

* Derby was the source of the joke about the wicked soldier who died and sent for his blankets from Fort Yuma.

When Bascom graduated, he was a brevet second lieutenant. A brevet is an honorary rank given generally as a reward for some service, or, in Bascom's case, as recognition of his graduation. He would have had to wait, however, for a place to open up so that he could receive his official commission. In the regular army, promotion was by seniority only. (He graduated July 1, 1858, and did not receive his commission until April of the following year.) West Point was not singling Bascom out, though. All but one of his graduating class received brevet ranks, and all of them had to wait a matter of months before official commissioning.

And so, after four years of academic and practical training, Bascom was "Brevet Second Lieutenant of Infantry as of July 1, 1858." What did he know? He would have been able to take sextant readings to locate himself on the planet, been able to identify geological formations and some of the botanical specimens he would find in the West. He could ride and shoot well enough, fence with a foil, and handle a saber—much good either of them would do on the frontier. He would have had an eye for terrain and been able to read a map. He would have had at least a passing knowledge of French and English grammar. He would have known something of chemistry. Given his low class standing, he would have been relatively weak in mathematics, but competent enough to graduate. He would have been used to giving and taking orders, and when he gave them, he would have expected to have them obeyed with no questions asked and no delay. "Hardee's Tactics" would have been his guide. He would have been intensely aware of differences in rank and seniority, a sensitivity drummed into him through four years of contact with professors, regular officers, and more senior cadets. He would not have received anything like a modern course in leadership—it was assumed that four years of drill and three years of ordering underclassmen about would translate into some understanding of it. The flaw in this theory, of course, is that the cadets were there because they wanted to be and had accepted the customs and traditions of the Academy. They believed in the concept of hierarchical leadership. Most of them, that is. The ones who could not accept the entire package resigned or were dismissed. Therefore, the cadets were practicing their techniques on willing subjects. Many of the men Bascom would command in the field would be of a somewhat different makeup and mind-set.

Bascom would also have ruefully understood the cruel fact of slow promotion based on the seniority system and the idea that it might be many years before he got his first lieutenant's silver bar, so that his only path to distinction lay in some independent action or some spectacular feat during battle. That might result in a brevet promotion, which was essentially the only distinction available. Then, too, he would have been eager for independent operations not only for the chance to distinguish himself but also for the simple opportunity to go off on his own, with troops under his command, and so escape the ever-present hierarchy of garrison life or campaigning, even though he would certainly never have challenged the concept or the correctness of hierarchies. If he had not believed in the concept before he came to West Point, he believed in the gospel when he left. Those who did not believe did not last. He might not have, and probably would not have, respected every senior officer he met—few young officers ever did—but he would have respected the idea of seniority, and that would be sufficient.

What were his instincts? How did he think? He left no memoirs or letters, so the answer is only speculation. But it seems fair to say that, having graduated and been assigned to the infantry, he would not have discarded the scientific habits of mind that were the basis of the curriculum. He did graduate, after all. He believed in a logical, linear way of thinking, a belief that was reinforced by four years of applying mathematical formulas to problems, marching in formation, and taking—and giving—orders. It's even reasonable to suggest that his lower class ranking would have bound him even more completely to the Academy's way of thinking. He survived there by playing by the rules. The difficulty would come when there were no rules to follow.

Despite his low class standing, Bascom was a reasonably consistent product of his culture. And when he graduated, he would naturally have felt a sense of achievement, and relief. But there's another question to consider: Would he also have felt a nagging sense of inferiority, a sense that his performance at West Point did not measure up, that he was assigned to the infantry because of his poor class rank? Would he have resented his more accomplished classmates who were assigned to the scientific corps? It seems hard to believe that there wasn't some small voice at the back of his mind telling him that someday a chance to prove himself would come along, and when it did, he would be up to the task.

At the outbreak of the Civil War, Secretary of War Simon Cameron was incensed at the defections of southern officers and cadets to the Confederacy. He blamed the Academy's training, "which drew little distinction between acts that were inherently wrong and acts that merely violated regulations," writes historian Jacob Kobrick, "resulting in the confusion of right and wrong and [in the words of Simon Cameron] 'in the decision of grave moral questions, [the substitution of] habit for conscience.'"[28]

It's not surprising that Cameron was exasperated, but it would be wrong to overemphasize his point. After all, no one would describe Robert E. Lee's decision as resulting from habit and lack of conscience. Like many of his colleagues, he agonized over deciding to fight for the Confederacy. Still, there seems to be a germ of truth in Cameron's observations. West Point did not turn out many philosophers or introspective poets, nor did it want to.*

---

* Edgar Allan Poe entered the Academy in 1830 and was dismissed a few months later for failure to attend formations, classes, and chapel. He was regular in his attendance at Benny Havens, though. Poe considered Benny "the only congenial soul in the entire God-forsaken place."[29] Manifestly, Poe's temperament was unsuited for the Academy.

Chapter Six

THE EDUCATION
OF A WARRIOR

*The parents and grandparents all advise the boy.
They tell him to run up the hills so that in emergen-
cies he can get along by himself, for in war time
they tell him nobody will go back for him, and he
must keep up. They advise all the boys that in case
of war they should have a strong feeling that they
will overcome the enemy; they tell the boy that the
enemy is as frightened as he is and that, if he puts
on a brave front and charges, the enemy may run.
And they tell the boys that after coming home from
a successful battle, their relatives and friends will be
proud of them. Cowards are talked about, told nasty
things before their faces, and are in disgrace. A girl
would not marry a lazy or cowardly man because
the women say he wouldn't be a good provider. The
boys all know this.*

—Anonymous Apache[1]

*It matters not by what process or method of schooling
the Apache has become the most treacherous, bloodthirsty, villainous and unmitigated rascal upon earth; it
is quite sufficient that he is so, and that he is incapable
of improvement.*

—Captain John C. Cremony[2]

IS GEOGRAPHY DESTINY? SO IT WOULD SEEM, ESPECIALLY IN THE CASE
of the Apaches, generally, and the Chiricahuas, specifically. "We
had a saying that the Indian follows the mountain and the white
man the streams," said Daklugie.[3] More than any other North
American tribe, the Apaches were mountain dwellers. No doubt
there was some aesthetic element involved in their preference. The
mountains in southern Arizona and western New Mexico are truly
beautiful, with health-giving weather and sunshine, clear air, and
a wide variety of plants and animals. Unlike the Rockies farther
north, the southern mountains are habitable through all four seasons. Winters can be cold, with dustings of snow, but centuries of
living there had taught the Apaches how to cope. A snug wickiup
and a good fire were ample protection against the cold. And while
the temperatures would dip in the darkness, the next day the sun
would shine and bring attendant warmth. The mountains were
well timbered and there were plentiful springs, if you knew where
to find them.

But living in the mountains was also a wise strategy militarily,
in terms of both defense and offense. Lieutenant William H. Emory
wrote:

> . . . the Sierra Madre and the Rocky Mountains, about
> the 32nd parallel, lose their continuous character and
> assume the forms that are graphically described in
> the western country as "lost" mountains—that is to
> say, mountains which have no apparent connection
> with each other. They preserve, however, their general

direction northwest and southeast, showing that the upheaval power which produced them was the same, but in diminished and irregular force. They rise abruptly from the plateau and disappear as suddenly, and by winding around the base of these mountains it is possible to pass through the mountain system in this region, near the 32nd parallel, almost on the level of the plateau, so that if the sea were to rise 4000 feet above its present level, the navigator could cross the continent near the 32nd parallel of latitude. He would be on soundings of uniform depth from the Gulf of California to the Pecos River.[4]

These "lost" mountains and ranges are unconnected with each other and overlook relatively flat desert floors. ("Desert" here is not meant to signify sand dunes or the like; the desert floors were mostly covered with grasses, mescal plants, and sage, with groves of mesquite trees and single trees interspersed. Here and there, though, the ground was barren and dotted only with ugly creosote plants and cactus.) From the summits, the Apaches could see travelers passing slowly through the desert far below. According to authors Carl and Jane Bock, "It is not uncommon in the southwest to have a clear view of the horizon and distant mountains sharp and well defined at a distance of up to sixty miles . . . ."[5] The clear air, devoid of haze and humidity, was a tactical advantage to the Apaches, whose sentinels perched on the summits could survey the countryside for three hundred and sixty degrees, and if the travelers below were enemy troops, their presence would be betrayed well before they offered any threat. The dust alone from their horses and wagons would be enough to signal their presence. If they were hapless emigrants heading west, there would be plenty of time to plan where and how to attack them. The mountains were not unlike medieval walled citadels from which marauding warlords could sally forth and to which they could retreat with their plunder when danger threatened. The main difference, of course, is that these mountain fastnesses were massive and intricate, unlike besiegable cities, and their byways were known only to the people who lived there in small family groups. When danger approached, they could scatter into any number of secure hiding places. In short, the mountains in southern Arizona and New Mexico are almost as impressive as the Rockies farther north, but they were not barriers to travel, nor were they snowbound in the winter. They were year-round sanctuaries. What's more, they lay across the border between the United States and Mexico—the Apache's commissary.

Did the Apaches become raiders because they quickly understood the advantages the mountains provided? Did the mountains give them the idea? Or did they arrive in the mountains with their warlike spirit and culture already in place? The questions are, of course, unanswerable with any certainty. But it's at least reasonable to surmise that the mountains were the source of many of their ideas and much of their culture. After all, the Mountain People, the gan, were their guiding spirits.

There were other advantages, though, to living where they lived. In the mountains, game was plentiful. Aside from raiding, the Chiricahua lived by hunting and gathering. The women were responsible for gathering edible plants, most notably mescal, as well as berries and nuts, primarily acorn and piñons, and the fruits of the cactus. (The acorns of the Arizona oaks, particularly the Emory oak, are far more palatable than the eastern version.) Many of these plants grew in the grasslands, foothills, and flat areas of the country. The march from Fort Buchanan to Cochise's camp in the Apache Pass was studded with agave plants, the source of mescal. And in season the women and children would dig up these plants and roast the heads, which were somewhat larger than cabbages, in a kind of ad hoc Dutch oven for three full days. (This is the same plant that provides the basis for tequila and alcoholic mescal, although the Apache women did not use it in that way.)

Hunting was the province of the men. The mountains where the Apache bands lived were well stocked with game of all kinds, although deer, both whitetail and blacktail (subspecies of mule deer), were the primary game animals, along with the pronghorn antelope, which lived in herds in the lower elevations. Elk and wild turkey were abundant as well as three species of quail—harlequin, scaled, and Gambel's. Ducks and geese would congregate in the Gila and Rio Grande bottoms and in the spring-fed wetlands called ciénagas. And there were plenty of small game animals—rabbits, squirrels, and even pack rats, which the Apaches were not above catching and roasting. They would not eat fish or pork, however, nor did they care for javelina, an ugly brute that resembles a wild boar. There were bears and mountain lions too, but the Chiricahua did not hunt bears, because they believed contact caused sickness. They also believed that bears were reincarnations of Apaches who had not lived properly and were in a kind of purgatory, so that killing a bear might mean killing a friend or relative who had strayed off the straight and narrow.[6] They would kill bears in self-defense but never eat the flesh or skin the animal.[7] They hunted the lions, though, because they prized the hide as material for quivers. On their forays into Mexico or against the ranches in Arizona and New Mexico, they would gather up livestock of any kind, including sheep, so that beef and mutton were staples of their diet. Mule meat was also a regular menu item; horse flesh, too. Flour and cornmeal were available either as trade goods or plunder. Some of the other Apache tribes also raised their own corn, squash, and beans, but the Chiricahuas did no farming of their own.

A boy's training to become a hunter and warrior began early in life, about the age of eight. His teachers were primarily his parents and grandparents. Physical fitness was considered the sine qua non for the warrior, not only as preparation for hand-to-hand combat but also for endurance on long-distance raids. The Apaches were famous for their conditioning, and they had to be, because after a raid they were often pursued by troops or civilian posses. Captain John Gregory Bourke's claim that they could travel seventy miles a day was supported by other army officers who had the frustrating task of trying to catch the raiders. (In this light, John Ward's belief that Cochise's band had attacked his ranch is not so unreasonable. Cochise's stronghold would have been merely a day's march away—for the Chiricahua, that is.)

The boys began developing their fitness with runs up and down the sides of the mountains or over long, flat stretches of desert. Often these were competitions with other boys. They were not allowed water during these excursions so that they would become inured to physical hardship and suffering and would develop adamantine stoicism in the face of pain. In the colder months, plunges into icy mountain streams added to their miseries, but toughened their bodies and resolve. "In such sports, in such constant exercise, swimming, riding, running up and down the steepest and most slippery mountains, the Apache passes his boyish years. No wonder his bones are of iron, his sinews of wire, his muscles India-rubber," wrote Bourke.[8]

Girls and women were also expected to be in good physical condition. "There were dangers in those days and the women had to exercise so they could stand anything," said one Apache.[9] The women knew that if the Mexican army or enemy tribes found them, they would be targets. Children too. U.S. commanders generally issued orders against killing women and children, but when the bullets were flying and attacking soldiers were frightened or enraged, innocents invariably suffered.* Moreover, Mexican troops were not at all fastidious when it came to killing Apaches.

While the girls trained under their mothers and grandmothers and learned the domestic arts, the boys were given weapons and taught to hunt. Their fathers and grandfathers explained the habits

---

* Once the war with the Apaches was under way, General James Henry Carleton, commander of the New Mexico Territory, issued the following statement: "There is to be no council held with the Indians, nor any talks. The men are to be slain whenever and wherever they can be found. The women and children may be taken as prisoners, but of course they are not to be killed."[10] Volunteer units and civilian posses, however, rarely had such scruples.

of the game animals and the art of using weapons. Bows and arrows were the staples, of course, but the boys also developed skills with the sling, and in fact were often set against each other in slinging matches—training designed to promote agility. (Geronimo told of ambushing and killing Mexican troops with rocks, saying that they were not worth wasting bullets on.)[11] When the boys were still little they would practice on small game, learning the art of stalking and shooting. Firearms and ammunition were difficult to acquire, so the boys would concentrate on more traditional weapons in their early training.

The Apaches had a pragmatic attitude toward horses. The children were expected to learn how to ride, and the adults were acknowledged to be competent horsemen, but they were different from the Plains Indians, who prized horses above all other wealth. To the Apaches, horses were transportation and, occasionally, dinner, and they did not acquire huge horse herds in the way the Comanches did.* Partly this was the result of geography, since the mountains where the Apaches lived would not have offered enough grazing to support large herds. Further, most hunting was done on foot, which was appropriate for the game they were after, unlike that of the Plains Indians, who hunted mostly buffalo and did so necessarily from horseback. (There were few, if any, buffalo in the Chiricahua ranges.)

"Unlike the Indians of the Plains, east of the Rocky Mountains, [Apaches] rarely become good horsemen, trusting rather to their muscles for advancing upon or escaping from an enemy in the mountainous and desert country with which they, the Apaches, are so perfectly familiar," wrote John Gregory Bourke. "Horses, mules and donkeys, when captured, are rarely held longer than the time when they were needed to be eaten."[12] We must balance

---

* When the army under Ranald Mackenzie attacked the Comanches in Palo Duro Canyon, Texas, they captured 1,424 animals, all horses except for 150 mules.

this statement from Bourke against his claim that Apaches could travel seventy miles a day when pursued. Obviously this would be impossible without horses or mules and the ability to ride them through difficult mountain passes and trails. And they were passionately fond of horse races and the gambling that went with them, so their horsemanship had to be reasonably advanced. Furthermore, horses and mules were valuable as more than transportation and menu items; they were sought-after trade goods and could be exchanged in Mexican or U.S. markets for firearms and ammunition, whiskey, tobacco, and assorted food staples, such as flour, sugar, and corn.[*]

It's been said that "fighting alters its character with the character of the ground."[13] Perhaps. But the character of the ground, in this case, the character of the mountains, was the key determinant in the development of the Chiricahuas' fighting tactics—and they never changed the way they waged war regardless of the nature of the country they were raiding. There is very little difference between the skills needed for successful hunting in the mountains and those needed for raiding and warfare—at least the way the Apaches practiced war. Stealth and patience, physical fitness, careful observation and stalking, caution, concealment, and marksmanship were the qualities boys were trained to acquire, whether the quarry was animal or human. (The tactics of the Plains Indians were similarly influenced by their hunting methods, which, in turn, were a function of geography, so that, in contrast to the Apaches, who were primarily stalkers afoot, the Plains Indians hunted and fought as light cavalry would have. These fundamental differences may go some small way in exonerating West Point from its failure to teach the tactics of Indian warfare. At the very least, such a course would have

---

[*] The Chiricahuas were passionately fond of smoking, both in ceremonies and for recreation. They would trade a horse for one cigarette. See Opler 441. Of course, the horse cost them nothing but a little effort.

had to deal with radically different situations—the Plains Indian horse tactics versus the Apache dismounted, hit-and-run guerrilla warfare. In either case, perhaps experience was the best teacher. On the other hand, some sort of introduction to what lay ahead could have accelerated the learning process for the youthful line officers sent to the frontier.)

"In point of natural shrewdness, quick perception and keen animal instinct, [Apaches] are unequaled by any other people. . . . To rob and not be robbed; to kill and not be killed; to take captives and not be captured, form the sum of an Apache's education and ambition, and he who can perform these acts with the greatest success is the greatest man in the tribe. . . . . They are far from cowardly, but they are exceedingly prudent. Twenty Apaches will not attack four well armed and determined men, if they keep constantly on their guard and prepared for action. In no case will they incur the risk of losing life, unless the plunder be most enticing and their numbers overpowering, and even then they will track a small party for days, waiting an opportunity to establish a secure ambush or effect a surprise." So wrote Captain John C. Cremony.[14]

He states what most of the soldiers on the frontier believed, but he is wrong about the extent of an Apache's education. There were many other cultural lessons to be learned—lessons about their religion, their origins, and their customs. They had a very strict code of conduct, and straying from that path brought on the opprobrium of the extended family and the local group. Further, the Chiricahua boys learned that everyone other than their fellow Chiricahuas was either an actual or potential enemy, even the other Apache tribes and the Navajos, and certainly all Mexicans and whites. This sort of indoctrination created a kind of tribal paranoia that reinforced the individual's joint commitment to stealthy caution and pitiless warfare. Wrote John Gregory Bourke: "For centuries he has been pre-eminent over the more peaceful nations about him for courage, skill, and daring in war; cunning in deceiving and evading his enemies, ferocity in attack when skillfully planned ambuscades have led an unwary foe into his clutches; cruelty and brutality to captives, patient endurance and fortitude under the greatest privations. . . . No Indian has more virtues and none has been more truly ferocious when aroused."[15]

It's also worth noting here that the Chiricahuas—with their stealthy tactics and prudence—are in marked contrast to the equally warlike Plains tribes. Lieutenant James Bradley, General John Gibbon's chief of scouts, said about his Crow allies: "[The] carelessness of these fellows at times is simply amazing. One would think that the Indian's life of constant danger would make caution and precaution so much his habit that he would never lay them aside, but it is quite otherwise. [I am on constant guard to prevent] some foolish or foolhardy thing that could have destroyed them all."[16] The Apache would have regarded the Plains Indian's delight in "counting coup" (that is, merely touching an enemy with a coup stick) as simply insane.

About the time a Chiricahua boy turned fifteen he was ready to become a novice raider. This was purely voluntary, but it was a rite of passage that boys wanted to undertake, for it was the way to become a man. The novice period consisted of four different raids. Depending on the local group's needs, these raids might come close together or be spread out over the course of a year. To prepare for the first raid, a boy was taken in hand by either a relative or perhaps a shaman and given four days of instruction on how to behave on a raid. He learned the taboos that must be observed and even a specialized vocabulary that he and he alone would use during the raid. The Apache language is extremely complicated and is made more so by the use of different forms of speech in different contexts, the novice raids being one of them.* Improper speech could

---

* Another example is the use of "polite form" with relatives of one's wife. Linguists refer to this as a fourth-person usage to differentiate it from common third-person usage.

bring dire consequences. (This idea that language was connected to events, and could create or deter them, runs throughout the Chiricahua culture.)

After teaching him the proper vocabulary and forms of speech, the boy's instructor gave him a cap containing the feathers of a hummingbird (for speed), an eagle (for protection against illness and misfortune), an oriole (to provide clear thinking), and a Gambel's quail (to frighten the enemy, as when a covey breaks cover).[17] The instructor also gave the boy a tube for drinking water, for his lips must not touch liquid, and a scratching stick to use when necessary. The other men on the raid referred to the novice as "Child of the Water," a reference to the supernatural culture hero who taught the Apaches the right way to live. On the morning of the first raid, the boy underwent a ceremony with his instructor in which the novice was sprinkled with pollen from the tule cattail. Called "hoddentin," the pollen was "used to strengthen all solemn compacts and to bind faith," wrote John Bourke.[18] The novice was therefore under the protection of ritual as long as he obeyed the complicated rules laid down by his teacher. Disobeying any of the rituals or violating any taboos had consequences ranging from the trivial to the dire. Touching water, for example, meant that the boy would grow a mustache—hardly a disaster, although the Apaches detested facial hair. If he ate warm food, he would have bad luck with horses. If somehow he should have sexual intercourse during the raid, he would forever be licentious. A novice had a lot to think about.

But the novice was also expected to act as a squire to the adult warriors. He did all the work around the camp, gathering wood, starting the fire, cooking the meals, tending the horses. He was careful to be respectful of the adults. He carried a bow and four arrows—four being a sacred number corresponding to the four cardinal points of the compass—but these were hunting arrows, with sharpened points instead of flint or metal arrowheads. The novice was not expected to participate in the actual raid but rather to find a vantage point and watch the action from a safe distance. It would damage the raid leader's reputation if any harm came to the novice.

Sometimes the raids would last many weeks, for the Chiricahuas traveled deep into Mexico and, if they were successful, they would gather livestock that had to be herded home. Sometimes these herds numbered in the hundreds—sheep, especially—so that the raiders, hampered by their plunder, were under constant threat of pursuit and retaliation. The novice was expected to participate in all aspects of the march to and from the target. But when he returned from his fourth novitiate, he was considered a man. "He is free to do what he will and to have his own views," an Apache explained to anthropologist Morris Opler. "He can smoke now, and he can marry."[19] That's an interesting sequence of new privileges, although for most adolescent boys, the idea of marriage might have had more appeal than the right to smoke. But no woman would care for a man who had not been successful as a novice, both because he would not be a good provider and because his prestige would be at a low ebb among the local group. Sexual pressure added to the peer pressure, and the desire to gain recognition from the group meant that boys wanted to perform well as novices.

And not only could he now smoke and marry and speak his mind, if not in that order, he could also fight. In fact, he was expected to be at the forefront of the next raid or war party, because it was time to see if he was reliable in battle. The popular image of the Apache then, if not still, was that he was not only extremely cruel and cunning but also exceedingly brave. Apaches were human after all, though, and some were afraid in fights and ran away as readily as anyone else. But peer pressure minimized this sort of thing. In many cases, the warriors were brothers in arms, literally. Certainly the small-unit camaraderie that military theorists have increasingly come to understand as a primary source of courage under fire was in operation among the Apache raiders, who seldom mustered more than a platoon-sized force. They were not warriors who were thrown together; they were warriors who had grown up together. Then there were the wise counsels of the elders, who understood that the enemy was just as susceptible to fear, and that surprise and aggressiveness often led to enemy panic. These same elders would have echoed Lord Moran in *The Anatomy of Courage*: "By cowardice I do not mean fear. Cowardice is a label we reserve for something a man does. What passes through his mind is his own affair."[20]

Raiding, then, was far more than just an economic enterprise, although that was certainly part of it. Raiding was deeply imbedded in the culture and flourished within a complex set of rituals and ceremonies, not only for the novices but also for the warriors. It was the means by which a boy became a man, in the same way that the elaborate Chiricahua puberty rituals and ceremonies transformed a girl into a woman. Raids were the path to becoming an individual who was respected in the community; they were the means to self-definition and were integral to the Chiricahuas' understanding of who they were. The Chiricahuas could have lived by hunting; they could have supplemented their diet with agriculture or gathering. Neighboring tribes in the Southwest were proof of that. The Chiricahua did not have to raid and steal in order to survive. They simply liked it, and over the centuries raiding became an integral part of their culture and identity.

From a Mexican or white perspective, of course, raids were nothing more than theft that was quite often accompanied by horrific violence. To them, explaining raids as a cultural phenomenon was either irrelevant or pious rationalizing. To their victims, Apache raiders were nothing less than vicious, murdering thieves. Yet within their own society, the Chiricahua were not sociopathic kleptomaniacs. In fact, all the army commentators who wrote about the Chiricahua reported with some degree of amazement that they were scrupulously honest in their own camps.

"At the time I was left alone with them . . . Cochise told me I could leave my belongings anywhere about there, and that nothing should be lost," remembered Lieutenant Joseph Sladen. "This proved to be literally true. . . ."[21]*

In short, the Chiricahuas were not inveterate thieves who disrespected private property. On the contrary, they had the highest regard for personal property. They just did not extend that courtesy to people they regarded as enemies.

There is an obvious disconnect between the image that the Mexicans and white settlers had of the Apaches (with good reason) and the more sympathetic observations of white officers who observed them around their campfires.

"The popular idea of the Indian, I know, is that he is phlegmatic in temperament, cold and reserved in disposition, lacking in vivacity, and entirely without a sense of humor," said Lieutenant Joseph A. Sladen. "These Indians [Chiricahua] were quite the reverse. They were always cheerful, demonstratively happy, and talkative; inquisitive beyond endurance; brim full of fun and joking, and ready to laugh heartily at the most trivial thing. They were especially fond of playing practical jokes upon each other, and the object of one of these jokes would laugh as heartily at his own discomfiture as would the bystanders."[22]

John Gregory Bourke echoes Sladen's comments: "In the presence of strangers the Apache soldier is sedate and taciturn. Seated around his little apology for a campfire, in the communion with his fellows, he becomes vivacious and conversational."[23]

How are we to reconcile these diametrically opposed views of the Apaches and the Chiricahuas—on the one hand, vicious and pitiless on a raid; on the other, amiable and sociable among their own kind? Perhaps it's not necessary, since both perspectives are correct.

"Rude tribes and . . . civilized societies . . . have had continually to carry on an external self-defense and internal cooperation—external

---

* Lieutenant Sladen accompanied General O. O. Howard to make peace with Cochise in 1872. He spent nearly two weeks in Cochise's camp.

antagonism and internal friendship. Hence the members have acquired two different sets of sentiments and ideas, adjusted to these two kinds of activity," wrote British general and military theorist J. F. C. Fuller. "A life of constant external enmity generates a code in which aggression, conquest, and revenge are inculcated, while peaceful occupations are reprobated. Conversely a life of settled internal amity generates a code inculcating the virtues conducing to a harmonious cooperation—justice, honesty, veracity, regard for each other's claims."[24]

In the case of the Chiricahuas, the sharp distinction between themselves and everyone else seems to have strengthened both sets of coexistent instincts and values—the savage warrior when out on a raid or on the warpath, the cooperative member of an affectionate extended family when at home. The Chiricahuas were living a double life, but their adversaries saw only one side. For most of them, that was more than enough. But humans are more than capable of holding multiple, conflicting sets of emotions and values, walling one set off from the other. To cite an extreme example, SS officers no doubt went home to loving families; Japanese soldiers on leave from Nanking enjoyed their domestic felicity. Despite their belief in their own superiority, the Chiricahua were no different in this regard. Clearly, this ability to maintain two radically different sets of values simultaneously has been the source of more than a little human misery—and misunderstanding.

It's also worth pointing out that the virulent hatred most southwestern civilians had for the Apaches—in contrast to the views of many regular army officers—was due to the fact that the civilians, American or Mexican, suffered the overwhelming majority of casualties from murder and kidnapping and the equally vast majority of property losses. A rancher who lost his cattle to raiders faced severe economic hardship, even if he was lucky enough to escape with his life. A soldier whose horse was stolen lost only something provided by the government. All of which means that it's hard to imagine many white civilians going into Cochise's camp and coming away with the same benign impressions as those of Lieutenant Sladen or Captain Bourke. That, however, does not invalidate the soldiers' perceptions.

For the Apaches, language had particular powers, as though there were a connection between what was spoken (and the way it was spoken) and subsequent events—as though certain forms of speech had the power to create, or ward off, an event. The specialized language of the novice was designed to deflect evil or bad luck during a raid. Similarly, adult warriors used a warpath language in which "a special set of nouns and noun compounds were employed in the place of conventional forms," explains anthropologist Grenville Goodwin.[25] This was not a complete substitution of vocabulary but, rather, highly selective. There was a warpath name for women and girls, for example, but none for men. Going to Mexico was called "grass, it catches on your toes," and there was a different phrase for returning home—"grass blown, swayed by the wind."[26] The term for heart was "that by means of which I live."[27] These terms were only used during raids or war. When the warriors returned home, they reverted to everyday usage and vocabulary. The Apaches believed that language was important not only to keep one's thoughts in order but also to summon the protection of the spirit world. The language of their ceremonies was strictly prescribed and deviation would arouse the ire of the spirit being called upon. Then, too, they had a specialized set of terms and modes of expression for their in-laws. Called "polite form," the terms and constructions were unique to the relationship. A father-in-law would be called "one for whom I carry burdens," a phrase that underscored the obligations of a son-in-law to his in-laws, obligations that were primarily economic: "A son may support the old people if he wants to, but a son-in-law has to support them," wrote Opler.[28] (In a somewhat bizarre corollary to the polite form, a son-in-law was expected to avoid all contact with his mother-in-law, literally to hide from her. This made for some awkward moments because, traditionally, the new bridegroom moved in with the extended family of his wife. He might also be asked to use the polite form with his wife's siblings. How a man with more than one wife managed these complex relationships is hard to imagine.)

This emphasis on precise language in different contexts contrasts rather dramatically with the English usages of the time—and of today, for that matter. "Savage" is an example of a word with multiple definitions that tended to obscure meaning and that, like today's "racism," conveyed nothing exactly but instead merely suggested something undesirable. Similarly, in the nineteenth century, the word "race" might be used to mean all of humanity (as in Mark Twain's "The Damned Human Race"), an actual racial category (Caucasian), a nation (the Mexican race), or a simple grouping of people, such as the Apache race. Not so with the Apaches. With their devotion to linguistic precision, they would have appreciated George Orwell's diatribe against flabby speech, especially in political contexts: "If thought corrupts language, language can also corrupt thought." Indeed, the very word "Apache" (and, even more, "Indian") undermined the white man's ability to understand these people by its generalized, amorphous character. The inability to discriminate among the tribes lumped under these hazy rubrics affected policy for the worse for decades. As Orwell argues, slovenly language leads to poor thinking, which in turn negatively affects behavior, often disastrously.

Language was also important to the ability of a Chiricahua individual to separate himself politically and rise to a position of leadership, and to maintain himself there. The Apaches were democrats of the old order. A leader was one who advised and advocated wise policies that benefited the local group. In this role he needed forensic skills as well as wisdom borne of experience. At home he was an adviser whose security in that role depended entirely on the quality of his advice. Leaders were not so much elected as recognized, and there might be more than one so designated. Cochise was almost unique in the sense that he had no rivals among the Chokonen. (This was true later in his life—after he had proved his value as a war leader.) Other bands often had several leaders.

Personal names also had significance. No one used a person's name to his face, except in dire circumstances such as the thick of battle. Cochise was actually named "Cheis," a word that signified the qualities of an oak. Where the prefix came from is unknown. But in either case, no one used his name in his presence. It was considered highly impolite. And it's interesting to speculate whether, in their first meeting, Bascom or Ward called Cochise by his name. If so, it was not a good start.

The Chiricahua had a word for the relationship between brothers—"shikisn." From his first exposure to training, the child learns, according to Opler, that "his [shikisn] is designed to be his companion in experience and adventure, his confidant, his defender against misrepresentation or direct attack. . . .If anyone is wronged or murdered, it is likely to be his [brother] who demands retaliation."[29] The word, therefore, conveys more than just a sibling relationship; it conveys sacred obligations that endure throughout a warrior's life. It will be remembered that one of the Chiricahuas hanged in Apache Pass was Coyuntura, Cochise's brother.

The Chiricahuas had a rough class system that seems out of character for people famous for individualism. The son of a chief was often chosen to succeed his father. Cochise's own son, Taza, became chief when Cochise was incapacitated with his final illness. But as in most things regarding the Apaches, there were differences between their class system and, for example, the European version. It was assumed that because a son's father was a chief, the boy would get the best possible training for leadership. It only made sense then to promote him when the time came. If he proved to be a poor leader and adviser, he could just as suddenly be ignored and deposed. A European duke, no matter how imbecilic or depraved, didn't run these risks. The Chiricahua also recognized and appreciated gradations of success and family, for although it was considered important that the wealthy share with the less fortunate (through hunting and raiding), still the wealthy warrior achieved his status through his own achievements and was therefore respected. Similarly, someone who was lazy or weak or morally deficient would be regarded as "worthless."[30]

In war, the leader exercised command and control. Raids were less structured affairs. Two or three warriors could decide to leave on a raid and do so for their own account and at their own peril. But war was a different matter. The object of war was not just plunder, but devastation, killing, and revenge, and the risks were commensurate with the goal. The war parties were larger, and managing them required someone who knew something more than how to steal a few cows.

As with most aspects of Chiricahua life, ceremonies played an important part in war. Before the war party left on its mission, there was a war dance (called "fierce dancing")[31] during which individuals joined in the dance to show their willingness to volunteer. No one was forced to go to war, but here again the peer pressure was strong, as was the almost universal desire of young men for fame and glory. And plunder. Often the subject was raised by the family of a slain warrior. Wanting vengeance, they would go to the leader and ask him to organize a war dance and subsequent war party. The dance was in effect a religious event, and the warriors sang out prayers that they would be successful and that they would come back safely. "The Apache is an eminently religious person, and the more deviltry he plans, the more pronounced does his piety become," wrote Bourke.[32] He described a war dance performed by over one hundred Apache scouts during a campaign in the Sierra Madres: ". . . in the first hours of the night [they] began a war dance, which continued without break until the first flush of dawn the next day. They were all in high feather and entered into the spirit of the occasion with full zest. Not much time be wasted upon a description of their dresses; they didn't wear any, except breech clout and moccasins. To the music of an improvised drum and the accompaniment of marrow-freezing yells and shrieks, they pirouetted and charged in all directions, swaying their bodies violently, dropping on one knee, then suddenly springing high in the air, discharging their pieces [rifles] and all the time chanting a rude refrain, in which their own prowess was exalted and that of their enemies alluded to with contempt."[33]

After the war dance there would be a social dance that included the women. Sometimes these war dances would last four days, although the dancing occurred only at night around the fire. The people would sleep during the day and then resume at sundown.

When the warriors returned, there was a victory dance that paralleled the war dance. These, too, could last four days. The Chiricahuas did not routinely scalp their victims. They might take one scalp to display during the victory celebrations, but the practice seemed to vary band by band. Some did not do it at all for fear of attracting the dead victim's ghost.

The education of a Chiricahua was broader than just learning how to hunt and fight. The Apache storytellers, both men and women, were the keepers of the tribe's traditions and culture and were, like many preliterate bards, known for their ability to repeat the stories exactly every time. Many of the stories had a particular point designed to educate the people in the proper way to behave, such as the need for piety, adherence to tribal customs, and willingness to share in the bounty of the hunt and the raid.

The stories were designed to keep the people on the straight and narrow or retrieve them if they had strayed, and many a story was rooted in a specific place, so that the place became a reminder of the story's lesson or moral. People must come and go but the places would remain as communicators of cultural meaning. These brief morality tales were introduced and ended with the name of the place where the events happened. In this way a specific place acted as a kind of metaphor of a cultural value: ". . . geographical features have served the people for centuries as indispensable mnemonic pegs on which to hang the moral teachings of their history."[34]*

Given the significance of places, it's easy to see why the Apaches detested miners and mining. To see a place that had significance changed utterly by men with machines and smelters was an attack not only on aesthetics and on Ussen's forbidden gold, but also on the culture itself. White people stored their cultural values in libraries and museums and universities; Apaches stored them in specific places in the landscape and in the stories that were rooted there and passed along from generation to generation. Seeing those places despoiled was the equivalent of watching vandals burn down a library. Of course, not all places could have significance, but many did, and as such they reinforced the Apaches' sense of history, not as something that happened in time but rather something that happened at a particular place. *When* something happened was not important; *where* it happened and *what it meant* were what mattered. This "spatial" understanding of history is clearly in sharp contrast to the white man's linear way of thinking. To Apaches, time did not matter; timeless lessons did. For Cochise and his people, therefore, Apache Pass, the physical location, was a critical and continuing reminder of the events that happened there and, as important, what those events meant—the innate treachery of the whites. Passing time did not dull the edge of that lesson. The pass itself was a factor in Cochise's undiminishing wrath and a means of keeping the story alive and fresh for the people.

The tent where Bascom confronted Cochise was likewise a powerful visual symbol, and it would be difficult to overstate the importance of visual symbols to Apache culture: "Western

---

* These observations are taken from Keith Basso's study of the Western Apaches, but it's reasonable to assume the Chiricahua had similar traditions.

Apache language and thought are cast in pervasively visual terms. . . . Thinking, as Apaches conceive of it, consists of picturing to oneself and attending privately to the pictures. Speaking consists in depicting one's pictures for other people, who are thus invited to picture these depictions and respond to them with depictions of their own. Discourse, or conversation, consists in a running exchange of depicted pictures, a reciprocal representation and visualization of the on-going thoughts of participating speakers,"* writes anthropologist Keith H. Basso.[35]

To put it another way, the Apaches would probably not agree with the philosophical notion "There can be no thought without language." They might recast that to "There can be no thought without images."

In this context, it seems fair to say that the visual symbol of the slashed tent in Apache Pass—conveyed in stories—operated powerfully on the Chiricahuas' tribal memory—more powerfully than a similar symbol might operate on white or Mexican groups, because of the stark difference in the way the Apaches thought and expressed their thoughts. By cutting his way out of the tent, Cochise had actually, symbolically, and dramatically rejected and escaped from a new and unwanted paradigm—the envelopment of his people by the white civilization. Indeed, the slashed tent is an important symbol whose meaning was well understood by subsequent Apache storytellers who called the Bascom incident "Cut the tent."

There were other kinds of stories too besides these morality or historical tales. Some dealt with myths and legends, others were merely for entertainment. Many were humorous, especially those dealing with the antics of the coyote, a complicated character and trickster who at times was risible and at other times troublesome.

---

* Readers will note the reference to Western Apaches but it is reasonable to assume that the Chiricahua operated essentially in the same way in their stories and conversations. They spoke the same language, after all.

But in almost all cases the stories had a point that was designed to educate the people, young and adults alike, on what it meant to be Chiricahua.

As mentioned, once a novice had completed his four raids, he was free to marry. And if he chose to do so he might take more than one wife, assuming he could support them and was willing to endure the domestic complexities polygamy entailed. Cochise had four wives, and when Lieutenant Sladen met him he was nursing a wound on his hand inflicted by the bites of one of them, which indicates that at least one of his wives had more than a little courage to accompany her sense of being somehow wronged. But Apache women were not shy about expressing their opinions on any matter. They were manifestly not the patient, submissive drudges Indian women were sometimes depicted to be, despite the fact that anything involving manual labor fell to their lot. While he was visiting a Chiricahua camp years later Captain John Bourke observed a fight between two women: ". . . they rushed at each other like a couple of infuriated Texas steers; hair flew, blood dripped from battered noses, and two 'human forms divine' were scratched and torn by sharp nails accustomed to this mode of warfare. . . . No one dared to interfere. There is no tiger more dangerous than an infuriated squaw; she's a fiend incarnate."[36]

Women could be shamans or storytellers. And they were often used as go-betweens to negotiate between the army and the Apaches. Cochise's sister, whose name has been lost, was said to be one of his most trusted advisers. Nor did the Chiricahua discriminate against enemy women during wartime. When the Chiricahua attacked their enemies—white, Mexican, or other tribes—they killed women as readily as they killed men—in part because they understood that enemy women could handle firearms and be as dangerous as their men, and in part because the object of war was killing the enemy, and enemy women were by definition not exempt. Sometimes they would keep women as captives and slaves, but they were not in the least chivalrous when it came to war. Revisionist historians who rightly decry the occasional army attacks that resulted in female casualties neglect to note that the Apaches were no better in this regard. In fact, they were worse. Describing an attack against a Mexican village during which the Mexican garrison was lured into an ambush and annihilated, an Apache fighter said: "Now we went into the town because all the soldiers were killed. When we got there we pulled the women out of the houses by their hair and killed every one in town."[37]

As mentioned, the U.S. Army's published policy was expressly to avoid killing women and children—a policy that the Chiricahuas would never have implemented. It's also fair to say that some of the worst atrocities against all the tribes were committed by civilian posses or by volunteer troops not under regular army command. The massacres at Sand Creek and Camp Grant come to mind. At Sand Creek, Colorado Volunteers attacked the Cheyenne; at Camp Grant, the victims were Apaches and the attackers mostly Mexicans, Pimas, and Papagos, led by a half dozen whites.

There were words to use with a power when you were fighting against your enemy. These made your enemy's bow break. . . . I don't know any words to make an arrow pass over or to the side of you.

—Anonymous Apache[38]

TO THE CHIRICAHUAS, THE IDEA OF THE SEPARATION OF CHURCH AND state would have been incomprehensible. They had no churches per se, or, for that matter, a formal state. But that is mere architecture, real or intellectual. The more fundamental source of their incomprehension would have been the idea that religion and everyday life were separate activities. Nor would they have had any sympathy for what's called secular humanism, atheism, or agnosticism. That would have struck them as ludicrous or dangerous, or, most likely, both. They had a way of living in which their regular affairs, whether peaceful or otherwise, were governed by contact with the spirit world.

> . . . there was no separate word for religion. Spirits, gods and demigods were believed to be everywhere and in everything. Religion was not an optional extra, it was the known and the unknown world. Gods were around every corner—the people . . . never knew when they would appear, in human form, or perhaps in the guise of a swan, a ram, a rainbow, a swallow, a waterfall, a gust of wind. All life marched to the beat of the great gods' drums. . . . this was the rhythm that men prayed fervently would never be interrupted. [They] were exhorted not to tamper with any ritual or do away with any of the practices their ancestors had handed down to them, and not to add anything to the customary ways.*[39]

There were several ways this contact was maintained. First, there was the concept of power.

"Supernatural power is, in the largest sense, the animating principle of the universe, the life force," writes Opler. "Since it is the office of the beneficial supernatural power to perpetuate life, it must find ways in which to heal, warn and guard mankind. These mediums are the familiar channels—the animals, the birds, the personified supernaturals, and others."[40]

The life force contacts the individual through various channels, such as an animal or bird. The contact may come in a dream or during a fast. For example, the image of a deer might appear to

---

* This is a description of Athens during the time of Socrates, but it could easily apply to the Chiricahuas. While it may seem incongruous to compare the ancient Greeks to the Chiricahuas, there are several important parallels, most notably the close connection and consistent interaction between the individual and the supernatural world.

the individual. The deer speaks to a hunter and offers to become his power. If the individual accepts, the deer then reveals to him the specifics of the ceremony that the hunter must follow in order to ensure hunting success. The hunter then has deer power and is responsible for performing his ceremony precisely as it was revealed to him, so that he and the rest of his group will have success. Another might be approached by a horse and thereby given power to control and heal horses. It would also give him success on a raid to capture horses. Someone who is approached by a snake would then have the power to heal snakebites by performing the stipulated ceremony over a victim.

In a sense, this relationship between the individual and a specific power is similar to a spiritual relationship with the Platonic idea of the particular animal or bird. And that idealized animal is the messenger of the life force and becomes the individual's guardian spirit in a relationship that suggests a kind of transcendentalism.* When in danger or in some sort of quandary or when simply wishing to express gratitude, the individual prays or simply talks to the representative of his power. That relationship endures throughout the individual's life, and it is mutually voluntary. If the individual does not perform the rituals properly, the power will become dissatisfied with him and punish him; but if, when approached initially, the individual does not want to accept a particular power, he does not have to. Powers can also be communicated with and perhaps manipulated by individual prayers that are separate from the defined ceremonies. Here again, though, the precision of language is important. Note too that power does not have to come in animal form. Lightning is a medium of power. Thunder too. (The displays of lightning during the monsoon season are spectacular—and dangerous. Individuals with lightning power performed a ceremony

---

* At the risk of stretching a comparison to the breaking point, one remembers Ralph Waldo Emerson's notion of establishing "an original relation to the Universe."

to protect people from being struck.) Even trees and rocks were considered to have life and therefore could be communicators of power. Then too there is the most valued power for a warrior— "enemies against power." This power provides protection in war and also success against enemies, whether in the form of befuddling them into allowing escape or in luring them into ambush or deflecting their bullets or arrows. It can also allow the individual to see into the future to learn the outcome of a raid. Women too could acquire this power: "Victorio's sister, Lozen, was famous for her power. She could locate the enemy and even tell how far away it was,'" said Daklugie.[41] "Enemies against power" had several facets: "The power for making the hail and wind on the enemy belongs to 'enemies against power,'" according to an Apache warrior.[42] Geronimo was said to be able to see into the future and also to control the wind so that he could create dust storms to confuse the enemy. To be truly successful, a war chief needed "enemies against power." Not surprisingly, Cochise was amply imbued.

The spiritual world, not the individual, always initiated contact through its various messengers: ". . . power requires man for its complete expression and constantly seeks human beings through which to 'work,'" wrote Opler.[43] But power did not come to everyone, even though an individual might wish for it. Cochise's second son, Naiche, had no particular power. (Naiche was one of the children with Cochise when he met Bascom.)

In addition to guiding the individual on the path to success in hunting or war, power was used to diagnose and cure illness. A shaman treated his patients by means of ceremonies, prayers, and songs. Wounds were treated similarly. A warrior wounded with an arrow would be sung over by a shaman who had arrow power.[44]

---

* Victorio was a chief of the Chihenne band of the Chiricahuas. His sister, Lozen, was the most famous and fearsome of Chiricahua women fighters. The Chiricahuas believed that if she had been with Victorio when he was ambushed and killed by Mexican troops, she would have been able to warn him.

Unlike similar shamanistic religions, the Chiricahua had "no hierarchy of religious leadership," said an Apache. "There were not a few shamans. Supernatural power is something that any Chiricahua can share. Most people have some sort of ceremony [indicating a particular form of power], little or big. Shamans aren't ranked; each person knows a different thing, so no one is better than another. . . . One thing, like the power to make someone run fast, is enough to make you a shaman. The possession of any ceremony makes a person a shaman. A little rite makes you a shaman just as much as a long elaborate rite."[45]

The Chiricahuas, then, were a collection of specialists who had access to the supernatural world by means of animal and natural mediums, who could be consulted by those needing their special gifts, whether for war, illness, hunting, or any number of situations. The shaman would then perform his ceremony in order to provide the requested result. If it didn't work, the client could try someone else. Not surprisingly, there were occasional false shamans, people who claimed power they didn't have. But the failure of their ceremonies to generate results eventually revealed them as frauds.

A Chiricahua who had somehow gone off the straight and narrow might use his or her power in a sinister fashion—to make someone ill or hamper someone's hunting or institute any number of antisocial acts. In such cases, he or she would be accused of being a witch and would be hung by the wrists and questioned until there was a confession. Once the person confessed, he or she would be burned alive to eradicate the evil.

Chiricahuas—all Apaches, for that matter—seemed to be much afflicted by witches and ghosts. While the witches were human, the ghosts arrived most often in the form of owls. They might be ghosts of dead enemies or of malicious people who had come back to spread disease and ill fortune. The Chiricahua believed the owls spoke their language and that the words could penetrate their bodies and cause sickness: "If you hear an owl you know a ghost is nearby, for the owl is connected with the ghost. The ghost uses him, goes into his body. Owls talk the Chiricahua language. They say different things to different people. To me it seems like they are saying, 'All your people are going to get killed.' The call of the owl is very powerful. It can get into your body and cause trouble," said an Apache.[46]

Here, then, is another example of the connection between language and events, in this case, dire ones.

As mentioned, the Chiricahua did have an idea of a supreme being—Ussen, the life giver. And it's difficult to say whether or to what extent contact with the Spanish and later the Americans affected their ideas on this subject.* Certainly the Chiricahua regarded Spanish missionary efforts with contempt. But, regardless, Ussen seems to be a rather remote idea. The myths suggest that Ussen created White Painted Woman, who mated with Water and gave birth to Child of the Water, the culture hero who slew monsters and released game animals into the world and taught the Apaches how they should live.** Once his task was finished, he retired from direct contact with humans, whereas other supernatural beings, such as the Mountain People and the Water Beings, were more directly involved in everyday life. Although they were supernaturals, the Mountain People looked just like men and were generally benevolent guardians, especially of the game animals. They were a source of power as well. The Water Beings consisted of a benign Controller of the Water, who, as the name suggests, managed rain and rivers and springs. His more malevolent colleague, Water Monster, was responsible for any disasters around the water such as drownings or flash floods, and was greatly feared.

The Chiricahua shared many of these myths with the other Apache and Navajo tribes, although, not surprisingly, they sometimes had different stories. For example, another culture hero,

---

* Anthropologist Morris Opler believes Ussen (or Yusn) is derived from the Spanish *Dios*.

** Other stories say that Child of the Water was fathered by Ussen.

Killer of Enemies, was a rather weak supernatural (and the creator of the white man) for the Chiricahua, whereas other tribes regarded him as the original giant killer.

The Chiricahuas believed in an afterlife. Interestingly, they also believed that it was exactly the same as the life they were living and it existed somewhere beneath the earth. One story told of an old woman whose ghost visited the afterlife and then returned to report, "The people were living there just as we live here. . . . All the people [I] met looked as they had in life, and [I] could see no difference between life down there and life here."[47] The story illustrates the Chiricahuas' complete satisfaction with their culture and their environment: Their idea of heaven was precisely the same as their experience of life. Some Chiricahuas referred to the afterlife as the "Happy Place."[48] By extension, then, this life too was everything they desired.

My father was a good man. He killed lots of White Eyes.
—Daklugie[49]

CHIRICAHUA SOCIETY WAS A DELICATE BALANCE OF INDIVIDUALISM, family and peer pressure, cultural and religious proscriptions and ceremonies, and leadership. Depending on the situation, one of these might be dominant or operate more powerfully than the others. Yet the Apache warrior was anything but the stereotype of the self-contained individualist who went his own way in any and all situations, heedless of any rules, a law unto himself, ungovernable. On the contrary, he viewed his life and well-being as largely dependent on his attentiveness to ritual acts and devices designed to evoke and maintain the goodwill of the supernatural beings he believed managed virtually every aspect of existence. He was mindful of his people's customs and his extensive responsibilities to his immediate and extended families, careful with his speech depending on the context, guided by his individual power, bothered now and then by ghosts and witches, and aware that enemies were all around. Like the novice on his first raid, the Chiricahua warrior had a lot on his mind. None of this excuses his virulent hatred of anyone outside his circle, or his capacity for incredible cruelty and violence toward his victims, innocent or otherwise. But it suggests that his mental, emotional, and imaginative world was far more complex than white observers understood (or cared about). The Chiricahua was routinely compared to the most dangerous of animals—rattlesnakes, lurking mountain lions, ravening wolves. Those comparisons trivialized the Chiricahua culture, reduced the warriors to simple two-dimensional cartoons of violence. The fact is, they had evolved a complicated way of living that was completely different from—and incompatible with—the European cultures that gradually surrounded them. It's tempting to wonder how a Christian minister who encountered these people would have assessed them. On the surface, he would have said that the Chiricahua were simply unenlightened and could be put on the right track by way of the Bible and some schooling. (Many ministers did say that.) But another part of him might have looked into the Chiricahua culture and wondered about their complicated beliefs and continuing communion with their spirit world, their devotion to family, and their social and religious mores—and their corresponding passion for violent raiding and bloody warfare. It might very well have been a frightening glimpse into the heart of darkness. Or if not the heart of darkness, then certainly the heart of otherness. That same minister might also have recognized that the Chiricahuas' capacity to maintain seemingly incompatible instincts and ideas was not so very different from the way the rest of humanity handled life. And that might have been even more disturbing to contemplate.

Cochise was more than just a product of this training, this life way. He was also an engine of its perpetuation. Along with his father-in-law, Mangas Coloradas, he was the principal protector of the Chiricahua way of life. Others would follow after his death, but none would surpass him in his devotion to the Chiricahua culture and his ability as a warrior and a leader of warriors.

Anthropologists are forever wondering about the roots of human violence. One school says it is fear of the stranger, the foreigner—the other—that stimulates violent reactions. Another posits the opposite view—that most violence is fratricidal, that civil wars are always the bloodiest. "Strangely enough," said Sigmund Freud, "the intolerance of groups expresses itself more strongly against small differences than against fundamental ones."[50] Regarding the Chiricahuas, either or both theories could apply. They would fight with anyone outside their immediate circle, whether the enemies were alien white men or other Apache tribes who differed from them in no way except geography. Were you to have asked Cochise why the Chiricahua were so warlike, what aroused their implacable wrath, he would probably have brushed aside the anthropologists' theories. Instead, he would have answered in one word—revenge.

Chapter Seven

BASCOM'S COMMISSION

The officers' code of honor . . . included "patience, fortitude, courage, temperance, chastity, probity and that large charity of self-forgetfulness which would sacrifice life for the protection of the weak and helpless."

—Army and Navy journal[1]

The men raised no tents, as it was near midnight '[ere] the horses were fed and groomed and the men got their supper, but the Officers, oh these gentlemen, they could not sleep these few hours without having their large wall-tents pitched, they did not have to put them up and the poor men, well what does an officer care how tired or worn out or even ill a man is, their imperial will would at all times have to be obeyed, humanity is something that is foreign to their feelings and a little kindness is but seldom or never shown to the rank and file.

—Private Theodore Ewert[2]

BREVET 2ND LIEUTENANT GEORGE BASCOM'S FIRST ASSIGNMENT WAS garrison duty at Fort Columbus on Governors Island, New York. Just off the tip of Manhattan, the fort had been built in 1795 and had seen its ups and downs over the years, its usefulness varying with political budget wrangling and the long periods of relative peace. When Bascom arrived, the fort was a recruiting and training center for the infantry. In the 1850s the army needed to do a good deal of renovation to repair leaking roofs and peeling plaster, but photographs of the period show it to be a handsome and imposing installation. At the time Bascom lived there, Fort Columbus was a masonry structure built along the lines of the classic European fortress, with high stone walls and a triangular bastion jutting out from each of the four corners. Inside the walls were four two-storied and colonnaded buildings, three for enlisted barracks and one for officers' quarters. These were arranged in a square around a parade ground. All things considered, Fort Columbus was a pretty civilized place, although an 1858 report lamented that the "permanent privies" were "quite inadequate for the number of men quartered in the work."[3] Despite that, Bascom no doubt looked back at his quarters there as nothing short of luxurious, especially by comparison to the forts on the frontier, and most especially, Fort Buchanan.

Aside from simply being there and waiting for a position to open up somewhere, Bascom would have practiced his skills in drilling new recruits, many of whom were recent immigrants from Ireland and Germany who had not been able to find work and had enlisted in the army as an alternative to starvation. In the 1850s more than half of the enlisted men were immigrants, and of those, 60 percent were Irish.[4] And although recruiters were ordered to accept only those with a "competent" command of English, many recruits had just a passing acquaintance with their new country's language.[*] (The acerbic Private Ewert was an immigrant from Prussia, and

---

[*] Many of the immigrants from Ireland spoke Irish and little, if any, English.

he was perhaps unusual in his ability to articulate, in English, his hatred of officers.)

The wave of German and Irish immigration in the 1840s and 50s aroused passionate nativist reaction. Most of the immigrants were Catholic, and their arrival sparked an anti-Catholic, anti-immigrant party called the Know-Nothings, so named because, as a secret society, the members were instructed to answer, "I know nothing," when asked about their party's activities. Membership in the Know-Nothings was restricted to Protestant men of British extraction. In this political climate it would have been impossible for some of these attitudes not to seep into the consciousness of the army and color the officially distant relationships between officers and enlisted men. What's more, the immigrants were almost by definition working-class people or peasants, and most, if not all, officers would have regarded them as socially inferior. This jaundiced view of immigrants, and especially Catholic immigrants, was reinforced by the celebrated desertion during the Mexican War of what became known as the Saint Patrick Battalion, or the "San Patricios," some three hundred or so men who deserted and then fought as a unit for the Mexican army—and fought well. The men switched sides for a number of reasons—solidarity with fellow Catholics, offers of land and money from Santa Anna, principled revulsion at what they saw as an unjust war, drunken impulse. Whatever their motives, the desertion and subsequent service for Mexico clearly signaled to Protestant America that foreign-born Catholic troops could be, and probably would be, unreliable. It was said they served the pope rather than their adopted country. The San Patricios represented an assortment of nationalities but an almost homogeneous group of Catholics. After the Battle of Chapultepec, some thirty of them were captured and hanged, including one who was dying after amputation of both legs. Another twenty were hanged elsewhere. Desertion during a time of war was a capital crime, but the usual method of execution was the firing squad. Hanging these San Patricios therefore appears to have been either vindictiveness or a means to send a message to other foreign-born troops who were assembled to watch the proceedings. The remaining captives, including their leader, John Riley, were flogged and branded on the cheek with a *D* for deserters. They escaped execution on a technicality, because they had deserted before the war was declared. The American population as a whole may have gained a sense of satisfaction at this outcome, but the execution did nothing to inspire confidence in foreign Catholic troops, despite the fact that during the Mexican War the overwhelming majority of foreign-born U.S. troops remained true to their colors.

The Civil War and the performance of immigrant soldiers, especially the Irish, would go some way toward removing both civilian and military prejudice. But in the 1850s the memory of the San Patricios and its attendant suspicions were still vibrant. Among the San Patricio deserters were members of the Seventh Infantry, Bascom's future regiment. And the regiment—especially the officers—would have a long memory. Regardless of anti-Catholic feeling, the army needed recruits, and immigrants kept streaming into the teeming inner cities, where they became a prime source of manpower.

Bascom endured eight months of garrison duty, drilling new recruits according to Hardee's manual of tactics, teaching them to march in straight lines and go through the manual of arms. But, in general, the training that Bascom and other officers could conduct was severely hampered by cost considerations and manpower needs on the frontier. In 1857, General Winfield Scott wrote, "Incessant calls for reinforcement from the frontiers compel us, habitually, to forward recruits without the instruction that should precede service in the field, and on joining their regiments, perhaps in the act of pursuing an enemy, it is long before the deficiency can be supplied."[5] During an inspection of muskets on the march to New Mexico, the officers in charge of 325 recruits found that 140 of them had loaded the bullet first followed by the powder charge.[6] Even those who understood how to load their muskets were given scant opportunity to practice their shooting, for ammunition was expensive. Little wonder then that their marksmanship was suspect. (It will be remembered that Cochise escaped on foot up the mountainside through a hail of bullets.) Also, the ammunition that was available to frontier forts had to be husbanded, because resupply could only get to remote outposts overland by wagon trains from depots such as the major supply center at Fort Leavenworth.

Since the troops' initial training was so spotty, it was up to their regimental officers in the field to make up for the deficiencies, but the officers were generally stretched so thin and so often engaged in active campaigning that there was hardly time to do proper training. What's more, the regiments were rarely quartered together. Instead, the remote forts were manned by a company or two, so that there was little if any senior commitment to training, and the junior officers in command of the companies were busy with operations in the field. The troops, like the officers, had to learn on the job. Fortunately for the service, there was a leavening of experienced recruits—men who had served in the army in their home countries. But the majority of recruits arrived on the frontier generally ignorant of their trade.

No doubt Bascom and his colleagues at Fort Columbus did the best they could with the material they were given. But it was not exciting or even interesting work. Now and then he probably took the ferry to Manhattan to assuage the boredom of garrison life with a dinner at Delmonico's. (Though the issue is debated, some food historians say that Delmonico's served the first hamburger, more or less as we know it: price, ten cents. Others say the dish was a favorite of immigrants coming to the United States aboard the Hamburg Line and that Delmonico's simply recognized a good thing when they saw it.) Unencumbered with a family, Bascom would have been able to afford an occasional spree. A second lieutenant's pay was forty-five dollars a month; in contrast, an enlisted man's monthly pay was eleven dollars. Whether Bascom also occasionally looked for female company is impossible to say. If he wanted a strictly commercial relationship, there were plenty of prostitutes roaming the streets of New York—farm girls escaping rural tedium, immigrant women looking to supplement their appallingly low wages, women who thought being on the streets or in a bawdy house was better than being in the sweatshops. Perhaps, as the nephew of an Episcopalian bishop, Bascom would not have been tempted by such offerings. On the other hand, his stay at West Point had been four long years.

In certain moments, Bascom's assignment to garrison and training duty may have seemed like a pretty soft job. But a young officer who had spent four years or more in theoretical preparation for war at some point must have looked forward to the chance to put all of what he had learned into action. Ordering troops around a parade ground was one thing; commanding them in action was another. Of course, the allure of combat often fades somewhat after the officer has experienced the real thing. But that does not diminish the appeal for an inexperienced officer like Bascom. He wanted to do what he had been trained to do.

Finally, in April of the following year, 1859, Bascom received his commission, along with orders to join the Seventh Infantry regiment. Nicknamed the Hay Balers, because they had fought behind bales during the Battle of New Orleans, the Seventh was in Utah at Camp Floyd, forty miles or so southwest of Salt Lake City.

They were there because of troubles with the Mormons.

> ... *thine enemy is in thine hands, and if thou rewardest him according to his works, thou art justified; if he has sought thy life, and thy life is endangered by him, thine enemy is in thine hands, and thou art justified.*
> —Joseph Smith, *Doctrines and Covenants*[7]

127

The Independence of Utah Territory has been declared, and the determination announced of adhering to no laws except such as the Mormons make themselves. This must bring them into speedy conflict with the United States—and this insures their final extermination. For once the general detestation and hatred pervading the whole country against the Mormons is given legal countenance and direction[;] a crusade will start against Utah which will crush out this beast of heresy forever.

—*San Francisco Daily Evening Bulletin,*
October 1857[8]

"Extermination" is a harsh word, to say the least. The word often appeared in newspaper editorials calling for a final solution to a troublesome Indian tribe. It is strange, though, to see it used in an article about white Americans—Mormons.

Certainly the origins and the beliefs of the Mormons were puzzling to the outside world, and their sometimes bizarre doctrines had something to do with the hatred the Mormons engendered.

The basic outlines of the Mormon story are these: An angel named Moroni visited Joseph Smith and told him about some golden plates that were buried on a hill near Smith's home in upstate New York. After several false starts over several years, during which Moroni was evaluating his protégé, Smith was finally allowed to dig up the plates and translate what was written on them in a language he called "reformed Egyptian." He used a "seer stone" that was provided along with the plates. The seer stone magically converted the language of the plates into English. Smith placed the stone in his hat and buried his face in the hat to shut out all light. The words then appeared on the stone in English so that Smith could read the text. He dictated the translation to a secretary who was shielded behind a curtain. This text became the Book of

Mormon. When he was finished translating, Smith returned the plates to Moroni and published the book in 1830.

From the perspective of the twenty-first century, Smith's use of the seer stone seems more than a little odd, but it was not at all unique during the superheated religious fervor of the Second Great Awakening, the evangelical, revivalist period of roughly 1820 to 1840 during which a variety of new sects, many of them apocalyptical or communitarian, flourished: "One interesting aspect of this religious excitement was the degree to which many Americans resorted to various forms of folk magic in expressing their religious beliefs," writes historian Joseph Rimini. "They used such things as amulets, talismans, divining rods, and seerstones or peepstones (akin to crystal balls . . .) for protection or to predict the future or even to hunt for treasure."[9]

As a boy, Smith was a dedicated treasure hunter; he had found an earlier seer stone while digging a well, and he used it to try to locate buried gold and other valuables.

The Second Great Awakening was alive with new religious interpretations, discoveries, and sects, many of them improbable to all but their converts. Itinerant preachers and prophets roamed the revival circuit, each seeming to outdo the others in whipping up frenzied reactions from the congregations. Writes Rimini, "The preaching by these sects was usually very animated, the responses quite frenzied. This was particularly true at camp meetings when men and women would shout their repentance."[10] Writhing on the ground, speaking in tongues, shouting, and weeping were all part of the desired response. Salvation was the goal; vocal and public repentance, the means.

Smith grew up in this atmosphere; he lived in the center of the Burned-Over District of upstate New York, so called because it was the epicenter of intense revivalism. Moreover, his mother and father were passionate believers who were members of no particular congregation. They were seekers after salvation but relied mostly on revelations and visions of their own. Small wonder then that Smith was drawn to prophesy and revelations.

Smith's message was ostensibly Christian, but with a number of twists. For example, after the crucifixion and resurrection, Jesus visited North America and preached to the Indians, who, according to Smith, were descendents of the tribes of Israel. (This became an important element in the future relations between the Indians of Utah and the Mormon settlers.) The Second Coming would occur in the United States, and although Smith did not set any dates, he was quite sure the time was close by.

As a prophet who believed he was on a level with the Old Testament prophets, Smith was given to frequent revelations. After one such, Smith announced that the Garden of Eden had actually been in Missouri, so that when Adam and Eve went out from the gates of Eden, they found themselves in what would become Jackson County. But his most important revelation came when he was just fourteen and it became the root of the subsequent troubles for him and his adherents, for in it, God visited him and revealed that none of the organized religions carried the truth. Worse, all the established religions and their preachers were "corrupt and an abomination in the sight of God."[11] Smith's mission would be to reestablish the true church. Not surprisingly, when he began preaching that message as an adult, the ministers of the other denominations bitterly denounced him, thereby giving their congregations a ready-made excuse for righteous hatred. Another revelation had to do with the sanctity of polygamy, or plural marriage. Many observers thought that particular revelation was especially convenient for someone with an eye for the ladies. Others thought it merely barbarous and inherently sinful. But it became part of the doctrine of the early Church of Latter-day Saints, as the Mormons called themselves. To be pedantically precise, the doctrine was restricted to polygyny, since only men could take multiple spouses. But regardless of what it was called, the Mormon doctrine of plural marriages outraged the rest of America.

To critics, the story of the origin of the Book of Mormon and Smith's various revelations seemed unlikely, to say the least. Speaking of the Book of Mormon, Mark Twain said:

"The book is a curiosity to me, it is such a pretentious affair, and yet so 'slow,' so sleepy; such an insipid mess of inspiration. It is chloroform in print. If Joseph Smith composed this book, the act was a miracle—keeping awake while he did it was, at any rate . . . . The book seems to me to be merely a prosy detail of imaginary history, with the Old Testament for a model, followed by a tedious plagiarism of the New Testament."[12]

Twain spoke for most of Gentile America in expressing not only his literary criticism but also his underlying opinion that the book's content was absurd.

In fairness, it's difficult to think of the basic tenets of any religion and not run across something that seems unlikely. Perhaps that was also a source of the vicious enmities that sprang up between sects; perhaps the improbabilities of someone else's faith exposed and highlighted the improbabilities in one's own and thereby created doubt, which had to be rejected. Or perhaps it worked the other way around: the improbabilities in the other person's faith just underscored the fact that he was a simple dupe, or a fraud, deserving of contempt, ostracism, or worse—especially when he went around denouncing other religions as corrupt.

The Mormons were just one of many new sects that sprang up in this period of religious fervor, although they seemed to stimulate the most violent reactions. The Shakers, for example, took a vow of celibacy—a certain guarantee of eventual extinction if recruiting declined.* No one seemed to hate the Shakers, though, perhaps on the theory that time would deal with them anyway. But were their doctrines any less unusual than those of the Mormons, who were positioned on the opposite end of the celibacy question? It doesn't seem so. Yet while Shaker celibacy did not seem to offend other Christians, the Mormon espousal of polygamy contributed to the

---

* The Shakers had been formed in England in the late eighteenth century but they flourished in the northeast United States during the enthusiasms of the Second Great Awakening.

bitter hatred much of Gentile America felt for them. The newly formed Republican Party adopted a platform calling for the abolition of the "twin relics of barbarism: slavery and polygamy"—an indication of the widespread antagonism the Mormon doctrine aroused.[13] The elevation of polygamy to a national issue on a moral level with slavery would soon come in handy with certain politicians in both parties. The Republicans were happy to link the two in order to discredit the Democrat southern bloc and its members' understanding of "popular sovereignty," which was their basis for states' rights and therefore the underpinning of legalized slavery. In other words, if the people in a state voted for it, that was their right. Democrats, on the other hand, saw an opportunity to leverage the nation's almost universal revulsion against polygamy to distract popular attention from the bitter debate between North and South. Thus the Mormons became unwitting and unwilling players in national politics and the divisive issues surrounding slavery.

The ever-skeptical Mark Twain also had something to say about polygamy when he passed through Utah on his way to the silver mines of Nevada:

> "I was feverish to plunge in headlong and achieve a great reform here—until I saw the Mormon women. Then I was touched. My heart was wiser than my head. It warmed to these poor, ungainly and pathetically "homely" creatures, and as I turned to hide the generous moisture in my eyes, I said "No—the man that marries one of them has done an act of Christian charity which entitles him to the kindly applause of mankind, not their harsh censure—and the man that marries sixty of them has done a deed of open handed generosity so sublime that the nations should stand uncovered in his presence and worship in silence."*[14]

---

* Twain would no doubt want to revise his opinion about modern Mormon women.

But not everyone—indeed, almost no one—had Twain's sense of humor or humanity when it came to the Mormons.

It's difficult to understand the intensity of hatred that the Mormons inspired in Gentile (non-Mormon) America. The closest parallel seems to be hatred of the Jews in prewar Germany and, indeed, most of Europe. But all of the first Mormons were by definition converts from something else, generally another form of Christianity. It was a new religion that began in 1830 with the publication of the Book of Mormon. Adherents were therefore indistinguishable from the rest of white, Protestant America (although Mormon ranks would swell in the near future with foreign converts). After their conversion, they gathered into close-knit communities that excluded nonbelievers. This clannishness, coupled with their unusual beliefs; their devotion to their prophet, Joseph Smith; their contempt for traditional religions; and their habit of voting as a single bloc, alienated their neighbors and generated fears that the constantly expanding Mormon population (through missionary conversion and immigration) would soon dominate local and state politics. All of these factors over time aroused an unreasoning fury that led to murders, looting, and arson. In the most hideous of these events, a mob (composed of the Missouri militia and sanctioned by the governor) attacked a group of eighteen Mormons in Haun's Mill, Missouri, and killed them all, including a ten-year-old boy, who begged for his life, only to hear his murderer say, "Nits make lice" just before blowing the boy's brains out.*

Mormons endured a series of physical atrocities and venomous political attacks in Ohio, Missouri, and Illinois. The final straw was the murder of the prophet, Joseph Smith, and his brother Hyrum, by a mob in Carthage, Illinois. With the assassination of their prophet, the Mormons realized they would have to leave everything

---

* This disgusting phrase surfaced again when John Chivington's Colorado Volunteers attacked the Cheyenne at Sand Creek. This suggests the phrase—and its underlying attitude—might have been in common currency and used to rationalize the killing of "enemy" children.

they had built up in Nauvoo, Illinois, and migrate again. And there was a considerable amount to leave behind, for in just a half dozen years or so, the Mormons had turned Nauvoo from a swampy wilderness into a thriving city of fifteen thousand, second in the state only to Chicago. Indeed, part of the enmity they aroused stemmed from envy of their commercial success. But they would leave their farms and businesses behind and this time they would go to a place beyond the reach of the Gentile "mobocracies." The attacks also developed in the Mormons an understandable sense of persecution that helped strengthen their solidarity, as well as their hope that they would one day be able to avenge the death of their prophet. Moreover, they had learned to distrust government, both at the state and federal levels, because the legal powers seemed to turn a blind eye to—and even in some cases sanction—the attacks against the Mormons. The Mormons felt quite rightly that they were American citizens who deserved equal protection under the law, regardless of their unusual beliefs. But too often they did not get it.

In July 1847, Brigham Young, Joseph Smith's successor, looked down upon the valley of the Great Salt Lake and said: "This is the place." Ten years later, there were a hundred towns and villages and forty-five thousand residents in Young's Utah, a place they called Deseret or, sometimes, Zion.[15] The desert had been made to bloom through hard work, discipline, religious fervor—and irrigation. Mormons from across the country and around the world (recruited by tireless Mormon missionaries) had journeyed there to escape persecution and to worship as they pleased—or, rather, as the church hierarchy was pleased to instruct them. Some had walked from the East, pulling handcarts; others had ridden in wagons drawn by oxen that had been paid for from the uniform allowance of the Mormon Battalion and by church tithes. The trails from the East were littered with the graves of those too weak to make it and the victims of disease and Indian raiders. Nor was this migration a single event; it went on throughout the decade of the 1850s as missionaries spread the word and converts came to Zion. Traveling by stagecoach along this same route on his way to Salt Lake City, Mark Twain wrote:

> We left the snowy Wind River and Uinta Mountains and sped away, always through splendid scenery but occasionally through long ranks of white skeletons of mules and oxen—monuments of the huge migration of other days—and here and there were upended boards or small piles of stones which the driver said marked the resting place of more precious remains. It was the loneliest land for a grave! A land given over to coyote and raven—which is but another name for desolation and utter solitude. On damp, murky nights, these scattered skeletons gave forth a soft, hideous glow, like very faint spots of moonlight starring the vague desert. It was because of the phosphorus in the bones. But no scientific explanation could keep a body from shivering when he drifted by one of those ghostly lights and knew that a skull held it.[16]

When Brigham Young first viewed the valley, Utah was part of Mexico. That may have been a comforting thought to him, for Mexico City was far away and careless in its management of this empty desert. In fact, the Mexican government essentially ignored Utah. But the war between the United States and Mexico changed all that, and Young must have had mixed emotions when he learned that the United States had acquired Utah as part of the Treaty of Guadalupe Hidalgo. On the other hand, he may have anticipated this very event, for he was an astute politician and no doubt understood the odds were against Mexico in the war. But he tried to make the best of the situation and petitioned Congress to allow Deseret to be admitted as a state. Congress was not interested. Worse for Young, in 1850 the United States declared Utah a territory, which meant Washington had the power to appoint the government. Bowing to the obvious political realities, the United States appointed Brigham Young governor, along with three other Mormons and six Gentiles to round out the officers of the territorial government.

This was the beginning of constant squabbling between U.S. officials and the Mormon hierarchy. Utah was in all respects a theocracy, regardless of what the bureaucrats from Washington said. The elders of the church, with Young at their head, ruled absolutely.* The officials sent from Washington were shunned. One by one, the Gentile officials returned home in frustration. Brigham Young ran the territory, and the federal officials could do nothing about it. As Mark Twain said, Salt Lake City was "the stronghold of the prophets, the capital of the only absolute monarch in America."

One of the most venomous and vociferous political appointees was Chief Justice W. W. Drummond. Thwarted like all the other federally appointed officials who tried to compete with Mormon hierarchy, Drummond returned to the States and took his revenge in the *New Orleans Courier* of April 3, 1857, where he wrote:

> A leading characteristic of the followers of the Mohamet
> seems to be a settled and abiding hatred of all "Gentiles,"
> as they are pleased to style all who do not subscribe to

---

* Among Gentiles it was widely believed that the Mormons maintained a shadowy group of secret police called the Danites, who kept people in line, often through violence. Zane Grey's classic, *Riders of the Purple Sage*, is an account of this anti-Mormon point of view. In that novel, the Danites are the villainous oppressors and enforcers, operating on the orders of a tyrannical church government. Sherlock Holmes also encountered them in *A Study in Scarlet*. The Latter Day Saints Church has steadfastly denied that a Danite secret society operated in Utah. No one disputes, however, the existence of Danites during the Missouri years.

their dogmas and conform to their unique and revolting creed. Although they come mainly from the northern portion of this republic they look upon the United States with no other feeling than hatred. Patriotic love of the country that gave them birth, and which they disgrace, has no place in their bosoms. . . . Could a correct side of those horrible transactions be known throughout the country, a crusade would be preached against this foul horde that would soon put an end to their sway.[17]

Drummond thereby positioned the Mormons as not only immoral devotees of a "revolting creed" but also essentially treasonous aliens. (Drummond was less effusive on the polygamy issue, because he had left his own wife and children in Chicago and arrived in Salt Lake City with his mistress; perhaps he felt he was on less than solid ground when the discussion turned to monogamy and its virtues.)

Despite the distractions of political contests with federal officials, Brigham Young also had a church to run. In 1856, this absolute monarch sensed a gradual falling away from the true path, and so he initiated a "Reformation." He sent missionaries to every village in the territory, regardless how small or remote, to catechize each person with a series of probing questions ranging from their devotion to the Mormon faith to their personal and business habits. After reaffirming their faith or confessing their lapses and promising to reform, believers received a second baptism. No doubt there was a political as well as religious motive for the Reformation, for solid faith in the Mormon Church—and Brigham Young—meant Mormon political solidarity as well. Indeed, there was virtually no difference between church and state.

There was a darker side to the movement as well. Dozens of shootings attributed to Brigham Young's orders and carried out by suspected Danite gunmen made Utah a dangerous place to be—for apostates or the occasional obnoxious Gentile. Whether these were

simple feuds or acts of revenge or robberies or political assassina-
tions has never been proved, even though some of the gunmen
later broke their ties with Young and accused him of ordering the
shootings. The targets were usually political and religious enemies
(essentially one and the same in Utah). Regardless of the truth,
federal officials certainly reported these incidents to Washington.
Those reports, coupled with wild rumors, strengthened the feeling
there that Young was running a growing "kingdom" in defiance
of federal law and keeping order by means of a secret police force.
And there seems to have been more than a little truth to that. Wallace Stegner writes: "In the years after 1856 the phrase 'to save' a
man came to the precise meaning of our modern euphemism 'to
liquidate.' There were almost surely not so many holy murders as
the frantic Gentiles charged, and perhaps not as many as the disgruntled avengers confessed, but there were enough. This was the
witch-hunt time of Mormonism, its Inquisition, and neither fanaticism's excesses nor the hierarchy's precise degree of responsibility
has ever been fully admitted or clarified."[18]

But the Reformation had effects other than weeding out apostates
and political enemies. Among the faithful, the movement generated
fervor akin to that created by the Second Great Awakening.

According to historian Juanita Brooks, "In general the effect of
this movement was to arouse the people to new religious consciousness, but for some who had lived through the persecutions of Missouri and Nauvoo [Illinois] and whose covenants included a hope
that God would avenge the death of the Prophet and the sufferings
of His Saints, the Reformation served to encourage fanaticism. It
also helped to cement their group solidarity and to make them feel
that Zion must stand against the sins of the world."[19]

This feeling that "Zion must stand alone against the sins of
the world" carried with it the growing idea that Utah, or Deseret
should become independent of the United States. After years of
squabbling with and being harassed by Washington officials, Young
began to think that independence might be his only choice. He

made a number of speeches on the subject, some recorded by the faithful: "President [of the LDS church] B. Young in his sermon declared that the thread was cut between us and the U.S. and that the Almighty recognized us as a free and independent people and that no officer appointed by government should come and rule over us from the time forth."[20] If Young said, "the Almighty recognized us," people believed it. He was, after all, the successor to the prophet, Joseph Smith.

Young made his pronouncement in the context of escalating tensions. In 1857, three federal judges were sent to Utah; all three were hostile toward the Mormons. When they arrived, the Mormons ignored them and continued to try cases in their own courts. The judges returned to the States, where one testified before Congress that "Brigham Young was a ruthless dictator who employed a band of 'destroying angels'[the Danites], that federal officials were constantly insulted, some had been killed,* and countless government records destroyed."[21]

Frustrated and exasperated by the Mormons' continuing intransigence and even violence against federal officers, and, perhaps as important, mindful of the widespread anti-Mormon sentiment in the country, President James Buchanan decided a show of force was in order, saying, "This is the first rebellion which has existed in our territory and humanity itself requires that we should put it down in such a manner that it shall be the last."[22] He may also have been trying to send a message to Southern secessionists. In contrast, his secretary of war John B. Floyd, who was a southern sympathizer, was eager to support Buchanan's position in order to "deflect public attention from slavery, weaken the power available to the Union in the event of trouble and fill his own pockets."[23] Floyd was widely rumored to be in business with the civilian contractors who supplied the wagon trains for army supplies.

---

* In 1853, eight government surveyors were killed by Indians, but Mormon complicity was widely suspected.

In May of 1857, Buchanan ordered the army to organize an expedition against the Mormons. Part of the expedition's mission would be to replace Brigham Young with a new federally appointed governor. The army would then remain there as a possible posse comitatus to be called as necessary to assist newly appointed civilian officials to enforce the law.

If the Mormons will only fight, their days are numbered. We shall sweep them from the face of the earth and Mormonism in Utah will cease.
　　　　　　—Captain Jesse A. Grove, U.S. Army[24]

THE MARCH WEST WAS THE FIRST TIME MAJOR FEDERAL FORCES HAD been mobilized and sent against citizens of the country. (Various Indian tribes were not considered citizens.) This was not a militia called out to control turbulent mobs; this was the regular army sent against fellow Americans. The "Utah War" is as puzzling as the bitter enmity that animated the campaign—the widespread political hatred of a sect that wanted to preserve its right to govern itself, but had been largely willing to do so within the context of the United States and its constitution. As Brigham Young said, in effect, he revered the Constitution of the United States but detested the rascals who were trying to administer it. Despite Buchanan's pronouncement of rebellion, the idea of independence was still a last resort for Brigham Young, and he had not yet declared it officially, even though he had reports that the army was on its way. Said Young, "We will wait a little while to see, but I shall take a hostile move by our enemies as an evidence that the time has come for the thread to be cut."[25] Independence was the final alternative that the Mormons preferred to domination by the Gentiles and their government—and the inevitable pollution of Gentile immigration. The Mormons didn't mind the wagon trains that came through on their way to California, and indeed they profited from them by selling supplies and services. But they didn't want anyone not of their faith to come and stay unless they were merchants or traders who could provide useful services.

The army expedition would involve twenty-five hundred troops, mostly infantry. The force assembled at Fort Leavenworth in July 1857. The plan was to follow the Oregon Trail to South Pass in Wyoming and from there to drop down through the northern passes into Utah. Along with the troops went an enormous supply train consisting of forty-one separate wagon trains drawn by oxen. Two thousand head of beef cattle also accompanied the trains. The trains were contracted from a civilian firm with strong political connections in Washington. The job of assembling the supply trains was enormous, because the firm had to scour the country for enough oxen to pull the thousand or so wagons that would carry three million pounds of supplies. The extent of the supply problem underscores the difficult logistical facts the army faced throughout the West. There simply was no way to provision a campaign except to bring supplies along—there were no settlements to speak of between Leavenworth and Utah, no railroads to carry supplies. The army had to be prepared for a scorched-earth policy on the part of the Mormons (a stated part of Brigham Young's defense strategy), so they had to take enough supplies to maintain themselves when they got to their objective, knowing that resupply would be difficult because their supply lines would be stretched very thin. The oxen and beef cattle would subsist on the grass between Kansas and Utah. The huge herds would need equally huge pastures along the way.

When the column got under way finally, it straggled for fifty miles, the trains traveling without army protection under civilian teamsters, the infantry units becoming separated and disorganized. They had a long way to go, and by the time they reached their destination, winter would be upon them.

Continue your conciliatory policy towards the Indians, which I have ever recommended, and seek by works of righteousness to obtain their love and confidence, for they must learn that they have either got to help us or the United States will kill us both.

—Brigham Young letter to Jacob Hamblin*26

THE MORMONS HAD A DELICATE RELATIONSHIP WITH THE INDIANS, although they got along much better with them than settlers in other regions, in part because the Mormons regarded the Indians as former Israelites and in part because the Mormon leaders understood the obvious value of peaceful relations and worked to maintain them. One of the tribes in the southern part of Utah, the Paiutes, was especially worrisome, because its members outnumbered the southernmost Mormon settlers four to one—and they had attacked isolated Mormon settlements in the past. The Paiutes did not seem very receptive to the Mormons' efforts to convert them, but for the time being they appeared generally content to maintain relatively peaceful relations. Part of their homelands lay athwart the Old Spanish Trail, which was the southern route to California that immigrants used when traveling late in the season. The northern route led through the Sierras, and winter arrived early in those mountains, as the Donner Party had learned in 1846.

When Brigham Young heard about the approach of the U.S. Army, he declared martial law and mobilized the Nauvoo Legion, some five thousand men of the Mormon militia. He also proclaimed that the people should be prepared to leave their homes, destroy everything, and take to the mountains. He sent messengers to Mormon settlements in California, calling the people back to Utah. He dispatched one particularly important church official, Apostle George A. Smith, to the southern communities to warn them to be

---

* Jacob Hamblin was Young's primary missionary to the Indians. He was also an explorer and rancher in southern Utah and Northern Arizona.

ready to fight. Smith's fervent message reminded everyone of past persecutions and stirred up a volatile mixture of panic and hatred. Perhaps regretting that he had poked the hornet's nest, Smith wrote: "There was only one thing I dreaded and that was a spirit in the breasts of some to wish that vengeance for the cruelties that had been inflicted upon us in the States. They did feel that they hated to owe a debt and not be able to pay it."*[27]

Young also sent emissaries to the Paiutes, soliciting their help against the invaders. The Paiutes were receptive to the idea, although, as it turned out, they were not in a mood to discriminate between the U.S. Army as the enemy and the emigrant wagon trains traveling through their territory, bound for California. Army or emigrant, they were all "merricats," the Paiute version of Americans.

One such train had come from Arkansas and Missouri. It was called the Fancher party and consisted of about 140 men, women, and children. Passing through Salt Lake City, they decided to head south to pick up the Old Spanish Trail, because it was getting late in the summer. Most likely, they were the first train to take that route that year.

The Fancher party had two elements—families from Arkansas and a group of rowdy Missourians who called themselves "the Missouri wildcats." As they traveled through the villages to the south, the wildcats made themselves obnoxious by claiming they had participated in the mob rampages against the Mormons, including the Haun's Mill massacre. One of them even displayed a pistol and claimed it was the one that had killed Joseph Smith. Under the emergency conditions then in effect, the Mormons had been ordered not to sell supplies to emigrant trains, not only because all supplies would be needed in the expected fight with the army, but

---

* George A. Smith was a cousin of Joseph Smith's and one of the twelve apostles of the LDS Church. His incendiary speeches in the southern communities therefore carried significant authority. A key Mormon precept was complete obedience to the dictates of the church hierarchy.

also because there was no need to sell aid and comfort to the enemy. And this lack of cooperation added to the contentious relationship between the travelers and the villages along the way.

In September, the Fancher party reached Mountain Meadows, a traditional resting stop in extreme southwestern Utah. There they would let their animals graze before heading across the difficult stretch of desert in Nevada. And it was there that the Paiutes ambushed them.

In the first attack, seven emigrants were reported as killed and three wounded, while the Paiutes lost several warriors and retreated. The emigrants then circled their wagons in classic style and threw up earthworks between them. The Paiutes meanwhile settled down for a siege. There was too much plunder in the merricat wagons for them to break off.

The attack posed a dilemma for the Mormon military in the southern district. Some were happy to have the Paiutes attack the train, for they would rid Zion of detested Gentiles, especially the Missouri wildcats. Some may have even believed that the wagon train contained the murderer of the prophet and that here was the opportunity for long-desired revenge. Others worried that the Paiutes, now that they'd been stirred up for war, might retaliate against Mormon settlements, if the chance to plunder the emigrants was somehow snatched from them. Also, there was the general atmosphere of fear and hatred of the Gentiles, the violent passions that George A. Smith's visits had aroused. And they were all aware of the approach of the U.S. Army in the north, coming to destroy everything the Mormons had built. All of those factors led to the conclusion that the Mormons should somehow support the Paiutes' attack. "The fervor generated by the eloquence of George A. Smith, the rehearsals of past sufferings and indignities, the imagined threat of being again driven from their homes, the repeated vows to avenge the blood of their martyred prophet had set fires to smoldering in even the calmest heart," writes Juanita Brooks.[28]

While the Mormon military leaders were debating what to do, three of the besieged emigrants tried to make a run to Cedar City, which was thirty-five miles back along the trail, but the Paiutes caught them and killed all three. It's said that a white man killed one of the emigrants, so it's possible some Mormons might have been involved already at this stage of the fight. One version of the story, in fact, has Mormon officer John D. Lee involved in initiating the attack, leading the Paiutes to the scene and participating in the fight from the start to the end.

Another version has Lee arriving at the battlefield after the first several days of the siege. Shortly thereafter, a group of Mormon soldiers arrived. The Mormons were in a tricky position, because the Paiutes' blood was up. They were angry about the loss of their warriors and they wanted both revenge and plunder. But the Mormons' blood was up as well. And certainly the prospect of acquiring the emigrants' wagons and cattle was appealing. In any event, the decision was made to kill everyone except the children, who were too young to give evidence of what they would see. There is still a mystery involved in exactly who made the decision to exterminate the wagon train—and exactly when it was made. It's possible, even likely, that higher military authority made the decision and that Lee was acting under orders. Certainly that was Lee's claim later.

Under a flag of truce, John D. Lee went to the wagon train and somehow convinced the emigrants to leave their barricades without their weapons. Lee told them that the Mormon militiamen would protect them from the Paiutes and guide them safely back to Cedar City. The youngest children would go in a wagon followed by another wagon carrying a wounded woman and three wounded men. The women and older children would follow these wagons on foot, while the men, each one escorted by a Mormon soldier, would bring up the rear. Why they agreed to this is impossible to say. Maybe they had run out of ammunition, so that their weapons were useless, although of course this was only a temporary situation until they could acquire more powder and ball. Maybe they were simply exhausted from five days of siege and not able to think straight. Maybe the idea that white men would be capable of treachery never dawned on them. Maybe they felt they had no choice. Whatever the reason, they agreed. They emerged from their barricades and lined up as directed and started walking east.

When the procession was under way and all the wagons abandoned, someone ordered, "Halt! Do your duty!" At that point, the Paiutes emerged from their hiding places and fell upon the forward party of women and older children, killing all of them. And simultaneously each Mormon militiaman shot the emigrant man he was escorting. It was over quickly, and at the end there were 120 dead, and only 18 of the youngest children had been spared. Though he later denied it, it seems that Lee himself assisted another Mormon soldier in shooting the wounded woman and men who were in the wagon.

Afterward, there were many variations of the story, many denials of complicity, and many explanations about who made the decision, and how high up in the church hierarchy the decision had reached. It was difficult to find a Mormon soldier who would admit to "doing his duty." And it was easy for them to say the Paiutes had done the vast majority of the murders. Today, the questions still persist and most likely always will.

The surviving children were distributed among Mormon families and some eventually returned to families in the States. The Mormons organized a burial party, but the shallow graves they dug soon attracted scavengers. Jacob Hamblin, who was not a party to the action, visited the scene a week after the massacre: "I went to the place of slaughter! Where those unfortunate people were slain. Oh! Horrible indeed was the sight—language fails to picture the scene of blood and carnage. The slain numbering over one hundred men, women and children had been interred by the people of Cedar City. At three places wolves had disinterred the bodies and stripped the bones of their flesh, had left them strewed in every direction. At one place I noticed nineteen wolves pulling out the bodies and eating the flesh."[29]

Lieutenant George N. Bascom.

OPPOSITE TOP: Troops getting ready to leave on patrol. The scene would have looked very much like this when Bascom and his men set out for Apache Pass. Note the jacal in the background. OPPOSITE BOTTOM: Infantry troops on the Arizona frontier. Their breech loading rifles and metal cartridges indicate that this photo is from a later period, but the men are representative of the kind of troops Bascom led. Spit and polish uniforms were not considered practical, necessary or even possible. ABOVE: Fort Bowie in Apache Pass, established in 1862. Note the absence of defensive structures.

Wittick Photo

"Naches"

85768

Nai-chi-ti. Son of Cochise
Chiricahua Apache Chief

OPPOSITE: Naiche, Cochise's son. There are no known pictures of Cochise, but Naiche was said to resemble his father. The photo was taken in 1882 during an interlude of relative peace, but Naiche would soon rejoin Geronimo to resume the war against the whites. He would fight until the end and be transported to the prisoner of war camp in Florida. ABOVE: Taza, Cochise's older son. Taza succeeded his father as chief but died of pneumonia during a trip to Washington, D.C. in 1876. Many Apaches rejected the pneumonia story, but there seems to be no evidence of foul play. Western tribal leaders were often enticed to visit Washington and other eastern cities in the hopes of demonstrating the futility of war against the white civilization. Sometimes it worked; most times, it didn't. But the object of bringing them there was to have them return and spread the word of the overwhelming power of the whites. There was, therefore, no motive for murder in this context; quite the contrary.

Felix Ward as an adult. Raised by the Western Apaches, he was known as Mickey Free, and he scouted for the army in the later Apache wars.

James Tevis, former Butterfield employee, Arizona Ranger and Confederate officer. He was obviously well armed—and needed to be. He knew Cochise personally and had nothing good to say about him.

TOP: Typical Apache dwellings, known as wickiups. Their materials and construction contributed to the mobility and elusiveness of the Apaches. Unlike the Plains tribes who carried their buffalo hide and lodge pole tepees with them wherever they traveled, the Apaches simply abandoned their dwellings when danger threatened or when it came time to leave, for whatever reason. The wickiups were made of bent branches covered with grasses and so had no intrinsic value and could easily be replicated elsewhere. The natural materials also provided a kind of camouflage, especially when the wickiups were nestled in mountain defiles. BOTTOM: Troops in a typically rugged installation. Note again the jacal in the background. Life in the frontier army was anything but comfortable.

TOP: Hog Canyon, site of Fort Buchanan. Some adobe ruins are in the background. The oak trees are similar to the ones used to hang the six Apaches in Apache Pass. BOTTOM: Infantry crossing the Gila River. The army's reliance on wagons for both supply and occasional transportation limited the troops' ability to move rapidly and to penetrate mountainous country. Later in the Apache wars the army would switch to pack mules for supply.

William Oury, Butterfield employee in Tucson and participant in the action in Apache Pass.

A Concord coach, much used, but still elegant in retirement.

A celerity wagon drawn by four mules.

TOP: An example of the rigors—and hazards—of travel by stage coach in frontier Arizona. BOTTOM: A typical stage coach scene in Arizona—an ideal location for an ambush.

OPPOSITE TOP: A Butterfield stage station in Southern Arizona. Creature comforts were not included in the price of the ticket. OPPOSITE BOTTOM: Tempting targets— emigrants passing through what could well be the western end of Apache Pass. ABOVE: Pack mules on the trail—the cynosure of Apache raiders.

The rugged terrain in southern Arizona was just one of the many sources of difficulty in finding, let alone fighting, Apaches. The giant saguaro cactus, while a western icon, is in fact indigenous only to the Sonoran desert region, which runs north and south from Sonora, Mexico to just north of present day Phoenix.

Why did it all happen? The tangle of combustible emotions certainly led to the tragedy, along with a legitimate fear of Paiute reprisals in case they were frustrated. Clearly, things got out of hand and the superheated rhetoric, caused largely by the coming invasion by the U.S. Army, led, as superheated rhetoric often does, to unintended consequences. Most historians agree that Brigham Young did not directly order the attack, but in a state that was based on obedience to higher authority, the highest authorities bear at the very least indirect responsibility for the outcome. When a ship runs aground, the captain is always responsible, whether he was on the bridge at the time or not. That indirect responsibility accounts in part for the official cloud of mystery that still surrounds many of the causes and the results of the massacre. Like most pioneers, the Mormons were experts at circling the wagons.

It took twenty years to bring anyone to justice for this crime. The Paiutes were not chastised, nor were any of the Mormon militia who were there, with the sole exception of John D. Lee. He and several other participants went into individual exile. Lee eventually ended up in Arizona in a lonely place on the banks of the Colorado River, at the end of Glen Canyon and the beginning of the Grand Canyon. Jacob Hamblin discovered the place, which is called Lee's Ferry today. It was one of the two places where it was then possible to cross the Colorado. There was a slight notch in the canyon walls that allowed wagons and horsemen to ascend and descend the cliffs that lined the river. (The other place, called the Crossing of the Fathers, is now at the bottom of Lake Powell.) Lee operated a ferry that carried Mormon emigrants farther south to establish new communities in Arizona.

But the rumors and stories of the massacre continued to circulate over the years, and federal officials finally put out a warrant for Lee and captured him while he was visiting one of his wives in Panguitch, Utah. He was tried once, but the jury could not reach a decision (four Gentiles for conviction, eight Mormons for acquittal). He was tried a second time by an all-Mormon jury and found guilty.* He was shot by a firing squad at the site of the massacre. Though he was certainly guilty, he always claimed he was acting under orders, and that seems evident today. Another of the participants, Philip Klingonsmith, a former bishop of the church who had also been in hiding, supported Lee's claims. Klingonsmith stated in an affidavit and also in testimony that the order to exterminate the emigrants had indeed come from higher authority, although he did not know how high. Klingonsmith was the first to break the ranks of silence. He was later found shot to death in Sonora, Mexico, thereby raising the suspicion of Danite retribution.

Many historians regard John D. Lee as a scapegoat, especially given the composition of the second jury, whose unanimous about-face certainly gives the impression that they were acting under orders.

The Mountain Meadows massacre probably would not have happened had it not been for the frenzy of fear and hatred engendered by the arrival of the U.S. Army at South Pass. The Paiutes might have attacked the Fancher party even without Mormon encouragement, but that's impossible to say. In any event, it's highly unlikely that the Mormons would have been directly involved, even given the antics of the Missouri wildcats. And so it seems fair to say that the Fancher emigrants were casualties of the so-called Utah War. They were also the only casualties from combat, if indeed that word applies.

The Utah War was unusual because no one other than a few fire-breathing officers wanted to fight. Brigham Young ordered his Nauvoo Legion to bottle up the northern passes and to harass

---

* An interesting historical oddity—Wells Spicer was one of Lee's attorneys. Spicer would go on to Tombstone, Arizona, where he would be the justice of the peace who conducted the hearing investigating murder charges against Wyatt Earp and his brothers after the gunfight at the O.K. Corral.

the "enemy" but not to shed any blood. (This order goes some way toward exonerating him from ordering the Mountain Meadows massacre, although there is an obvious difference between picking a fight with emigrants and picking a fight with the U.S. Army.) Young did not want to fight a battle with the army if it could be avoided. At the same time, he did want to prevent the army from entering and attacking Utah, so he decided to block the passes and harass the enemy's supply trains.

When the U.S. Army finally arrived at the northern passes in October, the supply trains were strung out along the trail and made easy pickings for the Mormon cavalry, who destroyed three separate trains, ran off herds of cattle, and burned the grass for miles around so that the remaining animals would have no feed. And, true to their orders, the Mormons did not shoot anyone. The army then had to change tactics and guard the wagon trains and move north to where there was grazing. In November, Colonel Albert Sidney Johnston* arrived to take command. With him were new federal judges and the newly appointed governor, Albert Cumming. Blocked by the militia from entering the passes and frustrated by a blizzard, Johnston went into winter quarters to await developments. The intense suffering the troops endured on the long march to Utah and during that winter, from reduced rations and primitive quarters, created a smoldering animosity toward their Mormon adversaries. When spring arrived, the troops would be looking to exact a little revenge for their miseries.

But although those animosities would remain, the Utah War was ultimately settled by negotiation. Buchanan saw that his campaign to stamp out rebellion had been an expensive overreaction that had turned into a fiasco, now called "Buchanan's Blunder." He decided to issue a blanket pardon for all Mormons, which must have caused Young to smile wryly; a pardon was neither here nor there

---

* An aggressive and well-respected officer, Johnston would go on to become a Confederate general, in command at Shiloh, where he was killed.

as long as his own power remained essentially in place. Young met with Cumming and agreed to accept the new government. He also agreed to the presence of the U.S. Army. They would establish an installation called Camp Floyd at a location about forty miles southwest of Salt Lake City—a face-saving distance that protected most of the faithful from too frequent a contact with the Gentiles.

But there was definitely some contact. As with all frontier forts, the establishment of Camp Floyd provided a boost to the local economy. Twenty-five hundred men need a lot of supplies, especially since many of their supply wagons had been burned and many of the beef herd they brought had either died from starvation during the winter or been run off by Mormon raiders. (It would not be at all surprising to learn that the Mormons sold some of the cattle back to the army.)

So ended the Utah War, probably the only war in history in which the sole casualties were civilians. A workable, if wary, truce now existed between the federal government and the Mormons. The new governor had become surprisingly well disposed toward the Mormons, and the army was far enough away. Brigham Young would remain the major power in Deseret, but he was willing to recognize the federal officials. His decision not to fight the invading army spared the territory and his people from devastation and numerous casualties. Still, there was some uneasiness between the two parties, and the shadow of the Mountain Meadows Massacre was still hanging over the territory. The army would be staying for a little while. Only the outbreak of the Civil War would rescue Deseret and its prophet from the unwanted embrace of the merricats in uniform.

Part of that army was the Seventh Infantry regiment, whose most junior officer would soon be 2nd Lieutenant George Bascom.

Chapter Eight

BASCOM GOES WEST

*That there are difficulties, and no inconsiderable ones,
to be met on this as on all other routes, no one doubts.
All accounts agree that traveling is not quite as pleasant
as in a Fourth Avenue car, or the fare as excellent as
that of the Astor House, or the climate and temperature as agreeable as the shady side of Broadway in
September.*

—Waterman Ormsby,
New York Herald, 1858[1]

CAMP FLOYD WAS NAMED AFTER JOHN B. FLOYD, THE SECRETARY
of war for President Buchanan and a man who had about him a
persistent odor of scandal. Accusations of payoffs in return for
lucrative government contracts swirled around him and his department. He was also accused of incompetence in his handling of
the Utah campaign. As Horace Greeley wrote: "[The army] was
at last sent on its way at a season too late to allow it to reach Salt
Lake before winter. No commander was sent with it . . . . It was
thus dispatched on a long and difficult expedition, in detachments,

without a chief, without orders, without any clear idea of its object or destination."[2]

Whether the pleasure of having a frontier fort named after him lessened Floyd's chagrin over these political attacks is difficult to say. It's possible he had a thick enough skin to shrug off the criticism while continuing to enjoy the considerable benefits of office.

After the Mexican War, Floyd's predecessors in the War Department had decided that the best way to handle supply transport for the army was to use civilian contractors. The War Department arrived at this conclusion after Kearny's expedition through New Mexico lost the majority of its mules and oxen and had to abandon many of the supplies. Kearny and his officers were unprepared for the difficulties of getting freight through rugged passages like Raton Pass. Subsequent army attempts to resupply the garrisons in Santa Fe went through similar tribulations, even though civilian freighters had been making this trip along the Santa Fe Trail for years without too many mishaps. As a result, the War Department decided to relieve the army of this business and rely on civilian freight companies.[3] As mentioned, the enormous supply trains supporting the Utah War were entirely under civilian management. The postmaster general also used civilian contractors to deliver the mail, an increasingly important and difficult operation now that the country extended to the Pacific.

Of course, there is nothing inherently wrong with the idea of civilian contractors providing goods and services to the military or the government. In fact, it is no doubt advisable to let various branches of government, military, and private enterprise do what they do best and not ask them to perform functions they are not equipped for by training or inclination. But there is no getting around the fact that these kinds of arrangements also offer encyclopedic opportunities for graft.

As he was traveling through the Utah Territory, Horace Greeley stopped at Camp Floyd in 1859 and, sniffing the wind, found it anything but fragrant:

Again, pursuant to a recent order from Washington the Assistant Quartermaster-General here is now selling by auction some two thousand mules—about two thirds of all the government owns in this territory. . . . Nobody here has recommended the sale of these mules . . . the army can never move without purchasing an equal number; and they can neither be bought here nor brought here for two hundred thousand dollars more than these animals are now fetching. Somebody's interest is subserved by this sale. . . . Who issues such orders as this, and for whose benefit? . . . [Also] there have recently arrived here thirty thousand bushels of corn from the States at a net cost, including transportation, of over three hundred and forty thousand dollars, or over eleven dollars per bushel. No requisition was ever made for this corn which could have been bought here, delivered, for two dollars per bushel, or sixty thousand dollars in all. The dead loss to the Treasury for this corn is two hundred and eighty thousand dollars, even supposing that the service required it at all. Somebody makes a good thing out of wagoning this corn from Missouri. . . . Who believes that that somebody has not influential and thrifty connections inside the War Department?[4]

Secretary Floyd's name was prominent among those suspected of making "a good thing" out of the purchase and transportation of army supplies, and he would later (in January 1861) be indicted for "malversation of office," a ten-dollar word for official graft. He resigned his office to stand trial, but the prosecutors entered a *nolle prosequi* (decision not to proceed) because they said there was not enough evidence. The decision was undoubtedly designed to make the scandals go away. There were other problems occupying official Washington in January of 1861, for South Carolina had seceded and other states were poised to follow.

Secretary Floyd would ultimately join the Confederacy, where he would be in command at Fort Donelson—a battle he would lose and the battle that established U. S. Grant's fame. Floyd disgracefully escaped on a steamboat on the Cumberland River and left his subordinates to accede to Grant's demand for "unconditional surrender." By that time Floyd's reputation was in well-earned shards on both sides of the Mason-Dixon.

But not so in 1859 while he was still pulling various levers at the War Department, and he probably felt at least a touch of pride in thinking about his eponymous fort in Utah. (After his difficulties came to light, the fort was renamed Camp Crittenden.)

The seventh infantry regiment was at Camp Floyd, and it was there that newly commissioned Second Lieutenant Bascom traveled in April of 1859.

On his way to Utah, Bascom would have stopped at his home in Owingsville to say good-bye to his family there, little knowing, of course, that it would be his final visit. Perhaps, though, like most soldiers leaving home for active duty in the field, he heard a small voice in the back of his head whispering that he was in fact leaving forever. Maybe he indulged himself in the sentimental images of a soldier's last farewell. He would not have been the first to do so.

Was there a girl he left behind? Let us say that there was. Going into harm's way he deserved to have someone to think about, whether she existed for real or only as a wishful product of his imagination. Perhaps she was the local belle. Perhaps she was there that last evening. If so, she no doubt admired his new uniform and his youthful beard, which covered his cheeks but not his upper lip. She might have thought his eyes particularly fine. In all objectivity, he was a good-looking young man.

It's easy to imagine the scene after dinner, Bascom and his family, and perhaps the local belle, gathered around the piano in the parlor, singing:

> *In the stillness of night,*
> when the stars mildly shine,
> My heart fondly holds,
> a communion with Thine;
> For I feel thou art near,
> and where'ere I may be,
> That the Spirit of Love
> *keeps watch over me.**

It was a time of such sentimental songs and a time in which people celebrated—in fact, made a cardinal virtue of—a level of sentimentality that to modern tastes borders on the maudlin. People wept over the death of Little Eva in *Uncle Tom's Cabin* and felt themselves good and virtuous for doing so. This was not so much catharsis as emotional indulgence. They sang melancholy songs and hung lithographs of children in prayer next to cross-stitched samplers saying "Bless This House."** But while the music and the lithographs would remain popular in the years ahead, for hundreds of thousands of families during the Civil War, the artificial, self-induced emotions of the antebellum days would be replaced by real sorrow, and the melodramatic tears over the death of Little Eva would give way to tears of genuine grief. Songs like "Just Before the Battle, Mother" were sung by both armies and were intensely sentimental, on one level. But when sung in the trenches or around

---

* "Thou Art Gone From My Gaze," a popular parlor song written by G. Linley and well known throughout the decade of the 1850s and the Civil War years.

** Mark Twain satirizes this sentimental style when Huck Finn visits the Grangerford home.

the campfire, these songs took on an additional element of deep and authentic longing, an intense mixture of homesickness and dread of what the future—indeed, the next day—would bring.

But all of that was in the future for Bascom and for several million other men, young and not so young. On the morning of Bascom's departure, his spirits would have risen, his unsettling premonitions would have gone, and once he had said his good-byes and was well and truly on his way, he certainly must have felt the excitement of facing the unknowable future and with it the chance to do something of value, finally.

He traveled by train as far as St. Louis, where he boarded a steamboat bound for the Missouri River and the landing at Fort Leavenworth, the great supply depot and jumping-off point for the frontier. The year 1859 was a high-water mark for riverboat travel on the Missouri. In fact, there were more steamboats leaving St. Louis for the Missouri than there were heading up and down the Mississippi. There were sixty steam packets working the Missouri trade and another forty or so tramp steamers catching the scraps of the freight and passenger business.[5] The business had grown dramatically during the decade because of the California Gold Rush and the Mormon migration to Utah, which implies that there were some reasonably prosperous Mormons who could afford the relative ease and comfort of steamboat travel, at least part of the way, in sharp contrast to their poorer coreligionists who walked to Zion hauling handcarts.

The typical packet steamboat was 250 feet long with a 40-foot beam. Side-wheeler or stern-wheeler, the boats could carry several hundred passengers and seven hundred tons of freight. Navigation on the Missouri River was tricky because of shifting water levels and numerous shoals and snags and brutal, ice-clogged winters. But in the hands of a competent pilot, a riverboat could recoup its construction cost in a matter of a few trips, given the passenger demand and the need for freight deliveries to growing communities along the river, to say nothing of the gigantic maw that was the army's principal supply depot at Fort Leavenworth.

In 1859, one of the redoubtable LaBarge brothers, John, piloted the steamboat *Chippewa* all the way from St. Louis to Fort Benton, Montana—a fur-trading post, not an army outpost.* It's tempting to think that Bascom might have been on that voyage, although, of course, he would have debarked at Leavenworth and therefore missed the rest of the record-setting journey. The odds are that he wasn't, though, because in April, when Bascom was traveling, the upper Missouri was probably still choked with ice floes, and the *Chippewa* was not able to reach Fort Benton until July.

Had Bascom come directly from New York by train to St. Louis and then by steamboat to Leavenworth, the whole trip would have taken something like eight days.[6] It was at Leavenworth that travelers on the two great trails, the Oregon and the Santa Fe, took their leave of civilization; they would not see it again until they reached their destinations, hundreds of miles away. The great wagon trains of emigrants and civilian freighters, loaded with supplies for the army and drawn by plodding oxen, departed in long, slow caravans of canvas-covered "prairie schooners." One emigrant extolling the virtues of the oxen said: "The ox is a most noble animal, patient, thrifty, durable, gentle, and does not run off. . . . The ox will plunge through mud, swim over streams, dive into thickets, and he will eat almost anything."[7]

Leavenworth was a busy place. Horace Greeley described the extent of the civilian contractors' operations: "Such acres of wagons! Such

---

* It's interesting to contrast the design of these private trading-post forts with the forts of the army. Trading-post forts, like Fort Benton, Bent's Fort, and Fort Bridger, were surrounded by walls with blockhouses at the corners. Army forts on the frontier generally did not have walls but were collections of buildings arranged around a parade ground. During the Utah War, the army wintered at Fort Bridger, although it was cold comfort, because the Mormons had burned all the buildings before retreating, leaving only the surrounding walls.

pyramids of axletrees! Such herds of oxen! Such regiments of drivers and other employees! No one who does not see can realize how vast a business this is, nor how immense are its outlays as well as its income. . . . They [the civilian contractors] last year employed six thousand teamsters, and worked 45,000 oxen."[8]

These civilian contractors' wagon trains were setting off in various directions to supply isolated forts that were scattered throughout the frontier. Manned by a few companies of soldiers, these outposts were largely dependent on the lumbering wagon trains coming from Leavenworth. Many of the forts were located to protect the supply and communications lines (mail and passenger traffic) and so preceded settlement by ranchers and farmers. In fact, in many parts of the frontier, the forts were prerequisites for subsequent settlement. These forts, therefore, had no local markets from which to supplement their supplies from Leavenworth. What's more, even if there were local ranchers to supply food and forage, horses and mules, they could not supply ammunition for small arms or artillery, medical supplies, uniforms and boots, and other materials specific to the army's needs. Also, army horses required grain and could not prosper on a diet of grass alone. If there were no local farms, the grain would have to come from supply trains.

Leavenworth was also a starting place for stagecoaches heading west, as they took over the job of transporting individual travelers. The stagecoaching business was expanding for two unrelated reasons. The first was the discovery of gold in the creeks around Denver. That started the Pike's Peak or Bust Gold Rush in the summer of 1858, and although many of the would-be miners traveled by hook or by crook, some were well heeled enough to take a stage, and, as is usually the case when a need arises, there were entrepreneurs ready to meet it. Ultimately, writes Frank A. Root, the "line was equipped with over fifty Concord coaches. . . . They were brought up the Missouri by steamboat and unloaded on the levee [at Leavenworth]. . . . It took a vast fortune to open up and stock the new route."[9]

The other reason for the growth of stage travel was the need to deliver better mail service to California by way of a central route that was faster than the southern route established and operated by the Butterfield line. Here again, North-South politics were an inescapable and contentious element in the discussions about how best to get mail to and from California. Northern politicians complained that the southern route was too long and wasted time in delivering the mail. Southern defenders pointed out that the southern route was free of weather problems and was therefore reliable twelve months of the year. Better to spend a few extra days on the road to ensure the mail would arrive regularly. It was an old and continuing argument that the Civil War would soon resolve.

The southern route operated by John Butterfield, the first of all the routes selected, still had the primary mail contract, for semi-weekly delivery. But it was not a monopoly. The postmaster general, Aaron Brown, though a southern sympathizer, was adding new lines. In 1858, Hockaday & Company was given a contract to carry mail from Independence, Missouri, to Salt Lake City. Another contractor, George Chorpenning, picked up the business in Salt Lake and carried the mail to Placerville, California, where other California contractors would then carry on to Sacramento and points beyond.

The central route went from Independence with a stop at Fort Leavenworth and followed the same road essentially as the army that invaded Utah—along the Oregon Trail to South Pass, Fort Bridger, and down to Salt Lake City and Camp Floyd, then through central Nevada to California. (The stagecoach route to the Colorado gold fields was more direct; Denver and Leavenworth are both more or less on the thirty-ninth parallel, and the country between the two is not blocked by mountain chains.) In any event, there was passenger and express service from Leavenworth west along the central route, and this was the way Bascom must have gotten to Camp Floyd from Fort Leavenworth. His alternative would have been to join a supply train, but he would have been too impatient to spend weeks traveling with a wagon train hauled by oxen.

It's safe to say that journey by stagecoach from Leavenworth to Camp Floyd would not have been Bascom's favorite part of the trip from New York. Western traveler Demas Barnes wrote:

> Coaches will be overloaded . . . passengers will get sick, a gentleman of gallantry will hold the baby, children will cry . . . passengers will get angry, the drivers will swear, the sensitive will shrink . . . and the dirt [will be] almost unendurable . . . Stop over nights? No, you wouldn't! To sleep on the sand floor of a one story sod house or adobe hut, without a chance to wash, with miserable food, uncongenial companionship, loss of a seat in a coach until one comes empty, etc., won't work. A through ticket with fifteen inches of seat, with a fat man on one side, a poor widow on the other, a baby on your lap, a bandbox over your head, and three or four persons immediately in front, leaning against your knees, makes the picture. . . . I have just finished six days of this thing and I am free to say, until I forget a great many things now very visible to me, I shall not undertake it again.[10]

Mark Twain made a similar journey along the same route as Bascom, but he was luckier than most because his coach was not crowded, and he could spread the mail sacks on the floor of the coach and so make a bed. (Twain traveled the route in 1861 when the southern route had been closed by the Civil War and all the mail transferred to the central route.) He also had something to say about the food at the stage stops:

> The station keeper upended a disk of last week's bread the shape and size of an old-time cheese, and carved some slabs from it which were as good as Nicholson pavement, and tenderer. He sliced off a piece of bacon for each man, but only the experienced old hands made

out to eat it, for it was condemned army bacon which the United States would not feed to its soldiers in the forts, and the stage company had bought it cheap for the sustenance of their passengers and employees. . . . Then he poured for us a beverage which he called "Slumgullion," and it's hard to think he was not inspired when he named it. It really pretended to be tea, but there was too much dish-rag and sand, and old bacon rind in it to deceive the intelligent traveler. He had no sugar and no milk—not even a spoon to stir the ingredients with.

We could not eat the bread or the meat, nor drink the "Slumgullion," and when I looked at that melancholy vinegar cruet I thought of the anecdote (a very, very old one even at that day) of the traveler who sat down to a table which had nothing on it but a mackerel and a pot of mustard. He asked the landlord if this was all.

"All! Why, thunder and lightning, I should think there was mackerel enough for six."

"But I don't like mackerel."

"Oh—then help yourself to the mustard."

In other days I had considered it a good, a very good anecdote, but there was a dismal plausibility about it here, that took all the humor out of it.[11]

There was, perhaps, some aesthetic compensation for the miseries of long-distance stagecoach travel. The coaches were generally "Concords," so called because they were built in Concord, New Hampshire, by the Abbot-Downing Company. (Because of the huge demand for their coaches, Abbot and Downing split into two companies in the late forties, but both still turned out coaches on the original plan.) The coaches were masterpieces of design and workmanship. Abbot and Downing had invented a new kind of coach suspension in which the body of the coach rested like an egg on leather straps called thoroughbraces. (Of course, the egg was secured fore and after and side to side.) The curving sides meant that the center of gravity was exactly between the wheels, so that the coach was less likely to capsize when going around a corner.[12] The action of the body was more like the pitch and roll of a ship rather than the violent jarring up and down and back and forth that was typical of other coach designs. The rear wheels were five feet one inch in diameter, the front wheels three feet ten. The wooden elements of the wheel were made of cured ash that was virtually immune to warping, and the iron tire was bonded to the wooden wheel circumference by intense heat, so that the usual warping and separation of the rim from the wheel—a common cause of crashes in other coaches—were rare with the Concord.

From the outside, the Concord coaches were, and still are, beautiful. No doubt at the start of his journey from Fort Leavenworth, George Bascom looked upon his coach with appreciation. The woodwork and joinery were perfect, the paint bright, red for the coach and yellow for the wheels and running gear; the horses, or mules, in their well-turned-out harnesses, sleek and full of energy, the driver and conductor colorful in outfit and language.*

As the miles unfolded, however, Bascom's appreciation for the romance of stagecoach travel as well as the aesthetic appeal of the Concord would gradually have given way to a more practical, and dispiriting, realization that he had eleven hundred miles to go—at an average of five miles a dreary hour. At that point, life became a simple matter of endurance. The empty prairie, low hills rolling endlessly, seemed to offer no prospect of ever coming to an end.

Two men operated the stagecoach. The driver was as often as not an easterner accustomed to the job of handling reins for six horses or mules, since stagecoaching had been in operation in the East for many decades and there were plenty of opportunities to learn the art. There was also a conductor. He was senior to the driver and was

---

* Horses were faster and easier to manage than mules, although mules were preferred in sandy or rugged sections of the route.

responsible for the mail and express packages being transported, as well as for the passengers. No doubt the conductor had a shotgun somewhere close by as well as some other armament. Sometimes there was a shotgun guard in addition to the conductor. The passengers were generally advised to be well armed, although in those days most intrepid travelers would have known that without being told. Even the normally pacific Mark Twain was "armed to the teeth with a pitiful little Smith & Wesson seven shooter, which carried a ball like a homeopathic pill, and it took the whole seven to make a dose for an adult."[13]

Each driver specialized in one section of the road, perhaps a seventy-five-mile stretch. When a driver finished that section going west, for example, he would rest at the stage stop and then relieve the driver of the eastbound coach and head back along the same route. This was an obviously sensible way to make sure the driver became an expert on the difficult portions of his section of road. The contingencies of bad weather, Indian or road agent attack, and accidents added enough variety to counteract the boredom of traveling the same route day after day. The stagecoach companies were very careful about the quality of their horses and the care they received. This was just good business, because, even burdened by a loaded stage, the horses were generally able to outrun grass-fed and undersized Indian ponies. Ambushes, of course, were another story.

The entire line was organized by divisions of about 250 miles each. A division agent handled all the needs of the stage stops within this length of road—acquiring and caring for the animals, providing food for men and animals, hiring and firing hostlers and blacksmiths, building and repairing stage stations; in short, looking after everything in his domain, including tracking down and dealing with troublesome bandits and Indians. "He was a very, very great man in his division—a kind of Grand Mogul, a Sultan of the Indies, in whose presence common men were modest of speech and manner," wrote Twain.[14]

The conductor was junior in rank to the division agent, but he was attached to the same division, so that his tenure as the man responsible for the mail and express lasted throughout the entire 250 miles. He stayed aboard even though drivers changed regularly.

The station keepers and hostlers were often a combination of low characters, fugitives, and dimwits who could find no other work and resorted to living in wretched conditions in the middle of nowhere, in places where the only excitement was likely to be the kind they didn't want. Sometimes they were old-time frontiersmen who knew something about the local Indians and how to deal with them. Even if they were reasonably law-abiding citizens, they were not drawn from polite, or even well-washed, society. The stations were approximately twenty to forty miles apart, and the coaches traveled between four and seven miles an hour, depending, of course, on the terrain. Except when it was time for meals, the coaches stopped only long enough to change the teams.

Bascom would have traveled on the Hockaday & Company stage line. About the time that Bascom was traveling, however, Hockaday sold his line to Jones and Russell. The Russell in this case was William Russell, who was associated with Russell, Majors and Waddell, the company rumored to have ties to Secretary of War Floyd, and the company that had furnished the supply wagons for the Utah War—and suffered from the Mormon cavalry's attacks.

One of the section agents on this line was the notorious Jack Slade, a man who brooked no banditry in his domain, which extended from Horseshoe, Wyoming, to Salt Lake City. After being ambushed by a local outlaw named Jules Beni (who founded the thieves' den known as Julesburg, Colorado), Slade recovered from his wounds and sought out Old Jules, captured him, tied him to a corral post, and used him for target practice, removing pieces of him one shot at a time, until finally putting an end to him and cutting off his ears as a memento.

Mark Twain remembers meeting Slade at a stage station: "The coffee ran out. At least it was reduced to one tin cupful. Slade was about to take it when he saw that my cup was empty. He politely offered to refill it, but although I wanted it, I politely declined. I was afraid he had not killed anybody that morning, and might be needing diversion."[15]

It's entirely possible, even likely, that Bascom had a similar encounter, because Jones and Russell kept Slade on as division agent after they bought out Hockaday in May of 1859—just about the time that Bascom was passing through. It's unlikely that Bascom would have heard of Slade's antics and adventures, so he would not have been as shy as Twain about accepting the last of the coffee. But even if he had heard of Slade—perhaps from a stereotypically garrulous driver—Bascom would not have demurred. As a young officer, he had his dignity to protect.

Slade was reported to have killed twenty-eight men—in the line of duty—and was apparently a valuable employee, except when drunk. He was never known to refuse an offer to "take a smile." Drinking finally put an end to him when he went on a violent spree in Virginia City, Montana, and the local Vigilance Committee hanged him.

Should the readers of your Journal in the States see these communications, they will understand that not-withstanding we are serving in the most God-forsaken country in the habitable globe, yet . . . with Valley Tan to drink and the Valley Tan to read, we are all right.
— Camp Floyd soldier's letter to the editor,
February 1859[16]

I say that the nausea the Goshoots gave me, an Indian worshipper, set me to examining authorities to see if

*perchance I had been overestimating the Red Man while
viewing him through the mellow moonshine of romance.
The revelations that came were disenchanting.*
                              —Mark Twain, *Roughing It*[17]

UNLIKE TWAIN'S "MOONSHINE OF ROMANCE," THE MOONSHINE
of choice at Camp Floyd was anything but mellow. Called Valley
Tan (as in tanning fluid), it was a species of locally manufactured
whiskey that was distilled under license by Mormons and sold to
the unwary or the undiscriminating, and therefore had a wide
market. Soldiers, teamsters, and assorted camp followers claimed
Valley Tan "improved" with each glass—a compliment that loses
something of its force the more you think about it. Indeed, the stuff
was described as liquor that "smells like gangrene starting in a mil-
dewed silo, it tastes like the wrath to come, and when you absorb
a deep swig of it, you have all the sensation of having swallowed a
lighted kerosene lamp."[18] No doubt, most of the soldiers who tried
it agreed with a local bartender who said: "There ain't nothing bad
about this whiskey; the only fault is, it isn't good."[19] During the
great Reformation of 1856, one of the reforms the Mormons were
required to adopt, or readopt, was abstinence from alcohol.* There
was no proscription about making it, though, nor did the church
hierarchy consider it wrong to sell it to the newly arrived American
soldiers or to the various rough-hewn Gentile teamsters, as well as
the gamblers, prostitutes, and criminals who predictably appeared
as Camp Floyd grew into a sizable installation. The Mormons saw
no inconsistency in this commerce; or, if they did, they were not
troubled by it, perhaps agreeing with Ralph Waldo Emerson that "A
foolish consistency is the hobgoblin of little minds." And in truth,
not all the Saints were as abstemious as they professed, though
most probably had more sense than to drink the local product.

---

* The precise wording of the catechism was: "Have you been intoxicated by
strong drink?" That leaves a little room for interpretation.

The other Valley Tan was a newspaper edited by Kirk Anderson, a Gentile, staunch critic of the Mormons, and tireless supporter of the army in Utah. The paper was a weekly that began publication in November 1858, after the army was installed in Camp Floyd. The *Valley Tan*, published in Salt Lake City, was the second newspaper in Utah Territory, the first being the *Deseret News* (founded 1850), which was the official organ of the Mormon Church. As an opposition editor, Anderson had strong opinions, stated them strongly and, like many frontier editors, went around well armed. He had good reason to, for, as he wrote in an open letter dated November 26, 1858, and addressed to the Salt Lake City mayor, ". . . at the corner of East Temple and First South, at least eight men in number, armed with guns, and who as we approached within a few feet of them, cocked their guns and placed themselves directly in front of us in a hostile manner, one of their number, viz. [*sic*] fired a pistol. We desire to enter [a] complaint against certain policemen (the above mentioned eight) for acting contrary to law."[20] All things considered, Anderson's "complaint" seems admirably restrained.

Not surprisingly, the *Valley Tan* ceased publication in November of 1860 after most of the troops at Camp Floyd had been sent on a campaign against hostile Navajos in New Mexico. Given the *Valley Tan's* editorial positions, two years seems like a remarkably long run, as well as a testament, albeit mild, to Mormon tolerance. (The *Deseret News*, on the other hand, is still in business to this day.)

Despite the fact that Deseret was an essentially Mormon theocracy, there were some Gentiles living there aside from the barely tolerated army and their civilian employees. Merchants, who saw a good thing from trade with and to the Mormons, had come early and established generally good relations with the Mormon hierarchy—a matter of mutual benefit, since the new merchants made a market for Mormon cattle and produce and brought in much-needed trade goods from the States. There were also some scattered ranchers and farmers throughout the territory who were either immune to Mormon proselytizing or, worse, apostate Saints. These latter were the particular concern of the great Reformation and the subsequent concern of alleged Mormon enforcers. As one prominent Mormon said, ". . . if men were found who were murderers and thieves and beyond the control of society and law, it would be better if they were disposed of."[21] "Beyond the control of society and law" is a broad category, and the question arises, whose law and whose tenets of society? That was the question that motivated the Utah War in the first place and would continue to make difficult the relations between Mormons, federal officials, and the army. Throughout the early days of Mormon Utah there is a continuing sense that Brigham Young's greatest worry was anomie, the breakdown of social norms and values; in this case, Mormon norms and values. The presence of a Gentile army and its civilian hangers-on, the steady stream of Gentile emigrants heading west, along with the problem of Mormon apostates, were all factors that could lead to the gradual dissolution of the Mormon prophet's vision and the society it created. Accordingly, Young used all the levers of his considerable power to combat those evils—without risking confrontations he could not win. In a strange way, he and Cochise had similar challenges—their cultures and ways of life were under attack from precisely the same historical and social forces. Both were vastly outnumbered. Both had the same kind of cultural paranoia that led them to protect their own and suspect outsiders. And both would die before they could realize they had lost.*

Aside from drinking Valley Tan and reading its namesake newspaper, the soldiers at Camp Floyd were kept busy erecting the camp buildings. The Cedar Valley was devoid of any vegetation except the ever-present sage and assorted desert plants that were useless for building materials or fuel. Soldiers had to go up into the surrounding mountains to cut logs and haul them to the

---

* Some might argue that the Mormon Church has been highly successful, but Utah today is hardly like the theocratic vision of the early church fathers.

camp, where they could be cut and split for firewood or sawed into lumber. Mormon workmen came to offer their services and, for three dollars a day, they turned out adobe bricks, ultimately producing 1,600,000 of them. Brigham Young and fellow church authority Heber C. Kimball had no scruples about selling finished lumber to the army, and the two of them made $70,000 from the sale. The presence of the army was an apparently mixed blessing.

Within four months, the army and its enterprising engineers were able to construct a fort consisting of three hundred buildings, most of them one-story adobes. "Scattered within this area were living quarters for civilian employees . . . as well as four hospitals, five guardhouses, numerous bowling alleys, canteens, sutler's stores* and scores of utility buildings," writes Donald R. Moorman.[22] Along with barracks for the enlisted men, there were officers' quarters, warehouses, workshops, corrals, and even a couple of theaters and beer halls. These latter were particularly appreciated by the German-born troops of the Seventh Infantry, who were no doubt homesick for the real thing. Undoubtedly, the beer brewed and served there was not of Hofbräuhaus quality, nor were there any buxom serving women carrying five steins in each hand. But it was better than nothing. These same troops also formed an amateur theater group that performed plays in their native language.[23] There was a lending library, a Masonic Lodge, and, against all odds, a small but active Temperance Society.

Getting this installation built was a prodigious undertaking. As the commanding officer, Albert Sidney Johnston, wrote to his son: "We have to provide storage for two years of provisions, quartermasters, ordnance and medical stores. These require 2000 wagons to [haul] them, each carrying about 5000 pounds—these

---

* A sutler was a civilian merchant with a license to sell merchandise to army personnel. Sometimes he operated out of a wagon, while on campaign or on the march. Other times he opened a store on the grounds of a fort.

buildings alone, 12 or 14, about 600 feet long, will be a heavy work to complete."[24]

The entire camp (which was really a large and traditionally designed fort) was organized in a broad rectangle with wide avenues running through the various lines of buildings. There were no walls surrounding the camp, but the artillery was positioned on the eastern edge, the most likely direction from which trouble might arise.

By November 1858 the construction was completed, just in time to shelter men and matériel from an early blizzard. Camp Floyd was now the second-largest population center in Utah.

No description of Camp Floyd would be complete without a word about Fairfield, a village on the right bank of the creek, immediately opposite camp. This village is habitually called Frogtown, and is inhabited almost solely by gamblers and grog-sellers, such as follow the movement of every considerable body of troops. There are scores of gambling places, and grogshops without number. It is, perhaps, safe to say that scarcely twenty men in the village earn an honest livelihood. When the soldiers are fleeced of their two [months'] pay, the keepers of these places pluck each other—one day rich, another poor. A gambler, well known here, was known to have had at one time $30,000, saved from his gains, but in a few months he left here "broke."

—*New York Times,* Jan. 17, 1860

BLIZZARDS OR SUMMER SANDSTORMS NOTWITHSTANDING, WHEN the troops were off duty, many of them heeded the siren calls coming from across Cedar Creek, and, more specifically, from the saloons and brothels of Frogtown.

Somehow Frogtown has escaped the notice of Hollywood myth-makers, which is strange since it was every bit as corrupt, seedy, and dangerous as Tombstone, Dodge City, or Deadwood. In some ways it was more dangerous, because not only was it the resort of gamblers, gunmen, and criminals (often one and the same), but also local Indians,* who enjoyed Valley Tan as much as the next person and who, when under its influence, rode "through the town on their ponies, whooping and yelling until they came into contact with drunken soldiers and then there would be some gunplay," according to local resident Ebenezer Crouch.[25]

Frogtown was a source of supreme irritation to the Mormon hierarchy because it was the epicenter of crime from which rustlers and murderers radiated out into the country, and it was also a magnet that drew Saints who might otherwise have remained pious but who could not resist the temptation of the brothels and gambling dens. Worse, these same brothels attracted some Mormon girls and women, who found life on the farm tedious and were happy, at least initially, to exchange their favors for some army gold: ". . . Fairfield was full of rottenness and evil of every description and I'm sorry to say our people of both sexes mixed up with them largely and . . . it did look [bad] to see young ladies whose parents were faithful," wrote local resident Charles Bailey.[26]

It was dangerous for anyone who ventured into Frogtown. As saloon keeper John Nelson said, "The law of six shooters was the only one in existence, and revolvers were called into requisition to settle all differences."[27] That wasn't quite true; there were law-enforcement officers in Frogtown. But their badges of office were hardly protection. One sheriff, a man named Coates, was attacked by a gambler and pistol-whipped. Coates managed to maintain his senses and stabbed the gambler with a hunting knife, which put

---

* Most frontier boomtowns did not welcome Indians as customers in the saloons.

an end to the gambler and also to Coates's career. He resigned and Frogtown had no sheriff for several months thereafter.

The criminal element got a serious increase in its ranks when the army, having finished building Camp Floyd, fired nine hundred civilians, mostly former teamsters, who had been employed in construction. These men were left without many resources or options, and since most of them were rough edged to begin with, they took to crime as a logical next step. Horse theft became epidemic. Even the menacing "Wild Bill" Hickman, a noted gunman, Mormon enforcer, and suspected Danite, had his horse stolen from outside the Frogtown saloon where he was drinking.[*]

Rustling on a large or small scale became thriving business because of California. Brimming with gold and expanding its population, the golden state was a ready market for horses, mules, and cattle, no questions asked.

The crime spree heightened the tensions that existed among the various power centers in Utah. Of course, the Mormon hierarchy was concerned on many levels, but that did not prevent them from protecting Mormons who were caught with someone else's livestock. In this, as in all their endeavors, the Mormons looked after their own. But tensions also existed between the federal officials and the army. The question was, who had the authority to call out the army as a posse comitatus? Governor Cumming maintained that he alone had that power. The federal judges—and, in particular, one John C. Cradlebaugh—claimed to have the authority. The army sided with Cradlebaugh (under instructions from the War Department), and during the judge's attempt to bring several murderers to trial, the army supplied several companies of troops to protect him and the courthouse in Provo, where the judge was

---

[*] The January 17, 1860, *New York Times* reported that Hickman and Lot Huntington, both Mormon enforcers, got into a gunfight: "Hickman was dangerously wounded in the groin, Huntington slightly hurt. Forty shots were fired, and it is strange no more were injured. The affair occurred Christmas Day, as the people were leaving the Tabernacle."

dealing with the frustrations of an all-Mormon grand jury.* Cradlebaugh also tried to bring indictments against suspected participants
in the Mountain Meadows Massacre, but here again the grand jury
would not cooperate, nor would Mormon witnesses to various murders testify against their own. Meanwhile, the presence of troops in
Provo, and in subsequent expeditions to try to arrest suspects in the
Mountain Meadows Massacre outraged the Mormon population.
The suspects, John D. Lee among them, were warned and went into
hiding.** Dozens of Nauvoo Legion soldiers took to the mountains in
guerrilla bands. Once again, the territory was on the verge of war.

Brigham Young complained to Governor Cumming that the
actions of the army were sending hundreds of men into the mountains and that this enforced neglect of their ranches and farms
was devastating the territory's economy. Young even suggested
that this was a conspiracy to require the army quartermasters
to import supplies from the States, since they could not rely on
local suppliers. (It's unlikely that there was such a conspiracy, but
certain politicians might have regarded this as a residual benefit
of the tensions in Utah.)

The situation was ultimately resolved when the federal government, eager to avoid more embarrassing contretemps with the
Mormons, instructed the judiciary and the army that only the
governor had the power to call out the army. Judge Cradlebaugh's
fangs were therefore pulled, and that was one of the main reasons
he did not or could not pursue his investigation of the Mountain
Meadows Massacre. Putting that investigation on the back burner
was something both the Mormon hierarchy and the federal officials
could agree on—in the interest of peace in Utah.

---

* One of the company officers was Henry Heth, a future Confederate general,
who, as he told the story, unwittingly initiated the Battle of Gettysburg when
he acted on a report that there was a supply of shoes in the little town.

** Cradlebaugh had accumulated some thirty names through informers, who
then begged not to be identified as such.

Bascom arrived at Camp Floyd when tensions were at their highest point. But in a matter of days, the instructions from Washington—that is, from President Buchanan by means of the U.S. attorney—defused the situation. So life returned to normal at Camp Floyd and Frogtown.

Still, Utah was a dangerous place when Bascom arrived there. Mormon settlers had been pushing north and encroaching on the hunting grounds of the Bannocks and Shoshones. (Obviously, a settler would want to establish himself and his partners on land near water, a commodity in short supply in the Great Basin. Like the Apaches in the Southwest, the tribes of northern Utah and Idaho bitterly resented any incursions that monopolized water. As any hunter understands, game animals are attracted to water holes and water courses.) The exasperated tribes retaliated with attacks against emigrants on the trails west and scattered Mormon settlements. They were abetted in these raids by so-called "white Indians," renegade white men who were either deserters from the army, failed miners, or former teamsters—or anyone else who preferred the handle of a pistol to the handle of a shovel or plow. Estimates run as high as 125 such outlaws who operated with the northern tribes to attack emigrant trains.[28]

The expanding settlements also caused more friction with federal officers. Legally speaking, the Mormons were squatters on federal land. All of Utah was a federal territory gained through war and subsequent treaty. There had been no homestead act to grant titles to settlers. The Mormons had occupied and settled their country essentially by right of conquest and maintained an uneasy peace and occasional conflict with the various tribes. But the question of titles to land—always of mind-numbing complexity—was not something anyone wanted to go into just yet. Still, the expanding settlements were an irritant to federal officials and brought the army into conflict with the Indians, who were never supposed to be the army's concern but who finally had to be confronted so that the emigrant trails to California and Oregon could remain open.

In the south, the Paiutes decided that their alliance with the Mormons versus the merricats had outworn its value, and they too began raiding, paying special attention to the mail stations of the overland stage lines. By 1861, half of the twenty Great Basin stations had been destroyed by Paiute raids.[29]

The army, always short on dragoons and cavalry (because of congressional parsimony), sent what mounted soldiers they had to the north to protect the emigrant trails. These actions resulted in some sharp skirmishes with the tribes, but the raids continued despite the presence of troops. Meanwhile, the infantry regiments at Camp Floyd were woefully inadequate to address the problems—not because of numbers but because of their virtual immobility.

But Indians, white or otherwise, were not the only sources of trouble. Gentile and Mormon criminals turned horse and cattle theft into a high art. What's more, as Camp Floyd had altered the balance of power in the territory, more and more Gentiles began to filter in, many of them gamblers and saloon keepers, who turned Salt Lake City into a semi-Gomorrah. Whiskey Street in Salt Lake City gave Frogtown a run for its money when it came to gambling, prostitution, and drunkenness. Shootings and knifings became an epidemic, to the point that Brigham Young asked the city council to authorize an increase in the city police force from forty to two hundred officers. And these officers were not in the habit of coddling lawbreakers: "Salt Lake police earned the reputation of affording every desperate prisoner the opportunity of escape, and, if embraced, to a 'halt,' and saved the country the expense of a trial and his subsequent boarding in the penitentiary. A coroner's inquiry and cemetery expenses were comparatively light," said local Mormon resident I. B. H. Stenhouse, a confidant of Brigham Young's.[30]

The tensions between the Mormons and the army continued. Now and then those tensions erupted into violence. In the summer of 1859, Sgt. Ralph Pike of the Tenth Infantry Regiment was shot and killed by a Mormon man who managed to escape, though there were plenty of Mormon witnesses to the shooting. (Earlier, Pike had assaulted the man in attempting to arrest him.) Then there was the case of Assistant Surgeon Dr. Edwin Covey of the Second Dragoons. Covey apparently did not share Mark Twain's opinion about Mormon women. His amorous adventures, along with some verbal vitriol in a hotel in Salt Lake City, offended the Mormon city marshal who, together with several deputies, tried to arrest him for disturbing the peace. The argument went into the streets, where the Mormon police opened fire and wounded Covey. Covey's colleague Lieutenant Saunders was also wounded in the altercation. Both men recovered, and Covey got his revenge while on the march to New Mexico, when he ran across one of the deputies who'd shot him, tied him to a wagon wheel, and flogged him senseless.

All of these incidents and many others less bloody stoked the fires of hatred between the army and the Mormons. The army was still smarting from the miserable winter encampment of 1857–58 and the frustration of not being able to shed some of the detested Mormons' blood. And the Mormons returned the hatred with interest. As the commanding officer, A. S. Johnston, said: ". . . no one who has offended this people regards himself free from assassination."[31]

Then there were the persistent rumors of inter-Mormon dissension. As mentioned, Bill Hickman was not only an original Danite in Missouri, but also a cattle rustler and gunman. His shootout with Lot Huntington on Christmas Day was nothing more or less than an episode in a gang war fought over the wages of rustling. Hickman survived and later wrote his autobiography in which he accused Brigham Young of operating a group of "destroying angels" who kept Mormons in line and dispatched apostates. By this time Hickman had been excommunicated, so there is some question about his motives and veracity. But his claims fed into Gentile suspicions about the shadowy organizations underlying Young's power.

And, of course, there was the still-lingering question of responsibility for the Mountain Meadows Massacre. The army had few doubts about who was culpable, and in fact when Company K of the First Dragoons visited the spot, they erected a memorial cairn with the inscription "Vengeance is mine I will repay saith the Lord." When he visited the same spot Brigham Young noticed the inscription and said, ". . . it should be, Vengeance is mine and I have taken a little."[32] Not surprisingly, Young's remark was deleted from the official "Journal History of the Church" that described his visit to the site.

Given this state of frontier violence, Bascom would have been well advised to avoid Salt Lake City and Frogtown and to attend to his duties at Camp Floyd. Between his arrival in April/May 1859 and the following spring, he joined a company in which he was the most junior officer. He would have been assigned routine garrison duties such as supervising morning roll call, ensuring those on sick call were marched to the doctor, sorting out disciplinary problems (generally the result of drunkenness, which, along with desertion, was the bane of the army), drilling the troops, supervising small arms practice (assuming enough ammunition was available), looking after the company's animals, posting guards, repairing equipment or company buildings—in short, ensuring that the tedious routine of garrison life continued according to the book.

Other duties included patrols into the countryside, for the army was busy surveying the territory to the west in the hopes of finding shorter routes to California. (Operating from Camp Floyd, Captain James H. Simpson of the army's topographical corps did succeed in discovering a new trail to California that would reduce the length of the journey by several hundred miles.) To protect these and other surveys and road improvement or wood-cutting parties, the infantry patrols would occasionally resort to riding mules—assuming there were enough available after the enforced sales of 1859 reported by Greeley. The army did not like mounting the infantry on mules, for, as General Scott said, such a practice "can only result in disorganizing the infantry and [converting] them into extremely indifferent horsemen."[33] The arrangement no doubt disgusted both soldier and mule. "A mule is an enduring animal, he will bear fatigue and cold, and heat and hunger and abuse; he will go without food and sleep, and the harder the toil and the greater the hardship, the more patient he becomes," said Lieutenant Joseph Sladen. "But no man can trust a mule. That is, he should not. What a mule has done is known. What he is doing may be seen, but what he will do the next minute, the mind of the philosopher cannot fathom." *[34]

Still, sometimes there were no other options, given the scanty resources of the dragoons and the vast territory to be patrolled and surveyed. The infantry used mules strictly as transportation— there was no thought of fighting while mounted. The infantry's long-barreled, single-shot, muzzle-loading muskets were not suitable for mounted warfare, and the very unpredictability of the mule's character made him a dubious partner in combat.

During these patrols, Bascom most likely had his first contact with western Indians. In all probability, they were Goshutes, a tribe that lived in miserable poverty in the deserts of the Great Basin. (The so-called Paiute War had not begun in earnest yet.) Captain Simpson described the Goshutes, or Diggers, as they were generally called: "They are the most wretched looking creatures I have ever seen. . . . They live on rats, lizards, snakes, insects, grasses, and roots, and their largest game is the rabbit, it being seldom that they kill an antelope."[35]

Mark Twain had similar impressions:

Such of the Goshoots [sic] as we saw, along the road and hanging about the stations, were small, lean "scrawny" creatures; in complexion a dull black like the ordinary American [N]egro; their faces and hands bearing dirt which they had been hoarding and accumulating for months, years and even generations, according to the

---

* As William Faulkner observed, a mule will work patiently and loyally for ten years just for the chance to kick you once.

age of the proprietor; a silent, sneaking, treacherous looking race; taking note of everything, covertly, like all the other "Noble Red Men" that we (do not) read about, and betraying no sign in their countenances; indolent, everlastingly patient and tireless, like all other Indians; prideless beggars—for if the beggar instinct were left out of an Indian he would not "go," any more than a clock without a pendulum; hungry, always hungry, and yet never refusing anything that a hog would eat, though often eating what a hog would decline; hunters, but having no higher ambition than to kill and eat jackass rabbits, crickets and grasshoppers, and embezzle carrion from the buzzards and coyotes[;] savages who, when asked if they have the common Indian belief in a Great Spirit, show something that almost amounts to emotion, thinking whiskey is referred to; a thin scattering race of almost naked black children, these Goshoots are, who produce nothing at all and have no villages, and no gatherings together into strictly defined tribal communities—a people whose only shelter is a rag cast on a bush to keep off a portion of the snow, and yet who inhabit one of the most rocky, wintry, repulsive wastes that our country or any other can exhibit.[36]

Twain, of course, was famously contemptuous of the Noble Savage theory in general and the Noble Red Man stories of James Fenimore Cooper in particular—contemptuous of both the content and style of Cooper's fiction. Nor was Twain much more tolerant of sentimentality or romanticism of any stripe. But that aside, Twain's description of the Goshutes, coupled with the similar impressions of Captain Simpson, indicate a level of degradation among the tribe that would make a profound impression on a young officer like Bascom, whose lack of experience with Indians would have intensified the shock. The Indians who hung around the outskirts of the frontier forts were generally not the finest specimens of their tribes, and contact with tribes like the Goshutes would have aroused both loathing and contempt among the officers.* Beyond question, the sight of the Goshutes would have reinforced the soldiers' belief in the superiority of the white race and culture. Perhaps, too, the very existence of a people like the Goshutes might have shaken a young officer's Christian faith—and in a strange way frightened him. Could these people really be a member of the human species, could they actually have been made in the image of God? This would be a glimpse of otherness that both disgusted and disturbed a man who a few short weeks before had been dining at Delmonico's. To borrow a line from Nietzsche: "If you gaze for long into an abyss, the abyss gazes also into you."

It's reasonable to suppose that Bascom, having seen the Goshutes, would have extrapolated an attitude toward Indians that would have reinforced his natural prejudices reflecting the widespread white view that all Indians were not only obviously inferior, but also essentially the same. What's more, he would have heard stories from troops who had been deployed against the more warlike tribes and would have been appalled by the reports of Indian brutality against emigrants—tales not only of murder and infanticide but also rape and mutilation. None of this would have served him well when he encountered a tribe that was certainly not degraded and was, in some ways, a superior fighting force and an equally complex, although radically different, culture.**

---

* The tribe was also notorious for selling their children to Mexican and Ute slave traders. Those who did not want to sell were frequently the targets of Ute slave raids—against which their only defense was to run away and hide.

** As the mail routes west developed and stage stations opened, the Goshutes felt the twin emotions of opportunity and cultural threat and began raiding the stations. In other words, they were not as timorous as the descriptions of them would suggest. But by the time they rose up against the whites, Bascom was in Arizona.

During his year of active duty at Camp Floyd, Bascom learned a number of lessons and lost a few illusions. He learned that the various tribes were primitive, treacherous, and violent—contemptible and shocking in their differentness. He learned that the Mormon civilians were equally untrustworthy and dangerous—that human beings, even though white, were capable of bizarre theories, strange behavior, and secret crimes by men allied with Indians to massacre emigrants. He learned that the saloons and brothels of Frogtown and Salt Lake City were populated by the dregs of society, a form of humanity he could hardly have imagined back on the banks of the Hudson. (Whiskey Street was a far cry from Benny Havens.) He undoubtedly heard rumors of political corruption and graft associated with the supply-freighting contracts. He knew of the federal government's indecision in its policies toward the Mormons; he knew that they had sent him and his brothers in arms a long way at great expense for little or no gain, and that they had sent too few dragoons and too many infantry because of their penny-pinching. He would have agreed with Albert Sidney Johnston, his commanding officer, who bitterly regretted "the folly of our people in selecting men for public office without regard to their education and training for the particular duties they are called upon to perform."[37] The Utah expedition would end up costing millions of dollars, but little of that money was spent on the right kind of manpower. Bascom also learned that the army was caught in the middle of a variety of competing interests and tensions—North-South politics culminating in attacks on "Buchanan's Blunder," disputes over whether the War Department or the Interior Department should manage the Indians, arguments between the territorial governor and the federal judiciary over who could call out the army as a posse comitatus. They had been sent to fight the Mormons, but ended up chasing Indians and protecting the emigrant trails, tasks that rendered their artillery and infantry virtually useless. Cynicism, disillusionment, and a drawing together as brother officers were the natural results. Taken all together, Bascom would have come to the conclusion that the army was the only institution of integrity in a world of violence, corruption, and incompetence. Whether these were all the right lessons is a different question, but certainly they were the lessons that the officers taught themselves. And certainly they were understandable conclusions.

By the summer of 1860, Bascom had been a soldier on active duty for two years; he was not, in short, "fresh from West Point." He had seen no combat, but he had seen a great deal of the country and a great deal of the darker sides of human nature. Any youthful ideals regarding the perfectibility of man or the integrity of the nation's political establishment or the nobility of its population, white or red, would have pretty much disappeared, replaced by images of Frogtown and the Goshutes and stories about Mountain Meadows.

By this time, too, Bascom knew all the men of his company very well. In theory, an infantry regiment could number as many as nine hundred men divided into ten companies. In reality, regiments numbered anywhere from three to four hundred men, and the ten companies were therefore less than half what they should have been.[38] But the reduced numbers at least gave a young officer a slightly easier job in getting to know the men in his company. He got to know which ones were reliable, which were useless, which could shoot well, which were likely to try to desert, which were shirkers, which were intelligent, which were dimwits, which wanted to please and which were troublemakers and complainers, which were drunkards, which were pious. His company, like most in the frontier army, was a mixed bag of nationalities—native-born Americans, immigrant Irish, German, and English. He would have understood that the most important asset he had was his company sergeant, an older man grown gray in the service, and Bascom would by this time have understood the man's strengths and limitations, would know just how far he could rely on him. Bascom would have valued the good opinions of all the men, even the useless ones, but he would not have pandered to them for popularity—that would have violated the code he learned at West Point. There was a strict dividing line between the enlisted men and the officers, a line dictated by the hierarchy the army believed in as an article of unshakable faith. Some of the enlisted men would have grumbled about this class consciousness, others would have accepted it without thinking. But whatever the men's attitudes on the subject might have been, those attitudes were to Bascom and the other officers irrelevant. The one thing he could not have known about his men, however, was how they could fight, how they would behave in combat. Of course, he did not know that about himself either.

And finally Bascom would have learned that the frontier was inherently inhospitable to the white newcomers. The deserts of the Great Basin—Twain's "repulsive wastes"—were wretchedly cold in the winter, wretchedly hot and dusty in the summer, and mostly empty. Water was scarce, as were fuel and forage. Enemies were all around, but the country was so vast there was almost no hope of coming to grips with them, except on their terms and on the ground of their choosing. There were too many places where enemies could hide, too many mountains, passes, canyons, too many natural obstacles for a civilized army, too many places for ambush. The only conclusion Bascom could have derived from this gloomy meditation on geography was, when you do manage to get hold of an enemy—white or red—don't let go, because you may not get another chance at him. What's more, Bascom would have noticed, perhaps with the help of his senior officers, that every time there was a confrontation with the Mormons, the other side backed down. In other words, firmness paid dividends—firmness combined with the necessary force to back it up.

Bascom undoubtedly felt frustrated by missing out on what little action the army had seen. The dragoons saw the bulk of it, while the foot soldiers were sidelined by the very nature of their branch of service. In wars between nation-states, the infantry was the "queen of battle." But war on the frontier was never going to be fought according to "Hardee's Tactics" or won by bayonet charges. This was contrary to the lessons Bascom had learned at West Point and therefore most likely a little disillusioning. But the attitudes he had formed at the Academy were still in place—the belief in the army, in the hierarchy of command—these would have been strengthened by the dispiriting sight of the rest of chaotic humanity, red or white. Writes historian Sherry Smith, ". . . on certain fundamental assumptions about savagery and civilization, the army's supposedly irreproachable conduct on the frontier, and the military's presumed special qualifications to manage Indian affairs, [the officers] found unanimity."[39]

In the summer of 1860, all of the elements of the Fifth and Seventh Regiments were sent to New Mexico. The transfer was part of the federal government's attempt to defuse criticism over the expenses of the Utah War. Troop levels at Camp Floyd were gradually drawn down until a mere three hundred soldiers were left to guard the trails and stage stations.[*40]

In April 1860, shortly before the troops' arrival in New Mexico, a large force of Navajos attacked Fort Defiance in northeast Arizona. With the arrival of the Fifth and the Seventh, the New Mexico department commander, Colonel Thomas Fauntleroy, organized a three-pronged campaign against the hostiles, consisting of most of the Fifth and all but four companies of the Seventh. Of those four companies, two went to the copper mines of New Mexico, and the other two went to Fort Buchanan under the command of Lieutenant Colonel Pitcairn Morrison.

---

* When the camp was finally abandoned in July 1861, because of the Civil War, $4,000,000 worth of supplies, equipment, and livestock was sold to Mormon buyers for a total of $100,000.[41] The apparently ubiquitous Philip St. George Cooke was the final commander who oversaw the fort's dismantling.

Morrison had received his commission in 1820, so he was on the verge of retirement. He was a rather senior officer—in rank—to be assigned to such a remote and undermanned post, and it's possible he was left out of the Navajo campaign because of his age. (That campaign was under the command of a brevet colonel and two majors.) It's also reasonable to assume that after forty years of soldiering, Morrison had lost a little of the edge off his zeal and aggressiveness. And perhaps he understood that even the cold comforts of a ramshackle fort like Buchanan were preferable to the rigors of a fall and early-winter campaign against elusive Navajos in a hostile terrain and environment. If so, he would have been right.

Also left out of the action was 2nd Lieutenant George Bascom. With Lieutenant Colonel Morrison and two companies of infantry, he was on his way to Arizona, his eagerness and drive still mostly intact and most likely in need of an outlet.*

---

* Accompanying the troops in the Navajo campaign were "sixty spies and guides" drawn from the Ute tribe. It's unfortunate that Bascom did not have the chance to watch a warlike but (occasionally) friendly tribe operate; it might have added some perspective. The campaign against the Navajos was only moderately successful; the campaign killed three dozen warriors and gathered up a thousand horses and seven thousand sheep, an economic disaster for the Navajos and a windfall for the Utes.[42]

Chapter Nine

RISING TENSIONS

[Cochise is] a very deceptive Indian. At first appearance a man would think he was inclined to be peaceable to Americans, but he is far from it. For eight months I have watched him and have come to the conclusion that he is the biggest liar in the territory and would kill an American for any trifle, providing he thought he wouldn't be found out.

—James Tevis, Arizona ranger and
former Butterfield agent[1]

However uninviting this [San Pedro] valley may appear, it is said to be very fertile, but so long as it is left, as now, a prey to merciless Indians, no one can settle there in safety. If there is any portion of the route calculated to impress one with the necessity of military protection for the route of this overland mail, it is this . . . running through the heart of the Apache country.

—Waterman Ormsby[2]

CRITICS AND POLITICAL OPPONENTS OF PRESIDENT BUCHANAN charged that John Butterfield received the contract for the overland mail because he was a friend of the president. Perhaps that was an element in the decision, but there is no doubt that Butterfield's energy and ability transformed an apparently hopeless task into an astonishing achievement.

In September of 1857, Butterfield received the contract to carry mail to and from California by means of the southern route. There were five other bidders, each of whom submitted proposals of routes to California along with their bids. Butterfield originally proposed a route that followed the thirty-fifth parallel, essentially coming south along the Santa Fe Trail and turning west at Albuquerque. But Postmaster General Brown, a pro-slavery Tennessean, rejected that route as being too exposed to winter weather and advocated the thirty-second parallel route instead—to the dismay and howls of protests of his and the administration's political opponents.

Brown preferred the southernmost route because he understood that a transcontinental railroad would ultimately be built and that the precedent of the thirty-second parallel established mail route would argue for that as the best way west. Though longer, it would unquestionably be the easiest roadbed to construct. That would strengthen the South's commercial advantage in trade with the West. In the meantime, the stage-line connection between the South and California would benefit both and leave the North frustrated. (It may be remembered that this same idea motivated the Gadsden Purchase in the first place.) The northern antislavery groups saw this route as purely a southern tactic to expand the economic well-being of the slave-holding states and, perhaps, to extend slavery. The northern newspapers cried foul, calling it "one of the greatest swindles ever perpetrated on the country by the slave holders."[3] The government, in the shape of Postmaster General Brown, could say with a straight face that politics had nothing to do with the decision, for although the southern route was longer, it did not have the weather problems of any proposed central route that would inevitably be blocked by snow in the Sierras. What's more, the character of the thirty-second parallel route, with its relatively flat desert floors winding around the "lost" mountain ranges, allowed for easier road construction and maintenance. Further, the weather along the thirty-fifth parallel, though better than farther north, was far worse than along the thirty-second. But North-South politics and the slavery issue were obviously key factors in the decision. And that means there was only one degree of separation between the slavery issue and the subsequent troubles with the Apaches in general—and Cochise's band, in particular—for the route that Butterfield would build would go directly through the Chiricahua homelands.

Brown had considered another bidder for the project but at this stage President Buchanan stepped in and suggested his friend Butterfield would be a better candidate, assuming he would agree to the new, more southerly route, which he did, although it would involve greater expense to build and maintain.

Butterfield had been born in 1801 in upstate New York. As a very young man, he learned the art of driving a stagecoach. (Many of the drivers on the Overland Mail were also from New York State. Almost all were from the East.[4] A natural entrepreneur, he was not content to be simply a driver. He branched out to establish stagecoach lines throughout New York State. Later, with several partners, he formed the American Express Company. So he was well prepared for the daunting job of building the Overland Mail from scratch.

Butterfield's service would essentially replace that from San Antonio to San Diego, which was known as the Jackass Mail, because some parts of the line relied on carrying the mail on mule back instead of coach. There was little if any passenger service on this line, primarily because the route led "from no place through nothing to nowhere." Also, the line, such as it was, went through dangerous Indian country and used mule back in precisely the stretches of country where even well-armed passengers would prefer the shelter of a coach and the security of stone or adobe stations instead of hostlers' tents and improvised stations.

The eastern terminuses of the Butterfield Overland Mail were St. Louis and Memphis, and the western was San Francisco. The route followed essentially the march of the Kearny Expedition in the Mexican War, except that Kearny followed the rugged Gila River trail, whereas the mail route would dip farther south. It would then travel across the southern Arizona desert to Fort Yuma, into Southern California, and turn north, bypassing San Diego, through the passes in the north-south mountain ranges to San Francisco. Called the Oxbow Route because of its dramatic southward then northward shape, it was just short of twenty-eight hundred miles long—roughly seven hundred miles longer than a proposed central route through Utah. The contract would pay Butterfield six hundred thousand dollars a year for twice-weekly mail delivery, allowing twenty-five days to make each trip.

The longer route would require more than Butterfield had anticipated on his proposed thirty-fifth parallel route—more stage stations, more horses and mules, more employees, and therefore much greater operating costs. That did not bother the government, of course—that was Butterfield's problem.

Another difficulty for Butterfield—which gave hope to his political and commercial opponents—was that from the date he signed his contract he had only one year to get the service up and running. That meant buying coaches, horses and mules, building stage stations, improving roads, such as they were, hiring division agents, conductors, drivers, hostlers—an almost unimaginable task, especially since there initially would have to be 139 stations (ultimately growing to 200), all of which had to be built, equipped, stocked, and manned within twelve months. Simply getting everything together and organized was what *New York Herald* correspondent Waterman Ormsby described as a "superhuman" task. From today's perspective, "superhuman" seems restrained.

Even supposing Butterfield was able to get everything in place in time, there was the problem of operating the line and meeting the twenty-five-day schedule, two a week, week in, week out, through all the seasons, east to west and west to east simultaneously. The weather in the Southwest might have been more benign than in the central routes in terms of snowfall, but weather was not always an ally to the Butterfield Overland Mail. Water was scarce except in monsoon seasons, when there was far too much of it. Then dry arroyos turned into brown torrents that threatened to sweep away horses and men.* Heavy rains cut new arroyos with perpendicular walls and deepened existing ones. Violent seasonal storms and flash floods regularly changed the terrain, washed out the riverbeds, and created instant creeks that eroded road grades and eliminated fording places, washed away constructed ramps to and from riverbeds, turned the trails and roads into sticky mud courses, and sent rocks and boulders tumbling down onto canyon roads. In summer, certain stretches in the Southwest ran through unforgiving deserts where the heat and beating sun wore out animals and men alike, and fine alkali dust grated in the mouths and noses and coated any skin not covered. The desert floor was unforgiving, with hard-packed stones that retained the sun's heat and tortured the hooves, and then the hard packs changed to shifting, deep sand that made it heavy going for the animals, slowing them to a walk. Dust storms caused by high winds could literally obliterate a driver's view of the road and make the animals fractious and difficult to handle. In winter, temperatures could plummet in the dry desert air, and snow was common above five thousand feet in elevation—the elevation at Apache Pass. There the snow would blow sideways from the harsh and frequent wind. It was not as bad as winter in the Sierras or the Rockies, but it was bad enough. In the winter of 1858, a sudden storm dropped three feet of snow on Apache Pass—an unusual but not unique event.

---

* Those who have seen a desert flash flood will understand that this is no exaggeration; more than one soldier serving in Apache country was washed away and drowned in just such circumstances. Rucker Canyon, Arizona, is named after Lieutenant John Rucker, who drowned while trying unsuccessfully to rescue Lieutenant Austin Henely, who had been caught in a flash flood.

To solve the water problem in dry seasons, Butterfield would have to rely on local pioneers to identify springs. Where there were no springs, his employees would have to dig wells. In at least one station west of Tucson, water had to be freighted in and stored in cisterns. Water dictated the route, which could not always follow the easiest or the most direct trail west. At Apache Pass, for example, coaches would have to climb through a rugged notch between the Chiricahua and Dos Cabezas Mountains simply because the only reliable spring for miles was located in the pass. Carrying water on the coach was impractical because of the weight.

The natural obstacles of weather and terrain would have been enough to discourage anyone, but then there were the Indians, and especially the Apaches. The stretch of road through Apache country was easily the most dangerous of the entire twenty-eight-hundred-mile trail, and the worst section of that was Apache Pass, for not only was the climb through the pass a chore for the animals, it was the favorite resort of Cochise and his Chokonens.

Butterfield initially constructed nine stage stations between Mesilla, New Mexico, and Tucson—a distance of three hundred miles through mescal-studded desert and the heart of Apache country. At an average elevation of four thousand feet above sea level and winding on a flat floor generally, past the lost mountain ranges, the route was not quite as desolate as it would become west of Tucson and just across the border into California, where there were miles of Sahara-like dunes. There was sparse grass in the eastern Arizona sections, though not enough to supply all the needs of the stations. Feed for the animals would have to be freighted in.

Objectively speaking, the odds were very much against Butterfield—against his meeting the one-year deadline and, even supposing he did meet it, against operating the line successfully and meeting the twice-weekly schedule—from both directions.

But he did it.

At the end of his year of preparation, he and his company had established the initial 139 stage stops along the route, bought

250 coaches, hired 800 men to man the stations, and acquired 1,800 draft animals—horses and mules. The first coach left San Francisco on September 15, 1858, and the sister coach left St. Louis the following day. They would meet on September 28 at the entrance of Guadalupe Canyon on the present-day Arizona–New Mexico line, and both would beat their twenty-five-day deadline for the trip.

The coaches on certain sections of the line were the standard Concords, but in places where the terrain was difficult, a Concord could be exchanged for a "celerity" wagon, a lighter, less expensive vehicle with a canvas roof and open sides that could be covered by canvas curtains in bad or dusty weather. Sometimes called a mud wagon, this vehicle could go places where the heavier Concord coaches would struggle. Many of the celerity wagons were built by Abbot-Downing and used the same kind of thoroughbrace suspension as the Concord. The seat backs could be lowered at night so that passengers could stretch out the length of the coach and sleep, assuming the coach was not full. Lighter than the Concord, the celerity wagons could be drawn by only four mules. Unlovely but practical, the mud wagons were to the Concords as mules were to horses.

The first passenger who made it from one end to the other—from St. Louis to San Francisco—was *New York Herald* correspondent Waterman Ormsby. Ormsby was only twenty-three and so had youth's resiliency. Even so, while he praised the efficiency of the operation (after he completed the journey) he did not sugarcoat the ordeal: "There's an old saying that every man must eat his peck of dirt. I think I have had a good measure of my peck on this trip, which has been roughing it with a vengeance."[5]

Discomfort aside, as a purely human achievement, the Overland Mail—its establishment and its operation—deserved Ormsby's accolade, ". . . whatever may be the difficulties in the way, the overland mail route may be considered as permanently established and its success placed beyond the possibility of a doubt."[6]

In the enthusiasm of youth and with the inability to see into the future, Ormsby could of course not know that two wars—one internecine, the other a collision of cultures—would put an end to the line in less than three years. Those wars would be fought differently—one, according to the rules of West Point; the other, according to the rules of the guerrilla. Unwitting historical allies, these conflicts would combine to destroy the southern route of the Butterfield Overland Mail. And a great deal more.

⊶◈⊷

The employees of the company, I found, without exception to be courteous, civil and attentive.
—Waterman Ormsby[7]

MOST LIKELY, ORMSBY MET JAMES TEVIS WHEN ORMSBY TRAVELED through Apache Pass during the initial trip of the Butterfield Overland Mail. Tevis was an early pioneer in Arizona who arrived there after participating in William Walker's infamous filibustering campaign in Nicaragua. Tevis could therefore legitimately fancy himself an adventurer, and his career bore that out. He was friendly with Captain Ewell at Fort Buchanan and went along with him when Ewell went to Apache Pass to meet with Cochise and recover some stock stolen by Cochise's warriors from a mining company near Sonoita. The Butterfield stage stop was under construction, and Tevis must have liked the look of things because he stayed on as an employee. Ultimately, he became the station agent for Apache Pass almost from its inception. (He took over from initial agent Anthony Elder, who had aroused the ire of Cochise and had to be transferred for his own safety, though in the end it did not help; two years later Elder was killed by Cochise's warriors near Stein's Peak, a station near the New Mexico–Arizona border.) Tevis would remain station agent at Apache Pass until late 1859.

Tevis was naturally wary of Apaches in general and Cochise in particular. On an earlier hunting trip into the mountains near the San Francisco River in New Mexico, Tevis and Moses Carson,

TERRY MORT

brother of Kit, were attacked by members of Mangas Coloradas's band and had to fight their way through rugged country all the way to Tucson. At least that was Tevis's story, although, like many old frontiersmen, he preferred his tales on the tall side, especially when he was the main character. Still, he did have some dangerous encounters with the Apaches, and so his willingness to live and work so near Cochise's favorite camping ground speaks well of his courage, as does his subsequent service as an Arizona Ranger and Confederate officer. (A few years later, Tevis would tell of being captured along with two companions by Cochise, who tortured the other men to death by hanging them upside down and lighting a fire under their heads. Tevis escaped with the help of a friendly Apache while Cochise was drunk and passed out.)

Given its location in the heart of Chiricahua country, the Apache Pass stage station was constructed of stone foundations and adobe bricks—with an obvious eye for defense. The corral was also surrounded by high walls that not only protected the stock from being easily run off but also served as a good defense in case of attack. Tevis describes the station: "A stone corral was built with portholes in every stall. Inside on the southwest corner were built, in an L shape, the kitchen and sleeping rooms. At the west end on the inside of the corral a space about ten feet wide was apportioned for the grain room and storeroom, and here were kept the firearms and ammunition."[8]

The mention of a grain room underscores the fact that the draft animals could not subsist and remain hardy on just the grazing in the area. (Because of the rough grades and the sandy soil that made up most of the road to and beyond Apache Pass, the Butterfield line in this section of the road used mule-drawn celerity wagons.) There was plenty of grass in the pass and the meadows beyond the western exit, but the mules needed grain as well. That meant it had to be delivered by freighters such as the train attacked by Cochise during the Bascom incident.

Because the station needed to be beside the Butterfield road, it was about one thousand yards from the spring, which was nestled

194

in a rocky defile surrounded by oak trees in an area that could not accommodate a road. As a result, Tevis (and, later, Culver) or one of the hostlers would have to make regular trips to the spring, leading a patient burro loaded with ten-gallon barrels.

The road to the pass from the east traveled through sparse desert with loose, reddish soil—hard going for the animals. Ugly and spindly creosote bushes, prickly pear, and cholla cactus were the only vegetation to speak of. The road climbed gently from the flat valley floor, which was about four thousand feet in elevation, to the summit of the pass which was over fifty-one hundred feet high. Once in higher elevation, the landscape changed dramatically. Apache Pass was and is studded with oak trees, willows, and black walnut trees, along with varieties of juniper, manzanita bushes, prickly pear, and mesquite trees. The trees and bushes stand as individuals amidst the tawny grass, so that the dominant color scheme is alternating yellow and green, accented by the gray-green of the sage and the light brown of the sandy soil. Here and there were sandy washes, formed by sudden monsoon rains and flash floods. All around the Butterfield road and station, the mountains rose up, with pockets of cactus and boulders, as well as oaks and junipers scattered here and there. The entire trip from the eastern desert floor to the western exit was something like fifteen miles, although the road through the Pass itself was only around four miles long.

Descending from the west side of the pass, the road flattened out and traveled through a beautiful grass-covered meadow, with the Chiricahua Mountains looming immediately to the south, the Dos Cabezas to the north. From there, the next station was in Dragoon Springs, about thirty miles away across the Sulphur Springs Valley.* Dragoon Springs lay on the eastern edge of the Dragoon Mountains, another favorite camping ground for Cochise and

---

* Later there was a station at Ewell Springs, at the base of the western exit to the pass. But that station does not appear to have been operating during the first months of the Overland Mail.

his followers. Like the Chiricahua Mountains, the Dragoons run roughly north and south and offered Cochise a handy jumping-off point for Mexico, as well as a number of superb defensive positions in the high-walled rock canyons. Hidden behind the rocks, high up along the cliffs above the narrowing canyon floor, a handful of Chiricahuas could hold off many times their number of troops.

In July 1857, a group of Cochise's warriors attacked a small emigrant train in Apache Pass and killed two men, wounded two women, and stole twenty head of cattle.[9] Oddly, though, there weren't many such incidents. During its brief existence, the Jackass Mail had been operating through Apache Pass without difficulty between the summer of 1857 and September 1858, the date when the Butterfield line took over. That may have been good luck or good timing or Apache forbearance—or it may have been because Cochise's band was off in Mexico raiding and, now and then, negotiating.

For years, if not centuries, the Apache bands had employed their own brand of foreign policy that played one political adversary against another. Until the arrival of the Americans, these adversaries were Spanish governors of the northern states, primarily Chihuahua and Sonora. When Mexico achieved its independence from Spain in 1821, the Apaches did not change their policies, although, of course, there was no uniform Apache policy, since the bands and local groups operated independently.

Despite the historic and consistent enmity between the Mexicans and the Apaches, there were occasional periods of peace. The Mexicans were naturally tired of the constant threat of attack, and now and then tried to buy off Apache raiders with guarantees of regular rations, as an alternative to the difficult and expensive business of trying to exterminate them. A military solution was especially hard to achieve once the American border could be used as a sanctuary. But Mexican attempts to cajole the Apaches with rations and trade goods were constantly frustrated by the decentralized social structure of the tribes. Peace with one band never meant a guaranteed peace with the others. While one group might be living quietly and enjoying Mexican bribes in the form of gifts and rations, another might be attacking a neighboring state and then selling the plunder to Mexican traders. Nor did the word of a chief necessarily guarantee the good behavior of individual warriors. A chief's power was moral, not legal, and if a few individual warriors wanted to rustle some Mexican beef or ambush an unwary peon and kidnap his wife, that was their business.

During brief periods when the Mexicans and the Apaches were able to make peace and get along, albeit warily, Janos in Chihuahua was a popular Apache market. There they found Mexican traders who were happy to receive plunder stolen from the neighboring state of Sonora. After the Mexican War, there was understandable anti-American resentment and rancor among Mexican officials, and they were quite willing to wink at Apache raiding across the border in Arizona and New Mexico and to provide markets and sanctuary for Apache raiders. The most egregious example of this business was Jose María Zuloaga, described by writer Edwin Sweeney as the "economic and political czar of northwest Chihuahua."[10] Despite the fact that he was involved in the earlier Kirker massacre, Zuloaga had a nimble conscience and was able to deal with the Chiricahua to receive their stolen goods and trade them for guns and ammunition. He did not care whether the plunder came from the United States, Sonora, or even other parts of Chihuahua—as long as it did not come from his district. He was also willing to supply occasional rations providing the Chiricahua left his business interests (which included mining) alone.

The arrival of the Americans and their new border came as mixed blessings to the Chiricahua. On the one hand, the border offered dual sanctuaries; on the other, it created the possibility of attack from two sides at once—the risk of being squeezed between two armies, in the unlikely event that the Americans and Mexicans could ever cooperate militarily. But even without that cooperation, the two powerful nations (certainly more powerful than the Apaches) would operate against the Apaches independently, and the resulting pressure would be difficult to endure. In other words, to have a secure sanctuary, the Chiricahua would ideally need to be at peace, however uneasy, with either the Americans or the Mexicans.

Cochise was ambivalent about which side to choose. He no doubt understood that the Americans would eventually offer the bigger military threat. He was used to the Mexicans and their way of doing things, used to fighting them and dealing with them. The Americans were a different story, one that he could not yet quite interpret. Their Fort Buchanan was nothing special, to be sure, but the mounted patrols under Captain Ewell were formidable enough to command respect. Moreover, Cochise had begun to sense that the American presence was growing faster than was agreeable. That realization was the source of mounting tensions between Cochise (along with his father-in-law, Mangas Coloradas) and the Americans.

His growing disenchantment with the Americans was both practical and cultural. He was aware that mining activity was accelerating in southern Arizona and the mountains of New Mexico. (Indeed, he had stolen the draft animals of the Santa Rita Mining Company as they were hauling mining equipment through Apache Pass en route to Tubac.) While these operations offered tempting opportunities for plunder, they were also siren calls to his and other bands' unruly warriors, whose raids brought short-term benefits but eventually aroused an unwanted response from the army. Then there was the Butterfield stage and the commercial traffic that accelerated as a result of the Butterfield improvements to the trail. The station itself, there in his heartland, must have been a constant irritant, if only because it symbolized the kind of change no Chiricahua wanted to see. The mining activity in the mountains along the Santa Cruz River was expanding, and American merchants from the East were starting to establish themselves in Tucson—still an unprepossessing Mexican village, but starting to grow. In 1859, placer gold had been discovered in Pinos Altos in the New Mexico mountains south of the Gila River—near Mangas Coloradas's country. In a matter of months, three hundred miners and the usual camp followers had established a new and typically rowdy and dangerous town.[11] If Cochise and the Chiricahua were beginning to feel a little hemmed in, it's understandable.

In view of the expanding American activity, some of the Chiricahua began to think they might need to hedge their bets, and they began to extend peace feelers to Chihuahua. The governor was interested enough to appoint Zuloaga to negotiate on the government's behalf. In the summer and fall of 1860, groups of Chiricahua migrated to Mexico, to Janos, Chihuahua, and to Fronteras in Sonora, and there made peace with the two Mexican states in exchange for regular rations. Cochise and a number of his followers stayed at Apache Pass, no doubt considering their options.[12] He had few reasons to trust the Mexicans. The Kirker massacre, after all, had occurred under precisely the same circumstances—a surprise attack against a group of Apaches who had come to a Mexican feast under the impression that a treaty of peace was in place. Were the Americans any more trustworthy? He could not answer that question quite yet.

> *I cannot see any other course but to feed them or exterminate them.*
> —Lieutenant Colonel Pitcairn Morrison[13]

> *To the credit of the agent it must be said that he made a praiseworthy but ineffectual effort to alleviate the pangs of hunger by a liberal distribution of hymnbooks among his wards.*
> —Captain John Gregory Bourke[14]

IN 1849, CONGRESS HAD TRANSFERRED MANAGEMENT OF THE Indians from the War Department to the Interior Department. Army officers were in virtually unanimous agreement that the decision would cause innumerable troubles—for the army, the white civilians on the frontier, and the Indians. They argued that they were the only ones who had any real contact with the Indians, that they had at least some understanding of how to handle them, that force and fairness were the twin pillars of a workable peace. Granted, most army officers leaned toward force and firmness as the first measures, believing that only after the Indians had been cowed—made to understand, in Sherman's phrase, "the iron hand of destiny"—would they see reason and submit to the inevitable, which meant ceasing their raiding and nomadic wanderings and settling down on a reservation to be wards of the state under the watchful eye of the army. If they could then learn to be farmers or craftsmen, so much the better. If not, it didn't matter as long as they stayed on the reservations. There was broad consensus on these ideas among professional officers, succinctly expressed by Maj. Alfred E. Bates: "Savages cannot be civilized without first being taught to respect the power which civilization promotes, and the only argument which avails with them is the one they employ—the argument of force."[15] If Bascom did not learn that lesson at West Point, he soon learned it while on duty in Utah and subsequently in Arizona. It was a prime subject for conversation in the officers' mess—as well as an ongoing topic for civilian editorial writers.

When the management of the tribes was turned over to the politicians at the Interior Department, the lid of Pandora's box opened—as predicted by the army. Graft, incompetence, venality, and political cronyism were let loose and would be the continuing hallmarks of the Interior Department's Office of Indian Affairs for decades. Civilian agents (often politically connected) were appointed to negotitate with the tribes and distribute rations for which the government allotted funds, and it is not surprising that some of these funds found their way into the pockets of the agents, either directly or indirectly through the sale of cattle and provisions earmarked for the tribes. When that happened, the rations delivered to the tribes inevitably fell short in the quantity and quality they were promised in return for their pledges to be peaceful. Captain John G. Bourke had more experience than he wanted with corrupt Indian agents: "Bad as the Indians often are, I have never yet seen one so demoralized that he was not an example in honor and nobility to the wretches who enrich themselves by plundering him of the little our Government appropriates for him."[16]

Not all agents were corrupt; some were simply inept or naïve. Others suffered from poorly informed philanthropy and ethnocentrism, religious bigotry and ignorance—not only of the tribes but also of life on the frontier, and all these factors combined to create a nightmare scenario in which promises were made and not kept, peace was made and not kept, and the collision of two utterly different ways of life brought out the worst in each other.

The army felt aggrieved and ill used in this system because they were the ones who had to clean up the messes made by the incompetence or venality of the agents. And they had a point. They also felt that because they were accustomed to maintaining strict control over their own funds and resources and operated within a strong chain of command, they were best positioned to administer the funds designed for the support of the tribes. The structure of the army and the code of the officers would virtually guarantee an absence of graft—not that all officers were preux chevaliers, but the strict oversight intrinsic to the military procedures virtually eliminated the opportunities for corruption. This was in contrast to the unholy combination of federal funding and civilian management that had proved during the Utah War to be a recipe for waste and graft. The army saw the civilian management of the tribes as similar to the use of well-connected civilian freight contractors, as indeed it was. Besides, the army believed that the Indians—the most warlike, anyway—only respected power, and the army was the only institution that could overawe them. Indians would have viewed any attempts at persuasive diplomacy or Christian forbearance by civilian politicians as contemptible weakness. What's more, the very real likelihood of graft leading to unfulfilled obligations would only infuriate the tribes and increase their distrust of white promises. Understandably so.

This discussion went on from the very beginning of 1849 until the end of the Indian wars. So it is not surprising to see it surface in the relationship between Cochise's people and the fast-expanding white population of Arizona.

By turning the management of the Indians over to the Interior Department, the Americans complicated the problem by adding a level of bureaucracy, and its attendant inefficiency. But, bureaucracies aside, the fundamental question of what to do with the "wild tribes" remained apparently insoluble, for the United States and Mexico alike. Each country undoubtedly wished the Apaches would move permanently across the border to the other. But the Apaches remained resolute commuters.

There was another and different voice added to the discussion about how best to deal with the Apaches—the white civilians who had settled in the territory. They had little patience with the "feed versus fight" discussion. For them, there was only one obvious solution. In the civilians' view, the Apaches were no different from a pack of wolves, and the idea of asking them to come in and be fed and, in return, to change their very nature, was absurd on the face of it. In fairness, the settlers were the ones who suffered the economic losses when their cattle were stolen, and they were the most likely targets for murders designed to enhance a warrior's prestige. It is not at all surprising that they would advocate the most extreme measures. And, of course, white attitudes were formed in the context of the nineteenth century's belief in a hierarchy of races and cultures. But the white and Mexican citizens of Arizona were not interested in discussing anthropological theory; ranchers, farmers, miners, and merchants could simply not tolerate savages who lived by raiding and warfare and posed a constant threat to life and livelihood. The settlers demanded blood and extermination. Sylvester Mowry's views on the subject have been mentioned, and it's fair to say that most, if not all, civilians in Arizona shared them. And it should be noted that Mexican civilians in Arizona, along with the Pima, Papago, and Maricopa tribes, felt the same way about the Apaches and advocated the same remedies.*

As an example of civilian attitudes, here is a section of an editorial from the *Tucson Star*:

> The very ground is moist with the blood of our murdered people. The very air rings with the shrieks of the victims of Apache atrocity. The glare of the frontiersman's burning cabin signifies the fact that the Apache is on the warpath . . . not because he is [in] want of food; not because the whites have molested him in any manner, but purely in the spirit of fiendish rapine and murder; not to seek food or shelter, but to seek victims to satiate his devilish disposition to kill and destroy. The Apache is by nature bloodthirsty, and having no sense of responsibility, gratifies his cruel, heartless thirst for blood by murder and rapine.**

There was very little in the way of creative thinking about policy alternatives, even among those charged with the official responsibility. No one could imagine options beyond sequestering Indians on a reservation and feeding them, or fighting them—in order to exterminate them or evict them permanently across the

---

* In one of the worst atrocities committed against an Apache tribe in Arizona, 6 white men, 48 Mexicans, and 94 Papagos attacked and killed some 118 Apaches, mostly women and children, in what became known as the Camp Grant Massacre in 1871. Two dozen or so captured infants were then sold into slavery.

** This article was reprinted in the November 29, 1885, issue of the *New York Times*. The startling point is that twenty-five years had gone by and attitudes and events had not changed. The headline reads "Whites Advised to Attack and Slaughter Them."

border. Both the army and the Office of Indian Affairs were in agreement on that, at any rate: "The irresistible conclusion, then, is that we must either feed these wild tribes or hunt them in their fastnesses until they are exterminated. The latter course we have pursued up to the present, at an outlay of three millions annually to the government; the former, it is confidently believed, can be made the more effectual plan at a cost of one twentieth of the expenditures heretofore defrayed, and without loss of life or property."

In this 1863 letter from Dr. Michael Steck, Indian agent for the New Mexico Territory, to his superior, the commissioner for Indian Affairs, he was merely reiterating the same ideas that had been bandied about since the treaty with Mexico—place the nomadic tribes on a reservation and feed them, as a cheaper alternative to extermination. Steck was considered an exception to the general rule of ineptitude and corruption among the Indian agents. He believed that the Apaches raided because they could not support themselves from hunting and gathering alone. It was either raid or starve. This was a rather benign view of the practice and overlooked the fact that the Apaches actually enjoyed raiding; it was not solely a means to an economic end but was part of their culture, a rite of passage and a major source of prestige. They were a warrior society, not a group of suffering scarecrows driven by want to thievery. But Steck was sincere in his opinion. He had been Indian agent for the New Mexico Territory since 1852; he made an effort to understand the Apache and Navajo cultures and languages and was widely regarded as competent and honest, albeit a trifle dovish. And, perhaps, easily hoodwinked.*

---

* Butterfield Station Agent, James Tevis tells a different story that suggests Steck was less than honest. Steck had sent Tevis a message saying he was coming with fifteen wagonloads of gifts and rations for the Chiricahua. He arrived with only three, which, according to Tevis, infuriated Cochise, who suspected Steck had sold the missing goods. As with many stories about this period and the Apaches, the truth is difficult to discern.

Steck traveled to Apache Pass in December of 1858 to meet with Cochise. It was their first meeting, and it seemed to go well because Steck brought presents—cattle, corn, kettles, cloth. Steck returned to Apache Pass in January along with Captain Ewell in an effort to retrieve horses stolen from the Sonoita area. The meeting was a graphic example of the army's policy of force and firmness, and Cochise responded diplomatically by returning the horses and even releasing a Mexican captive taken from Sonora.[17] It was at this meeting that Steck, Ewell, and Cochise arrived at an understanding (most likely tacit): the Chiricahua were welcome to live in Apache Pass. The army would not bother them as long as they resisted the temptation to raid American settlements and the Overland Mail. What they did in Mexico was no concern of the U.S. government's. That there was a deal of some sort is strongly suggested in an editorial by Edward Cross (Mowry's dueling opponent). Cross criticized agreements and even treaties with Apache raiders as "legalized piracy upon a weak and defenseless state [Sonora], encouraged and abetted by the United States government."[18]

Steck returned with more presents in April, after which Cochise assembled his warriors to make plans for a raid into Mexico, but not before going on a tiswin spree. Tiswin was an alcoholic brew made by the Apache women from corn. Warriors would fast before imbibing in order to increase the effect of the drink, which tasted, according to Tevis, like liquid yeast. During the spree, Tevis was constantly harassed by intoxicated Chiricahuas. As Tevis said, "When any government train is here they are as gentle as lambs, but as soon as the train leaves, the devil seems to let loose among them."[19]

Assuming that Tevis was reasonably reliable, there is the inescapable conclusion that Cochise and his warriors were dangerously unpredictable. It may be fashionable in some circles to portray Cochise as a wise elder statesman among the Apaches and to posit that he navigated between various threats to his people with care and wisdom. But settlers like Tevis and army officers at the time were more ready to believe that the Chiricahua and their leader were violently erratic, and especially so when under the influence of tiswin. It seems eminently reasonable to accept the possibility that both views were correct, depending on the time and context. In fact, Cochise becomes more three-dimensional, and perhaps more interesting, when his capacity for violence and cruelty is acknowledged. He was known to have a furious temper, and a man afflicted with turbulent passions makes a formidable warrior but not much of a statesman. On the other hand, many of the descriptions of Cochise's character are based on contacts with him made in 1872, after more than ten years of war. He was therefore more than a decade wiser and more famous and influential with his people. But the passage of time must also have made him less resilient. It was then that he made peace, and kept it. But in the years leading up to the Bascom Affair, he was less a wise leader and more a warrior, less a Roman statesman and more a fearsome Achilles, out for blood. It would caricature him to imply that he could not and did not evolve as a chieftain. Even a war lover at some point may grow weary of war.

After days of drinking tiswin and, presumably, after a period of rest and recovery—the Chiricahua version of sermons and soda water—Cochise and his warriors raided Fronteras, Sonora, capturing a man who was working in the fields and two boys. Under a flag of truce, and displaying their prisoners, they lured the soldiers from the presidio and offered to parley. The offer, though, was a ruse designed to allow warriors to slip behind the soldiers and cut them off. The soldiers saw the trap and scurried back inside the walls, at which point the Apaches killed their adult captive, lancing him to death, and carried the two boys back to Apache Pass, where Tevis ransomed them for ten sacks of corn.[20] This incident is important because of the tactics Cochise used; he would use the same tactics when confronting Bascom in Apache Pass—take a prisoner, offer to parley under a flag of truce, and spring a trap. Taking hostages was a common tactic by all sides in this ongoing war between cultures. Captain Ewell had used a similar one in order to recover a young girl captured by Apaches: he had several Apache prisoners, and he turned one of them loose to tell the kidnappers that, if they did not return the girl, he would hang the others. The Apaches agreed, and an exchange was made. Hostages, in other words, were a common currency; both sides took them, both sides used them. The Bascom incident at Apache Pass set no precedent in this business and, in fact, followed one.

Cochise's actions also illustrate the value he and his warriors placed on human lives—five sacks of corn each. Tevis had nothing to gain from this transaction other than the exercise of common humanity, and, objectively speaking, he comes off far better than Cochise, for whom captives were nothing but trade goods, chattel.

Given the Chiricahuas' ultimate extermination—cultural if not actual—they are usually portrayed as victims of inexorable history, or white rapacity and duplicity. Certainly there is some merit to that point of view. But it is also true that had Cochise and the Chiricahuas lived up to their part of the bargain—raiding only into Mexico and leaving the American settlements alone—their destiny might have been different. What was disorganized Mexico going to do about the raiding? Certainly not come across the border and attack Apache Pass and thereby risk another war with the United States. Diplomatic relations were hardly cordial between the two countries and virtually precluded a cooperative campaign against the raiders. Alternatively, the Chiricahuas might have moved to Mexico, made a deal there, and restricted their raiding to the United States. But this would have been a riskier strategy, because eventually the United States would have grown impatient with the attacks and gone across the border in force. (As indeed they did later in the Apache wars, to say nothing of Black Jack Pershing's pursuit of Pancho Villa.)

For whatever reason, though, the Chiricahuas continued to raid on both sides of the border. They regularly attacked American mines and ranches. Now and then they ambushed soldiers traveling from Fort Buchanan to Tucson.

The Chiricahuas' relationship with the Americans was complicated, because other Apache tribes, such as the Coyoteros and Pinals in the mountains north of Tucson, were also heavily involved in raiding. That inevitably led to confusion among the whites about who was really responsible, incident by incident. The problem was compounded when, in March 1859, Steck and Ewell met with the Pinals at Canyon del Oro, northwest of Tucson, and concluded a treaty in which the Pinal Apaches promised to stop raiding American settlements in exchange for gifts and regular rations. The white citizens, in the person of *Daily Arizonian* editor Edward Cross, decried the treaty and called it "a contemptible farce."[21] But Steck apparently had faith in the agreement, and that in turn may have increased the level of suspicion against the Chiricahua when future raids took place. And suspicion of the Chiricahua generally meant suspicion of Cochise.

When confronted with charges of theft or attack, Cochise could sometimes legitimately plead innocence—as indeed he did in the Felix Ward case. At other times, warriors from his local group were, in fact, responsible, and here again the whites ran into the age-old misunderstanding about exactly how much power a chief had over his warriors. There was no law; there was custom. And custom favored the raiders. It is more than possible that Cochise winked at these excursions and when confronted merely shrugged and said he could not always control the young men, who were by nature wild and undisciplined—even though, of all Apaches, Cochise was believed to have the power to command his warriors. Now and then he would return a few stolen animals as a sign of his good faith. Such gestures were like paying commission.

In fairness, though, even with the best will in the world, a chief had no means to control his warriors if they decided to steal away— the country was so vast that communications with roving warriors was virtually impossible. A chief might make a temporary peace while some of his warriors were away and not likely to return for weeks. Unlike the army, the Chiricahua had no ironclad chain of command—nor did they want one. All Cochise or the other chiefs could do in the face of a warrior's depredations was make restitution after the fact. And certainly that was the position Cochise and other Apache leaders would take when confronted. Whether that position was disingenuous or not was a question no one—the army, Indian agents, Mexican governors—could answer with any certainty. Ironically, the contact army officers such as Ewell or civilians such as Tevis had with Cochise would have impressed them with Cochise's character and dangerous forcefulness—qualities that would make them doubt his claims not to have total control over his people. That, in turn, would contribute to the general impression that any outlawry anywhere could be laid at his doorstep. In later years, ethnologist Dr. John B. White met Cochise, noticed these same qualities, and drew similar conclusions: "This chief may be said to have been about the only one who really exercised control over any of the Apaches. He was a fine looking man, about five feet ten inches in height and well proportioned . . . of manly and martial appearance, not unlike our conception of the Roman soldier—possessing great physical endurance, and one well calculated to command the respect of a band of savage warriors."[22]

Given the white perspective that assumes hierarchies of government and command, these conclusions are understandable enough—and, to a large extent, fair. But they also overlook the Chiricahua culture—raiding and warfare were intrinsic parts of who they were. Warfare was an essential aspect of their being. Cochise might have made a temporary peace for tactical reasons, but telling his warriors not to go on raids would have been like telling them not to hunt, or, worse, not to be Chiricahua. Now and then he might have grown tired of fighting, now and then he might have felt the need for sanctuaries, now and then he might have needed time to refit and regroup, but a permanent peace with no raiding was a cultural impossibility and something he would not have considered even if he could have enforced such a thing, which ultimately he could not. And, just as important, it was part of who he was as well. He had become chief because of his prowess in raiding and warfare, not in spite of it.

It's also worth remembering that the Apaches drew a distinction between raiding and warfare. For the white victims and for the army, this was a distinction without a difference. As far as the white settlers were concerned, they were already at war with the Apaches, including the Chiricahua. People were being killed and taken captive; property was being stolen or destroyed. That was close enough to war to satisfy the settlers—as well as the Mexican population and the peaceful tribes. Perhaps the army would have been more sympathetic to the Apache distinction, since for the army war was something fought between massed men in formations, with artillery preparation and bayonet charges, whereas chasing Indian raiders was little more than police duty. But parsing these ideas was basically irrelevant. The army had been sent to the ends of the earth to protect the growing settlements, and that is what they tried to do. Whether they called it war or constabulary work hardly mattered. But to the Apaches, the distinction was important, which is one reason, in their minds, Cochise's war with the whites began after the Bascom incident, whereas in the white settlers' minds, the war, or whatever it was, had begun long before, with the advent of Apache raiding in Arizona. From the white perspective, the Bascom incident was just one more minor event in a long and continuing saga of Apache violence and criminality. And had it not been for the unlucky timing of the Civil War and the attendant removal of federal troops, that's probably all it would have been.

It should also be noted that in the years before the encounter with Bascom, Cochise was just one of several chiefs operating in the Chiricahua territory. His formidable political power would develop in the future as he led a war against the whites—after the Bascom incident. But at this time he was chief of his local group and living in close proximity to at least two other local groups, one under a chief called Esconelea, the other under "Old Jack." These groups were sometimes at odds with each other, and it was

Esconelea who, according to James Tevis's account, rescued Tevis after Cochise had captured him with the intention of torturing him to death. The story illustrates the fragmented political situation among the Chokonen, to say nothing of the larger divisions among the Chiricahua, who, in turn, nursed enmity against other Apache tribes, such as the Western Apaches. (And this enmity was long-standing and enduring; the Western Apaches would supply many of the scouts who tracked hostile Chiricahua for the army.) Small wonder then that the white settlers, army officers, and agents were frustrated in their attempts to deal with the various tribes. That partially explains why the most aggressive of the whites, such as Sylvester Mowry, echoed Simon de Montfort's orders during the Albigensian Crusade against heretics. Though some in the city de Montfort was besieging were good Catholics, he said, "Kill them all; God will recognize His own."

In the winter of 1860, Cochise and a war party attacked Sonora and, moving from village to village, terrorized the Mexicans and added some fifty murders of men, women, and children to his score. On returning to Arizona, Cochise and his men stole some stock from the Dragoon Springs Station and, later, attacked the long-suffering Santa Rita Mining Company near Tubac and escaped with its entire herd of animals. The indefatigable Captain Ewell tracked Cochise to Apache Pass and was able to recover some of the stock, although Cochise blamed the raid on another band from whom he said he had acquired the animals with the idea of returning them. Some historians and commentators have made much of Cochise's ironclad honesty and his detestation of liars, and that may have been true within his own circles. But he would have thought nothing of dissembling to an enemy, either actual or potential. That would have been perfectly consistent with his and other Apaches' tactics in raiding and warfare, which were based essentially on deception. That is, of course, not unique to the Apaches. In modern war it's called disinformation, and is regarded as a military art form. No doubt Cochise would have approved. On the other hand, Cochise would have been incensed to have been called a liar, even if the charge was true: "Cochise was very proud of making his word good, and no greater offense could have been offered to him," said Daklugie.[23]

As tensions mounted, the men at the Apache Pass Overland Mail station began to hear rumors of an impending Chiricahua attack. Amicable Chiricahuas (and there were some) gave these hints, which were then picked up in local news reports such as this: "[F]riendly Indians at Apache Pass [have] given intimations of extensive preparations for a total extermination of the Overland Mail line through their country to be followed by a descent upon the settlements."[24] Whether there was any truth to this is another question, but it illustrates the increasing tensions between the Americans and Cochise's people. These were further heightened by several incidents in which Cochise's warriors were killed in the act of stealing cattle. One of them was killed near Sonoita Creek, not far from Ward's ranch.[25] The death of any warrior was a tragedy to the local group and always required some measure of revenge. If the actual killers could not be found, anyone else—in this case, any other white people—would do.

Raids continued in Arizona, relations deteriorated, and more and more Chokonen migrated to Mexico while Cochise continued his operations from Apache Pass. Butterfield Agent James Tevis left the Overland Mail. Indian Agent Steck distributed rations in March 1860, but could not promise more until the following November—a semiannual distribution that irritated Cochise, who was accustomed to the Mexican policy of weekly distributions. (Later, Steck had a number of his mules stolen by Apaches while he was traveling in New Mexico on agency business.) With friendly relations unraveling, and presents from the U.S. government slow in coming, Cochise began to think that peace with the Americans was a game not worth the candle. Accordingly, toward the end of 1860, Cochise sent a trusted sister-in-law, Coyuntura's wife, Yones, as an emissary to Fronteras, Sonora, to ascertain the possibilities of a peace arrangement with the governor, Pesqueira.[26] Chiricahua women frequently acted as diplomats and negotiators. Certainly this had nothing to do with believing that their enemies would treat women with any kind of chivalry. As mentioned, women were killed in attacks as readily as men and children. Nor were women less likely to be taken hostage. But perhaps Cochise and other leaders felt that the Mexicans (or Americans) would be less wary of a woman. Or maybe she was just smarter than other possible ambassadorial candidates. Whatever the reason she was selected, Yones set out for Sonora in December, accompanied by her nine-year-old son and another Chiricahua family. She gained some initial indications that the Sonorans were amenable to the idea of peace with rations, but by the time the official word came from the governor, the fight at Apache Pass had occurred, and the war was on.

Chapter Ten

FROM FORT BUCHANAN TO APACHE PASS

... had the southern planters put their negroes in such hovels, a sample would, ere this, have been carried to Boston and exhibited as illustrative of the cruelty and inhumanity of the man masters.

—General William T. Sherman,
on frontier forts

How in the world any girl of ordinary sense can think of marrying a line officer I cannot imagine, for they must make up their minds to spend a life of exile, deprivation and poverty.

—Captain Randolph Marcy,
in a letter to his daughter

CAPTAIN RICHARD EWELL WAS FAMOUS IN THE ARMY FOR HIS eccentricities. Something of a hypochondriac, he preferred, of all things, a dish called frumenty, a concoction made primarily from boiled wheat. He supplemented this with vegetables, including potatoes, from his garden at Fort Buchanan. When he came west, he brought with him his childhood nurse, a slave named Nancy, who looked after him and prepared his meals. He was known as Old Baldy, for obvious reasons. A bald head is not an eccentricity, of course, but rather an affliction to be regretted, which he did, and therefore shaved off the remainder of his hair in order to preserve it. (His later photographs indicate a change of mind, for he is bushy everywhere but on the top of his head.) He was intense in all his activities and given to verbal outbursts and noisy non sequiturs, and he was chronically restless and had trouble sleeping. Later, when he married a widow, he would introduce her as "my wife, Mrs. Brown." But he was even more famous for his gift for profanity: "His profanity did not consist of single or even double oaths, but was ingeniously wrought into whole sentences. It was profanity which might be parsed, and seemed the result of careful study and long practice," said an admiring brother officer.[1] Given the period and its manners, it's likely he toned down his fulminations around Mrs. Brown, but he held nothing back among the troops. "[W]hen vexed he was not very particular about his language and would cuss the soldiers very lustily," said James Tevis.[2] But despite his odd mannerisms and volcanic curses, Ewell was popular with his men. He knew what he was doing, and he looked out for the welfare of his troops, the two primary keys to effective leadership. And he was widely respected by his superiors as a frontier cavalry officer. Since he came from a distinguished Virginia family, it's entirely possible that his long service on the frontier was responsible for at least some of his eccentricities—more so than genetics. If so, he would not have been the first officer to have been affected.

"Take a boy sixteen from his mother's apron strings, shut him up under constant surveillance for four years at West Point, send him out to a two company post upon the frontier where he does little but play seven-up and drink whiskey at the sutler's, and by the time he is forty five he will furnish the most complete illustration of suppressed mental development of which human nature is capable. . . ."[3] So said Lieutenant General Richard Taylor, CSA who was not a graduate of West Point and did not think much of the Academy's products. He thought even less of the management of the frontier army. Ewell (West Point '40) did not tumble into these pitfalls, but many other frontier officers did. U. S. Grant's experience as a junior officer in California was common—the boredom, the separation from his home and loved ones, the wretched living conditions caused him finally to resign his commission, although not before he had acquired a taste for strong drink, a taste that stayed with him.

Life at a frontier fort was anything but salubrious. The men and officers alike were "living the best years of their lives in remote frontier posts with rare glimpses of the refinements of civilization, having little reward in sight but a sense of duty done, growing gray in junior grades under the slow promotions of peace conditions, kept poor by the necessities of frequent changes of stations," writes historian John C. Waugh.[4] After eighteen years of service, Ewell, though highly regarded in the army, was still just a captain. He had some ambitions for wealth, although he understood he would not get rich or even very comfortable on army pay. So he and several other officers at Buchanan invested in a Patagonia silver mine, which they bought from a Mexican herdsman. This was the same mine that Sylvester Mowry would buy in 1860 after it had passed through other hands and out of Ewell's. The mining business did not make Ewell's fortune, but it gave him something other than his garden to occupy his mind and relieve the boredom of life at Buchanan—for it was exceedingly dull and uncomfortable there, except when he led troops on patrols or campaigns against the Apaches. Then it was quite the opposite of dull.

Life at a frontier fort like Buchanan was even worse for the enlisted men. Even immigrant Irish soldiers, having escaped the poverty of the famine years and the expulsions of "the clearances," during which their tiny hovels were demolished by landlords wanting grazing land, probably viewed their new homes at places like Fort Buchanan as something of a step down. (The regular meals provided by the army, though, were a welcome step up. Otherwise most would not have enlisted; eleven dollars a month, every month, were welcome too.)

The establishments dignified by the term "fort" were usually just ramshackle collections of buildings arranged around a parade ground. Generally, there were no walls or palisades, so that forts looked less like imposing military installations and more like frontier villages sprung from nothing and expecting to return there sooner rather than later.* Ghost towns in waiting. Oddly, few officers on the frontier seemed concerned about the possibility of attacks. (That may explain in part why the Navajo attack on Fort Defiance generated such a vigorous response.) But the very designs of these forts indicated how little the frontier army feared the Indian, especially in the 1850s. True, the Indians preyed on civilian settlements and traffic, but the officers were not particularly worried about their personal safety or the safety of their troops while in garrison. And events proved them right, most of the time. This attitude was in line with their view of their assignment, which most officers considered mere constabulary work involving occasional patrols punctuated by long periods of inaction, routine, and boredom. Apaches and other hostile tribes were not soldiers as the officers understood the term. They were mere bandits or wild beasts, depending on the officer's particular view of things. After all, the subject of fighting Indians never really came up at West Point. A few officers found them interesting, but almost all believed them to have one foot on the edge of inevitable and justifiable extinction—especially the incorrigible tribes like the Apaches. The more warlike they were, the more likely their eventual disappearance from history.

---

* This was especially true in the early frontier days. Fort Bowie in Apache Pass—built in 1862 and rebuilt in 1868—developed over the next two decades into an impressive installation featuring even a two-story house with a mansard roof for the commanding officer. There's nothing much left of the fort today, however—just a few gradually eroding adobe walls.

It's not difficult to understand this attitude. Indians as a general rule did not favor direct attack, except when they believed they had overwhelming numbers. That was nothing more than good sense because the army had a continuing advantage over the tribes in firepower. If the tribes had understood how poorly trained many of the troops were, however, they might not have feared the massed musketry of the army. But they had no real way of knowing that. They simply saw men in uniform, armed with modern weapons, and they quite logically decided that direct confrontation in combat made no sense. They were without question better guerrilla fighters and, on the plains, the better light cavalry. But when there were major confrontations, the army's massed firepower, plus the advantages of light howitzers that could scatter and kill Indians from what seemed to the Indians an unimaginable range, generally made the difference.* Besides, as noted earlier, the raiding parties of Apache tribes consisted to a large extent of kinsmen. They were careful with each other's lives, whereas an officer viewing the body of one of his soldiers would most likely feel saddened at the death, but would not consider the casualty a tragedy, or something calling for blood atonement. There were plenty more where he came from. Starvelings in Ireland or Germany were ready to take his place and they were on the way. What's more, there weren't many casualties among the troops; the Mexican War cost the army 13,780 dead, although only one in eight died from wounds, the rest died from disease. Still, the numbers were staggering compared to the casualties in the wars against the tribes.** And that in itself reinforced

---

* In two major fights against hostile tribes, the mountain howitzers were decisive—against Cochise and Mangas Coloradas in 1862 and against the Comanches and Kiowas at Adobe Wells, Texas, in 1864. Mountain howitzers fired explosive shells. The weapons could be disassembled and packed on mules and so were ideal for frontier service.

** A single day's fighting in the Civil War would inflict more casualties—on the army—than all the Indian wars combined. The civilian toll in the Indian wars was another story entirely, to say nothing of the devastation of the native tribes.

the officers' belief that they were nothing more than frontier policemen. A murder here or there, some mules stolen, a half dozen Apaches killed in a three-week scout—this was not war. There was, therefore, really no need for scientifically engineered forts, no need for ramparts or bastions. And it's impossible to escape the conclusion that this attitude also indicated a level of contempt for the native adversaries. Of course, the Indians could be dangerous, but only if you were foolish enough to let them set the terms. And, finally, after the expensive blunder known as the Utah War, Congress was in no mood to pay for elaborate fortifications.

Quite often the soldiers themselves built their forts, especially in areas where civilian labor was in short supply—which was most places. It's not surprising then that the quality of construction was uneven, often because of the paucity of materials and know-how. (At West Point, cadets studied military and civil engineering, but they had no courses in house building and probably had never heard of an adobe brick until they went west.) Troops were expected to go into a country and make something out of nothing. Nor did this kind of work do much for the troops' morale. Even immigrant soldiers who were used to hard labor might grumble about spending more time with a hammer and saw than a rifle or saber.

And, because of the remote locations of these posts, the question of supply was always vexatious. To supplement the sometimes undependable shipments, the soldiers planted vegetable gardens for themselves. They also spent hours cutting hay for their animals and wood for their fireplaces. Critics complained that the army was establishing farms instead of forts and was spending more time hoeing and harvesting than fighting Indians.[5] Some of the soldiers had enlisted to escape the shovel and the hoe and honestly would have preferred an occasional patrol to the mind-numbing labor of the field, even if the patrol involved a brush with the Indians. Or maybe even because of it. But the opportunities for action were sporadic. Historian Robert Utley estimates that a soldier could expect one Indian fight for every five years of frontier service.[6]

But that's an average throughout the West. Apache country offered somewhat better opportunities . . . or risks.

The army's problem, as usual, was funding. When the United States acquired its vast new holdings, it also acquired vast new responsibilities, which would grow geometrically as settlers trickled and then poured into the territories. New settlements and lines of travel and communications had to be protected, and of course that was the army's job.

By the mid-1850s, there were some fifty army posts scattered throughout the Trans-Mississippi. Many were near growing towns; others were placed along travel routes to protect emigrants on their way west. Still others were placed in an area where Indian raids and depredations were common. It was hoped that the mere presence of troops would act as a deterrent, but it didn't take long for hostile Indians to realize that forts manned by a few companies of infantry were hardly to be feared. Cavalry, however, was a different matter.

The question became how best to protect the growing migration of white settlers into the territories. Inevitably, there was a political dimension to the problem. As frontier forts sprang up, Congress became increasingly appalled by the cost of manning and maintaining these far-flung posts. The shock came primarily because Congress's experience with funding had been exclusively in the settled parts of the country. The military posts in the East were within easy reach of the railroad or riverboats, or they were on the Atlantic Coast and could be serviced by oceangoing vessels. This meant the problem of transporting supplies was negligible and relatively inexpensive. Further, the forts were in populated areas, so that the local quartermasters could rely on civilian suppliers for many of their requirements. But when the new posts began sprouting in the Southwest, there were no rivers and no railroads to offer avenues of supply. The nearest seaports were in California or the gulf ports of Texas. Supplies had to be freighted overland from central depots like Leavenworth. Nor were there many settlements to provide local produce and livestock. Aside from the Mormons in Utah, the first Americans into the territories were generally miners, who were useless as possible sources of supply and, in fact, created many of the problems with the tribes that the army was sent to address.

Faced with ballooning costs caused by a combination of geography and Indian hostilities, Congress looked for various ways to manage the problems. That took them into the realm of military strategy, rarely a politician's strong suit. Various ideas were bandied about. One suggested strategy was to consolidate smaller forts into a handful of large installations manned by cavalry that would periodically ride forth into Indian territories to show the flag or punish marauders. This idea was rejected for two reasons—the cost of maintaining large units of cavalry and, more important, the inherent flaw in the plan. Hostile Indians, seeing a column of soldiers, would simply fade away and wait until the soldiers left, at which point the hostiles could begin raiding emigrant wagon trains again. Large units of cavalry—or infantry, for that matter—could not be kept permanently in the field. Supplies and equipment would eventually run out and require a return to base, at which point the gleeful tribes could resume normal service.

An alternative strategy was to position forts along the routes of communications and near settlements, such as they were. That meant many forts manned by sufficient numbers of cavalry to deal with a highly mobile enemy. Congress didn't care for this approach, once again because of the expense of maintaining cavalry. Yes, they would go along with a number of smaller forts, but these would have to be manned by infantry primarily.

Then there was the question of negotiating with the tribes as part of the feed-or-fight discussion. Treaties made with the tribes offered annuities in exchange for land and/or peace. These annuities would be administered by the Office of Indian Affairs through its agents. But Congress's parsimony effectively scuppered this strategy as well, as did the venality and/or incompetence of some

Indian agents. Too little was offered; even less was delivered. Meanwhile, the small peacetime army was scattered throughout the frontier and organized in small cantonments, manned by ill-trained soldiers and not enough of them, officered by professionals who had not been trained for jobs they were given. As John G. Bourke said, "The army has always been too small to afford all the protection the frontier needed, and affairs have been permitted to drift along in a happy-go-lucky sort of way indicative rather of a sublime faith in divine providence than of common sense and good judgment."[7]

In short, Congress's response to the key strategic question was to fall between two stools. Feed or fight? Do both, it answered, but did not provide sufficient resources to do either. Small wonder then that most frontier officers regarded politicians with contempt and would have echoed President John Adams's remark that "in politics the middle way is none at all."

The decision of where to locate a frontier fort was a military question but, inevitably, a political question as well. White settlers, especially ranchers, farmers, and merchants, wanted the forts near them, not just for protection but as markets for their produce and livestock. Throughout the history of the Indian troubles, there were repeated accusations that local civilian populations exaggerated the Indian threat in order to maintain and expand the military presence—for economic reasons. Many of those accusations came from politicians and editorialists operating at a safe distance from the frontier. But there was some truth to the charge—witness the economic windfall to the Mormons from Camp Floyd's brief existence. A fort meant good business. In some cases, the forts preceded civilian settlement (which followed quickly), but in others, as in southern Arizona, there were already villages such as Tubac and Tucson as well as several intrepid ranchers along the Santa Cruz

River and Sonoita Creek and a number of mines scattered in the surrounding mountains.

In the autumn of 1856, Maj. Enoch Steen was ordered to take four companies of dragoons to southern Arizona and establish a fort there for the protection of the growing population of ranchers and miners. (In a matter of a couple of years, these dragoons would be replaced for the most part by infantry.) Steen initially considered Tucson but quickly rejected it because of the lack of grazing and grain supplies. He was also disgusted by the quality of the local population. A later traveler described it as ". . . a city of mud boxes, dingy and dilapidated, cracked and baked into a composite of dust and filth; littered about with broken corrals, sheds, bake ovens, carcasses of dead animals, and broken pottery . . . the best view of Tucson is the rear view on the road to Fort Yuma."[8] (This account was from J. Ross Browne, who had waxed rhapsodic over the glories of the Mowry Mine.)

After rejecting Tucson, Steen went south along the Santa Cruz Valley until just a few miles above the border with Mexico. He established Camp Moore and at first supplied the fort with produce and livestock from Sonora. Soon, however, that source of supply dried up because of squabbles with the Sonoran governor, Pesqueira (the same man Sylvester Mowry later praised for reestablishing Apache scalp bounties and the same man who would consider the peace feelers initiated by Cochise's sister-in-law, Yones). Pesqueira was incensed over yet another Yankee filibustering expedition and closed the border to trade.* At that point, Steen began ordering

---

* The 1857 filibuster expedition was under the command of Henry Crabb, who was an unsuccessful California politician and member of the Know-Nothing Party. He took one hundred or so men into Sonora in what was little more than a piratical attempt to grab Mexican land. Some reports implicate Pesqueira in the plot; he was trying to unseat a political rival. In any event, Crabb and all his men were killed, some in battle, most by firing squad, thereby relieving Pesqueira of having to explain anything. Granville Oury was one of the Crabb filibusters who missed out on the battle and survived; Oury was the brother of William S. Oury, who was the Butterfield agent in Tucson and figured in the Bascom incident.

supplies from ranches and farms along the Rio Grande River in New Mexico—a long distance to haul freight, but closer than other options, such as California. He could also supplement these shipments with livestock from local ranchers.

Steen's commander in Santa Fe rejected the site of Camp Moore because of political outcry from Tucson merchants and directed Steen to find a site closer to Tucson. Steen chose a site discovered and recommended by Captain Ewell in the area of Sonoita Creek. Steen said this was as good a place as any, with water and decent grass and the best weather in the entire Gadsden Purchase. If the Tucson merchants were unhappy, he said, it was only because they were losing potential whiskey sales. Steen may have been pleased to frustrate the Tucson "whiskey peddlers," but he was also fully aware that drunkenness was one of the two chief evils afflicting the frontier army, the other being desertion. (In 1860, one in eight soldiers deserted throughout the frontier army.)[9] Both he and his men would be better off in semi-isolation at the fort they would name Buchanan.

The new location was closer to Tucson than Camp Moore, but it was still a good fifty miles away, which, in wars against the Apaches, might as well have been a thousand. The new location insured that the army would not be able to prevent an attack against the major settlements and could only react once an attack had occurred. In that sense, the citizens of Tucson, Tubac, and the Santa Cruz Valley had a legitimate complaint, as events would prove. The settlers in the Sonoita Valley, however, were better pleased. Most likely, it would not have bothered Steen if the Apaches burned Tucson to the ground.

Fort Buchanan was located in Hog Canyon—named possibly because someone saw a javelina there; or perhaps named after the pigsty built and occupied to provide the soldiers with their eternal favorite—bacon. The pigsty, of course, did nothing for the air quality, nor did the manure piles, or, for that matter, the concentration of soldiers and animals. The buildings—barracks, officers' quarters, workshops, hospital, and stables—along with the sutler's store—were constructed of local live oak and built in Mexican style with the oak boards or unfinished logs standing upright and chinked with mud. The buildings were called *jacales*, a Spanish word roughly translated as "shack." The roofs were made the same way, or sometimes with a kind of thatch made from brush and branches. That was acceptable in dry weather but less so during summer monsoons and winter rain or snow. Then the dry chinking predictably turned to dripping mud. In the warmer months, loathsome centipedes shared the men's barracks along with an occasional tarantula. Rattlesnakes were also frequent visitors. Harmless but unlovely geckos hung on the sides of the buildings, motionless and waiting. But the worst discomforts came from the ciénagas, which were spring-fed pools of standing water that formed marshy areas and bred malaria-bearing mosquitoes. It may seem strange that malaria would be a problem in the high grasslands of southern Arizona, but in 1858, Assistant Surgeon Bernard J. D. Irwin's report shows that every man was suffering from some touch of the disease. The only people to have escaped were some employees of the sutler, and Nancy, Captain Ewell's old nurse.[10] The fact that these were all civilians indicates that troops also encountered malarial insects during patrols. These insects could breed in playas as well as ciénagas. Playas are temporary wetlands in the flats caused by rainstorms. These evaporate after a while and generally leave an alkali residue, but mosquitoes don't need much time to breed. The playas were to the east of the Sonoita Valley, but well within the army's patrolling areas. (Apaches, too, suffered now and then from malaria, which they called "shaking sickness.")

Fort Buchanan was not unique in its comprehensive discomforts. An officer described the first Fort Bowie (built in Apache Pass the year after the Bascom incident): "The quarters, if it is not an abuse of language to call them such, have been constructed without system, regard to health, defense or convenience. Those occupied by the men are mere hovels, mostly excavations in the side hill,

damp and illy ventilated, and covered with decomposed granite
taken from the excavation, through which rain passes very much
as it would through a sieve. By the removal of a few tents, the place
would present more the appearance of a California digger [Indian]
rancheria than a military post."[11]

Diseases of all sorts were a constant complaint in all the forts
on the frontier. "On the average each soldier had to be hospitalized
three times a year, and each year one in thirty three men died of
disease," according to historian Robert Utley.[12] This percentage is
small compared to the toll disease took on the army in the Mexican
War—especially among the volunteers—but it is still a sad com-
mentary on the quality of life in the frontier army. The poor diet
of salt pork, beans, dried peas, rice, and hard tack contributed to
various illnesses that were aggravated by fatigue from long hours
on patrol—when there were patrols. When the post garden didn't
produce enough fresh vegetables, scurvy was the inevitable result.
Colds and pneumonia were common, as well as the "old soldier's
disease," dysentery. Alcoholism and the occasional bout of venereal
disease, acquired locally or imported from an earlier post, rounded
out the list of usual maladies.

Because of illness, Maj. Steen was relieved at Fort Buchanan
in the spring of 1858 by Maj. Edward Fitzgerald, but Fitzgerald
was suffering from tuberculosis and lasted only a few months. In
effect, then, Captain Ewell was in command of the fort much of
the time.

Assistant Surgeon Bernard J. D. Irwin, who was assigned to
Fort Buchanan, was generally regarded as competent, but that was
according to the standards of the day. The quality of medical science in those days was not up to many of the tasks it confronted.
But Irwin at least was a medical doctor and an experienced soldier
as well. He was born in Ireland in 1830, so he had something in
common with a number of immigrant soldiers at Buchanan. Commissioned in 1856, he would play an important role in the Bascom
incident.

Fort Buchanan was an uncomfortable eyesore made all the more unattractive in contrast with the surroundings, for Hog Canyon, like all of the canyons in the area, was a lovely grass- and tree-filled opening in the foothills. With its gently sloping sides dotted with live oaks and junipers, it hardly deserved to be called a canyon at all, and seemed more like a small valley in a landscape of rolling hills. To the northwest, the peaks of the Santa Rita Mountains added some aesthetic grandeur to the scene. The green trees stood all along the sides of the surrounding hills, and in the mornings and evenings the soldiers could hear the sounds of Gambel's quail calling to each other. Now and then a soldier would flush a covey of harlequin quail that was foraging at the base of the oaks. Men who were adept with a shotgun could supplement their diets with quail or the occasional duck that visited the ciénagas, though this kind of sport was more the province of the officers than the enlisted men. Deer and javelina were plentiful, but a soldier on a hunting expedition needed to be aware that there were others who were more experienced hunting those same deer and perhaps the soldier too. The weather was generally good and certainly better than almost any other place in the territory. The sun shone nearly every day and the temperatures were mild most of the time, although the Sonoita Valley had four seasons of weather. As a wry soldier might have said, if it weren't for the malaria, the Apaches, the miserable housing conditions, and the terrible food, life at Fort Buchanan wouldn't have been too bad. No doubt the troops regretted the absence of saloons and brothels, but their health was bad enough already from malaria and scurvy, and if they wanted the occasional drink or glass of beer, the sutler's store could provide that at least. As for female companionship, there were the senoritas of the Mexican families working at the mines and ranches, and it would be surprising if enterprising soldiers had not found ways to make occasional contacts. But professional "soiled doves" were just a fond memory from Frogtown.

Despite the peace treaty concluded by Steck and Ewell with the Pinals, raids continued. In most cases it was impossible to say who the raiders were. That mystery, combined with the army and white settlers' inability to distinguish among the various Apache groups, resulted in the decision to initiate a campaign against the Pinals, who shared with the Chiricahua the dubious distinction of being blamed for most depredations. Accordingly, in the autumn of 1859, and then again in the winter of that same year, the army organized a contingent of dragoons at Fort Buchanan and penetrated the Pinal country north of Tucson. Agent Steck protested, saying that the incursion would alarm and radicalize all the tribes in the area, but his protests were ignored. Neither campaign netted many Apache casualties, although the December campaign did in fact frighten the Pinals into coming to Fort Buchanan to make peace with Ewell. Of course, these peace overtures and agreements meant nothing to the other bands who lived in much the same territory.

Ewell was wounded in the hand during a skirmish with the Pinals and the following year he was transferred to Fort Bliss, no doubt taking Nancy along with him. When he left, Arizona lost a man who had genuine experience with the Apaches and knew when to fight and when to parley. In fact, he was as close as possible to the ideal of the army's firmness and fairness policy. But now he was gone, to be replaced by Lieutenant Colonel Pitcairn Morrison. Ewell's two experienced and trustworthy subordinates, Lts. Isaiah Moore and Richard S. C. Lord, were also gone, transferred to a new fort in the San Pedro Valley at the juncture of Arivaipa Creek and the San Pedro. Called Fort Breckinridge, the post was established in May of 1860. It was sixty miles north of Tucson and eventually manned by two companies of dragoons under Lord and Moore. Moore was the senior man, having been commissioned in 1853, while Lord's commission dated from 1856. Moore was in command at Breckinridge. Both officers were investors in the Patagonia Mine with Ewell, the same mine that was later sold to Sylvester Mowry—an obvious indication that Mowry and the officers at Buchanan were closely associated.

The strategy of assigning these dragoons to the newer post seems to reflect the difficulty of the terrain there. The mountains that border the narrow river valley are brutally rugged, rocky, and strewn with saguaro cactus and other forms of spiny plants. Although it was initially established by infantry, under Lieutenant John Rogers Cooke, the fort was not located in the kind of terrain that was conducive to infantry operations and made the Sonoita valley and surrounding countryside look like an Eden by comparison. Additionally, it was just to the south of the Pinal Mountains, home of the Coyotero or Pinal Apaches. (Sometimes the two terms—Pinal and Coyotero—were used interchangeably; other times they referred to two cognate groups living in the same area.) The dragoons, therefore, were thought to be in position to block a major Apache raiding trail as well as to intimidate the Coyotero and Pinals living in the mountains north of the fort. There was some logic in this, for it is undoubtedly true that all the Apache tribes feared the horse soldiers far more than they feared the less mobile infantry, for good and obvious reasons.

In October of 1860 the two companies of the Seventh Infantry under Morrison arrived at Buchanan. That, plus the transfer of the two companies of dragoons to Breckinridge, meant that the balance of power in terms of mounted troops had shifted northward to Breckinridge. (Breckinridge would be renamed Camp Grant and would be the site of the 1872 Camp Grant Massacre.) Though Breckinridge was more than a hundred miles from Buchanan, the dragoons would have been able, if necessary, to support action against the Chiricahua in Apache Pass by following the San Pedro River Valley south-southeast before turning east to the Dos Cabezas, rather like tracing the hypotenuse of a right triangle.

If the Coyoteros were troubled by the presence of dragoons in the territory, it did not prevent them from raiding. And in January of 1861 they attacked the ranch of John Ward in the Sonoita Valley.*

---

* Other accounts say the raid took place in October 1860—an example of the conflicting stories that characterize this incident. January seems a more likely version, though, because, in all likelihood, the army would not have waited three months before responding.

The raiders might have come down the Santa Cruz River Valley and turned east to Sonoita Creek, or they might have eluded the troops at Fort Breckinridge and come south along the San Pedro, turning west to Sonoita. In any event, when they got to Ward's ranch, they captured a few head of cattle and then headed east, most likely intending to follow the San Pedro River Valley back north. Just after the raid, it was easy enough to slip by the infantry troops at Fort Buchanan. And no doubt by this time, the Coyoteros had devised a route that would bypass Fort Breckinridge, when they got closer to home.

It was this eastward movement that caused so much of the subsequent trouble, for to the east lay not only the San Pedro River Valley but, beyond that, the Dos Cabezas Mountains and Apache Pass. The Coyoteros were laying a trail that would lead the army, mistakenly, to Apache Pass.

And along with the cattle, the Coyoteros took a twelve-year-old captive, Felix Ward.

> *[Bascom was ordered] to demand the immediate restoration of the stolen property, [and in case Cochise should fail to make restitution, the officer] was authorized and instructed to use the force under his orders to recover it.*
>
> —Lieutenant Colonel Morrison's Order
> Number 4 to Lieutenant Bascom[13]

THE APACHE RAIDERS STRUCK WARD'S RANCH ON JANUARY 27, 1861. It's curious that they did not kill Felix, for he was obviously at the age at which Apaches killed captive boys. (Other raiders had murdered Pete Kitchen's young son.) Here again the Apaches displayed some capriciousness, as they had in the past. There is some suggestion in the oral traditions that the Apaches had come for

Felix specifically, because his father was actually a Coyotero. That may explain why he was spared, or it may be a piece of romantic fiction.

Once John Ward reported the raid to Fort Buchanan, Lieutenant Bascom was ordered out to locate the trail of the raiders. Some accounts suggest that Ward himself had already followed the trail and that Bascom and his troops merely verified the easterly direction. In either case, the troops returned to the fort, satisfied that the trail led eastward toward Apache Pass and that Cochise's band must therefore be responsible. They began preparation for a patrol designed to recover the boy and the cattle. It will be remembered that Apache Pass was a good seventy miles from Buchanan.

To the army this was nothing but more police work. Property had been stolen, a boy had been kidnapped. It was just one more incident in a long line of similar ones, many of which could be fairly laid at the feet of the Chiricahuas and Cochise. This was not war as any of the soldiers understood it. As mentioned, more than a few officers believed that the Apaches were not warriors at all, but simple thieves and murderers—nothing more than land-based pirates. Nor did this particular incident seem any more outrageous or unusual than any of the other raids that had been occurring in the Santa Cruz and Sonoita Valleys. No one would have regarded it as having any particular significance. It was neither more nor less than another chapter in the ongoing business of dealing with Apaches. In fact, in the scheme of things, it was less important than the raids on the mining companies, which were run by men with some political influence, unlike John Ward, who was a subsistence rancher and a doubtful sort of character.

Still, the army recognized it had a job to do. Morrison may have looked at it as an opportunity to "strike a blow" against the notorious Cochise, but that seems unlikely given his status in the army; he had requested a leave of absence,[14] and at age sixty-five he was more interested in returning to civilization than in gathering the dubious laurels to be gained by killing a few Apache thieves.

If he wanted those laurels, or if he had any professional ambition or energy left, or if he considered the incident all that important, he should have, and probably would have, led the patrol himself. But his prospects for further advancement at his age and in the peacetime army were virtually nonexistent, and his one ambition by this time would have been to get out with everything intact.* And so he assigned the task to his most junior lieutenant, whom he "authorized and instructed" to use whatever force might be required. On the other hand, Morrison did assign a fairly large force to this mission, possibly to balance Lieutenant Bascom's lack of Indian-fighting experience.

Obviously, when it comes to the use of force, there is a vast difference between "authorized" and "instructed." "Authorization" allows considerable room for judgment. "Instruction" leaves far less room. Bascom may well have gone into the assignment with the firm conviction that if Cochise did not surrender the cattle and the boy, he would be expected to use the force at his command, and that not doing so would be regarded as a failure, or worse. And, in his first independent command of any consequence, he would not have wanted his record to show a failure. Besides, given his West Point training, with its belief in formulaic solutions and the virtues of following the exact letter of any orders, Bascom would have appreciated the lack of ambiguity and regarded the situation in Apache Pass as a fairly simple "if-then" proposition. If Cochise returned the boy and the cattle, then fair enough. If Cochise refused to make restitution, then Bascom would apply the force at his command. Either way, Bascom would have done his duty properly. He was not on a diplomatic mission and did not see, and did not care to see, any other options.

Parsing military orders often turns up examples of unintended consequences. At the Battle of Gettysburg, for example, Lee's orders

---

* The Civil War changed things for Morrison, as it did with so many professional officers. Morrison served a few more years, but finally retired while the war was still raging. During the war, his assignments did not involve a combat command.

to Ewell to take Culp's Hill "if practicable" must have contributed to Ewell's failure to do so.[15] To his credit, the always-professional Ewell later said that it took a great many mistakes to lose the Battle of Gettysburg, and "I myself made most of them." But certainly the question of practicability must have given him pause. And it's fair to wonder what might have happened if Lee had simply said, "Take Culp's Hill." Period. (Not fully aware of the situation, Lee felt he had to make the order discretionary. Still, the point remains.) One of U. S. Grant's greatest virtues as a commander was his ability to write clear orders—a skill that must have come naturally to him, because it was not a subject that was given much attention at the Academy. Of course, the ability to write clearly depends on the ability to think clearly, and in the heat of battle, thinking clearly is difficult at best. But in Morrison's case, there was no emergency; he simply wrote orders that changed the tone of the coming encounter at Apache Pass. It's also possible that he used the words "instructed to" as a standard prevention against indecisiveness in a young officer, perhaps as a way of stiffening a young man's resolve. Regardless of Morrison's thinking, the wording of Order Number 4 had a profound impact on what would happen in Apache Pass and therefore on what would happen in Arizona for the next ten years. Many would die, perhaps in part because Bascom was not only "authorized" but "instructed."

As Ben Franklin observed, "A little neglect may breed great mischief."

On January 29, 1861, Lieutenant Bascom and fifty-four soldiers from the Seventh Infantry mounted their mules and headed east. John Ward went along, not only because he was an interested party, but also because he could be an interpreter. If the idea of infantry on mules seems ludicrous in retrospect, the soldiers probably did not give it much thought. Undoubtedly, they had ridden mules now and then while on duty in Utah, and they were exceedingly glad not to have to walk the seventy miles between Buchanan and Apache Pass. And ludicrous or not, Bascom would have looked back on the line of men following him and felt a genuine sense of pride. He had led patrols in Utah, but they were little more than training exercises or protection for working parties. This was closer to the real thing. It was only a police action, to be sure, but it was action nonetheless.

The troops were armed with their long-barreled, muzzle-loading .58-caliber rifled muskets, and they carried their lethal pointed-socket bayonets sheathed in their belts or on their saddles. The column also took along several wagons to carry the tents, food for men and animals, and extra ammunition. They were prepared for a patrol lasting twenty-five days, and they were well prepared for a fight, if it came to that.[16] Their line of march would initially take them through rolling yellow grasslands. Studded with agave (mescal) plants, the road led east to a pass between the Mustang Mountains and the Whetstones. If the actual raiders who kidnapped Felix Ward had in fact headed east, they would have taken this same trail. Beyond that pass, the land, while still fairly flat, would change character somewhat and take on the harsher look of a desert floor. Ugly creosote plants, scrubby sage, and cactus took over from the grama grass and agaves. But soon in the distance they would see the line of willows and leafless cottonwoods that bordered the San Pedro River, and they no doubt camped that evening along the river that they would then follow northward next day. That first day's march would have been about twenty-five miles, slightly above average for a cavalry march. Infantry, unused to a day in the saddle and the gait of mules, no doubt greeted the arrival at a campsite with undisguised relief.

If the Coyoteros who had made the raid turned north along the San Pedro to return to their camps in the Pinal Mountains, they either covered their tracks well or Bascom missed seeing their trail continue north. He did not have any Indian trackers with him, an omission that later Indian fighters, like General George Crook, would deprecate. Bascom must have missed the continuing northward track—if it was there at all—for on the next day he continued along the river but only until parallel to the northern edge of the Dragoon Mountains. At that point, he turned east, away from the river, and made camp at the Dragoon Springs stage station. They were now in Cochise's homeland—the Dragoon Mountains being Cochise's other favorite camping place and the site of his stronghold, though the troops were still a good thirty miles from the pass. Bascom would have been careful to post a strong guard over the camp and the animals that night. The mules would have been fed from supply wagons rather than allowed to graze. There was no sense taking the risk of losing them to Apache raiders. That would have been a serious blot on Bascom's record. The sentries would have been especially sensitive to the night sounds—the howls of coyotes, the calls of the night birds. Were they real or were they something else? Bascom may have spent a restless night, this second night in command, and he would undoubtedly have checked on the sentries more than once. Nightmare scenarios would have occurred to him—the loss of his animals and equipment, the loss of his men from Apache devils screeching as they attacked in the darkness. (Not that Apaches ever did that, but Bascom did not know better.) He would have felt some indications of the proverbial loneliness of command. But perhaps he was then able to reject all of that as melodrama. He had his men around him, men he knew individually, men whose strengths and weaknesses he understood. This would all work out well, and at least he had his tent to sleep in, erected by his men. Perhaps they used their bayonets as tent posts for him and for their own shelters. Bayonets were often used that way. One in particular, though, would be used differently in Apache Pass.

The next day's march would take them across the Sulphur Springs Valley to Ewell Springs (named presumably after the redoubtable "Old Baldy") at the western base of the Dos Cabezas

Mountains. The Ewell Springs station was established in 1857 by the Jackass Mail, and some reports suggest that the Butterfield Overland Mail also used the station, which seems reasonable, although Waterman Ormsby does not mention it in his account nor does it appear on his accompanying map. The trip from Dragoon Springs to Ewell Springs was some twenty-five miles, and Bascom followed the Butterfield road skirting along the southern edge of the flat Sulphur Springs Valley. Whether there was a functioning stage station at Ewell Springs or not, it would have been the logical place to camp on the third night, for, as the name implies, there was reliable water there.* The following day would take Bascom and his men up the Butterfield trail into Apache Pass.

---

* There was a Butterfield station there in 1862, perhaps added after Bascom's patrol. It was burned by Cochise and his warriors that same year.

Chapter Eleven

MEETING THE OTHER

Stranger in a strange country.
> —Sophocles, *Oedipus at Colonus*

Keep strong, if possible. In any case, keep cool. Have unlimited patience. Never corner an opponent and always assist him to save his face. Put yourself in his shoes—so as to see things through his eyes. Avoid self-righteousness like the devil—nothing so self-blinding.
> —Sir Basil Henry Liddell Hart

COCHISE UNDOUBTEDLY KNEW OF BASCOM'S APPROACH. THE SIGHT of soldiers coming through the pass may have been an annoying reminder of the growing infestation of white men, but it was nothing to worry about particularly. Army patrols, though smaller than this one, often came through guarding wagon trains. In fact, there was just such a patrol at that point camped not far from the stage station. It consisted of thirteen troopers under Sgt. Daniel Robinson, yet another Irish professional soldier. Robinson was returning from escorting a wagon train to Fort McLane, a new installation near the mines at Pinos Altos. By this time, there were some two thousand miners and hangers-on at Pinos Altos[1], and Fort McLane had recently been established to protect this exploding population. James Tevis, who built a house there and was working a claim (and employing fifty Mexican workers), described the new mining town: "After the town was begun, houses went up thick and fast. Saloons, dance halls and a ten pin alley were in operation with gamblers galore. Sundays were used for dueling and all difficulties were settled on that day, unless contending persons were full of whiskey, in which case the killing was quickly done."[2] Once again, miners were leading the way, and after them quickly followed the more dubious blessings of civilization—environmental disruption, whiskey, gamblers, prostitutes, shoot-outs, and even ten-pin alleys.

Pinos Altos was squarely in the midst of the homeland of Mangas Coloradas, Cochise's father-in-law, chief of the Chihenne band of the Chiricahua, and Cochise's close colleague in raiding and war. It's not hard to imagine Mangas's and Cochise's reactions to the messy arrival of detested miners and their degraded camp followers. And in fact, Mangas would attack the mining town and partially destroy it in 1862, once the army had been withdrawn because of the Civil War. His objects were economic, cultural, and aesthetic, for Pinos Altos was both an actual and symbolic blot on Mangas territory. But for now, both chieftains chose to bide their time while allowing their warriors to do their normal work of picking off the unwary and stealing livestock—once again drawing a mental and military distinction between raiding and open war with the whites.

In any event, traffic through Apache Pass, whether civilian or military, was nothing Cochise felt he needed to worry about overmuch. He understood it was the other way around most of the time—white travelers needed to worry about him.

When Bascom arrived at the stage station he met with Wallace and
Culver, neither of whom seemed very worried about the Chiricahua;
indeed, the two men believed they were on reasonably friendly terms
with them. At the station they also met two Chiricahua women,
mixed-blood Mexicans. One was an old woman worn down by labor,
but the other, Juanita, was young and attractive. Juanita, apparently,
was the apple of Wallace's eye. Whether she returned the emotion was
a question that would be answered in the next few days.

After questioning through the interpreter, both women denied
any knowledge of the Ward boy. At Bascom's request, they went off
to find Cochise and tell him that Bascom wanted to have a chat. As
a way of defusing Cochise's possible suspicions, Bascom also may
have mentioned to the women that his troops were merely passing
through on their way to El Paso.

Bascom then moved his troops a couple of hundred yards up
Siphon Canyon, which was more or less at a right angle to the Butterfield Road. He pitched his camp there and ordered Sergeant Robinson
to move his camp and join him. From this location Bascom had a good
view of the stage station and the adjacent road. This was on Sunday,
February 3, a day when the miners, gamblers, and assorted criminals
at Pinos Altos were presumably settling their disagreements with
pistols and looking forward to the beginning of a new workweek.

It's at this point in the story that it fragments into something
Faulkner or Kurosawa would appreciate. There were plenty of men
there to see what happened, but few of them later agreed on what
actually did happen. What follows is a reconstruction of events based
on most accounts of the facts and some interpretation of the princi-
pals' motivations and thought processes, Bascom's in particular.[*]

---

[*]   The primary sources for the basic events are Edwin Sweeney's excellent biography of Cochise and Sergeant Robinson's article in *Sports Afield* (written
many years after the encounter) and Robinson's report "Apache Affairs in
1861."

239

> . . . march through the woods and in some inland
> post feel the savagery, the utter savagery, had closed
> around him—all that mysterious life of the wilder-
> ness that stirs in the forest . . . in the hearts of wild
> men. There's no initiation either into such mysteries.
> He has to live in the midst of the incomprehensible,
> which is also detestable. And it has a fascination,
> too, that goes to work upon him. The fascination of
> the abomination—you know, imagine the growing
> regrets, the longing to escape, the powerless disgust,
> the surrender, the hate.
> —Joseph Conrad, *Heart of Darkness*.

COCHISE DID NOT COME IN THAT FIRST DAY. THE NEXT DAY, BASCOM
issued a second invitation, this time delivered by Wallace, who did
not especially relish the assignment when Bascom asked him to
go to Cochise's camp. That may indicate that his relationship with
Cochise was at best tenuous, which would be not at all surprising.
It may also indicate that Wallace was leery of the intentions or
capabilities of this officer, someone he did not know very well. In
fact, this was their first meeting, so Wallace can be excused for
wondering if Bascom was trustworthy. After all, the stage station
was in a precarious position and existed at the sufferance of the
Chiricahua. So, too, the road through most of southern Arizona. An
army officer like Ewell, who had a sense of balance, was a welcome
visitor and ally. But what of this new man? The last thing Wallace
or anyone at the station needed was an unnecessary contretemps—
something that got out of hand and ruined the delicate relationship
with the Chiricahua. Wallace, after all, was a stage driver, a man
who must have felt very keenly his vulnerability as he sat exposed
atop the celerity wagons, guiding his mules and knowing that every
bush throughout his seventy-five-or-so-mile route might hide an
assailant—and being certain that, throughout the whole of his way,
he was being watched.

But whatever the source of Wallace's misgivings, he went as requested. Perhaps he had hopes of seeing Juanita.

Cochise finally arrived in the afternoon of that second day. With him were his wife and two children; his brother, Coyuntura (husband of the intrepid ambassador Yones); and two or three warriors, at least two of whom were nephews. (Subsequent events strongly suggest that there were three other warriors, not two, as sometimes reported.) Some accounts mention only one child, but in either case, Cochise's second son, Naiche, was there. They were not armed. At least, they were not carrying visible weapons—no rifles, lances, or bows. Obviously, they were not expecting trouble.

Given that it was February and they were in a high mountain pass, Cochise and the others would have been dressed for the weather in their thigh-high deerskin moccasins with distinctively turned-up toes. Covering these would have been breechclouts that hung below the knees. They most likely wore woolen shirts taken in trade or as plunder from the Mexicans. Around their necks they wore silver and beaded necklaces. They carried blankets, perhaps obtained in trade with the Navajos, whose woven crafts were prized throughout the Southwest. (The Chiricahua were remarkably unskilled in craftsmanship in comparison to other tribes. The only useful items they made—aside from weapons—were waterproof baskets.) All wore their hair long, to the shoulders, parted in the middle, and held in place by a scarf. Dark-skinned and somehow Asiatic-looking, they were no doubt exceedingly strange to the eyes of an eastern soldier—strange and alien. And, unquestionably, a little unsettling at first.

All accounts of Cochise portray him as an imposing figure. (There are no known photographs of him.) Indeed, he could be, and often was, a frightening presence, even to his own people. Said Lieutenant Joseph Sladen, "He carried himself at all times with great dignity and was always treated by those about him with the utmost respect and, at times, fear."[3] At this stage of his life, he was in his late forties, still vigorous, and no doubt menacing, especially when alarmed or annoyed. He had a ferocious temper, and legend has it that he was never known to laugh. That seems a little unlikely, given the Chiricahuas' domestic habits and reputation for improbable lightheartedness among their own, but it underscores the fact that Cochise was serious to the point of solemnity, not one to suffer fools or tolerate slights.

This was the first time Bascom had been in such close contact with an Apache or any Indian beyond the unprepossessing Goshutes of Utah. It would not be surprising if Bascom felt a little uneasy at first. He was staring into the eyes of someone entirely different from anyone in his experience, a nearly perfect representative or embodiment of "otherness." Everything about Cochise—his dress; his long, black hair streaked with silver; his prideful demeanor—all of this and more must have been startling and weirdly fascinating to Bascom. There in front of him was the perfect barbarian, someone who might have stepped out of Caesar's *Commentaries*, and if Bascom at that moment thought of himself as a young Roman proconsul meeting a wild Germanic chieftain, he might be forgiven. Such imagery would have been useful in supporting a young officer's resolve.

Further, Bascom and Cochise literally did not speak the same language. Not only was that a practical barrier but it was another metaphor, in this case for the misunderstanding that characterized relations between the whites and the Apache—indeed, the Indians in general. As Captain Bourke said later, "No one had ever heard the Apaches' story, and no one seemed to care whether they had a story or not."[4] The obverse was also true, though—Cochise had no understanding of the complexity of white culture. His only contacts had been with a few miners, transient emigrants, corrupt traders, and a few Butterfield employees and soldiers. Few of these inspired much admiration or respect. He had no idea of the size of the gathering storm.

Indeed, this first meeting between the two men seems a useful emblem of the entire confrontation between the native tribes and the army. And the fact that John Ward was there, representative of the white civilians, completes a historically meaningful tableau of enmity, suspicion, and misunderstanding. Some might say it could have been a tableau suggesting the possibility of reconciliation and coexistence, but none of the three men there would have believed that. Each was looking into the face of an enemy, either actual or potential. Bascom, symbolic guardian of the inchoate westward movement, sometimes described as Manifest Destiny, was twenty-four-years-old and mindful of his tender dignity, mindful of the army's dignity too, and mindful of his orders. And facing him was this older Apache, this visitor from another time or place. He looked different, he dressed differently, he spoke an impenetrable language, and was said to be a murderer and thief. Unquestionably, he had personally shed human blood with an edged weapon, which meant he had looked into the eyes of his victims as he was killing them. Bascom had never done anything like that; he had yet to injure, much less kill, anyone, even at a distance with a rifle shot. Though soldiering was his profession, the only firing he had ever done or heard was on the practice range. That is not to suggest, however, that Bascom was the stereotypical "shavetail fresh from West Point," as almost all accounts have described him. He had been on active duty for several years and was by now comfortable in his uniform and his role as an officer. The shine on his gold insignia would have faded well before this time, and he would have felt a certain pride in that, for it was the sign of a veteran. He would have been as protective of his personal and professional standing and authority as Cochise was of his own, even though (or perhaps because) this was the first time he had had an opportunity to do anything beyond the routine.

Adding to the strangeness and the possible sense of slight disorientation Bascom might have been feeling was the mise-en-scène. They were in Cochise's homeland, which was rugged and unwelcoming to any who had not been born there. The army tents in Siphon Canyon looked, and were, out of place—their temporary

243

nature a comment on this mission. They had sprouted like toad-stools after a rain and would disappear even faster. Bascom was a visitor in a strange land, a land that was very different even from the grass-lined canyons of Fort Buchanan, only six dozen miles away. The mountains here were closer, looming, and darkly oppressive. The country was beautiful in its way, but it was not the kind of beauty a Wordsworth would celebrate. It was not the romantic beauty of the snow-covered Rockies, beloved of artists. It was not nature in a kindly mood. On the contrary, it was nature at its most indifferent—rocky, spiny, vertical, cold. To an overactive imagination, the place seemed almost sinister, with endless numbers of shadowy places for ambush, along with a bemusing diversity of plants and trees, for this was the meeting ground of the Sonoran and Chihuahuan Deserts, two very different ecosystems. They overlapped, like hostile tribes invading each other's lines. Apache Pass was the place Bourke must have been thinking about when he described "a region in which not only purgatory and hell, but heaven likewise, had combined to produce a bewildering kaleidoscope of all that was wonderful, weird, terrible and awe-inspiring. . . ."[5] There was nothing to attract a white man, nothing comfortable or familiar. Perhaps some mountain man might have liked the look of the place because of its utter absence of civilization, but most emigrants would have been happy to pass through quickly and keep going. The future of this sliver of Arizona involved no farms, no ranches. It was a place fit only for a way station, a remote and precarious outpost for people to work their way through and nervously at that. No white man would have gone through there, if it hadn't been for the spring. To live there the employees of the Butterfield stage station must have had more than their share of courage—either that or a desperate need for money. Or a profound lack of imagination. Or, most likely, some combination of the three.

Bascom invited Cochise into his tent and offered coffee. It's possible Ward got things off on the wrong foot by using Cochise's name, and thereby insulting him; there's no reason Ward would have been versed in the niceties of Chiricahua manners. But that would not have mattered to Cochise; an insult was an insult, even when delivered out of ignorance. It was bad form to mention names out loud. "Never during all our intercourse with this chief and his band did I hear of him spoken of or addressed by his name, Cochise. The Indians invariably referred to him as 'he,'" said Lieutenant Sladen.[6]

Coyuntura joined his brother in the tent, while the rest of the family apparently remained outside. Inside the tent, Bascom got right to the point. Through Ward, Bascom accused Cochise of the theft of cattle and the kidnapping of the Ward boy. Cochise denied the accusation and said the Coyoteros had carried out the raid. Bascom must have wondered exactly how Cochise knew that. The claim seemed suspicious. But Cochise offered to find out where the boy was and return him. It would take about ten days, he said. In his report, Bascom says he agreed to this suggestion, but other accounts say he rejected it and told Cochise he and his family would remain prisoners until the boy and cattle were returned. Bascom was directly calling Cochise a liar and doing so through an interpreter in a language Cochise imperfectly understood and Ward imperfectly spoke. Or perhaps Bascom actually did agree to the offer and only meant to keep the others as hostages until Cochise came back. As we have seen, hostage taking was a routine tactic used by the army and the Apaches alike—even during peaceful negotiations. But such a response could easily have been misunderstood in translation. Or perhaps an angry Ward misspoke or used a tone of voice that alarmed or angered Cochise, a tone that conveyed something different from what Bascom intended. The Chiricahuas were far more attuned to the nuances of tone and language than the Americans. Words had power. Perhaps Ward dipped into his knowledge of Spanish curses or insults. Writes Opler, "A curse is a grave affront because of the acknowledged potency of verbalism. . . . [because of] the general respect for the efficacy of words. . . ."[7] And even though Spanish was Cochise's second language, he would not have departed from his belief in the power of the word. Indeed, it's hard to escape the conclusion that Bascom's first mistake in this patrol was using an angry and aggrieved Ward as interpreter, a man who had been described by contemporaries as entirely "worthless." Bascom was relying on Ward to understand his literal words as well as his intended message and to translate them into his imperfect Spanish, learned from his Mexican wife, and then to articulate the words and nuanced meaning to a man he considered a bitter enemy. It was a task worthy of a seasoned diplomat and well beyond the linguistic, intellectual, and political skills of a man like John Ward, who, it will be remembered, was run out of San Francisco by vigilantes—an indication that his powers of persuasion were limited.

On the other hand, it's entirely possible that Ward accurately translated Bascom's words and that Cochise read Bascom's tone even though he did not understand his words. Since he had come west, Bascom had been nurtured on the army's notion of firmness and force as the twin pillars of Indian management. Bascom would have had implicit belief in the efficacy of those ideas and would have considered himself the representative of the army and its policies, and therefore deserving of respect. Writes historian Sherry Smith, "An enlisted man who refused to obey orders met swift punishment. An Indian who refused to obey an officer's command posed more of a problem. He might respect neither the officer nor the army, itself. In this context, physical force (or the threat of it) could prove the only apparent recourse to preserve the officer's dignity."[8] Human behavior routinely exposes the fact that the less entitled to respect some people feel themselves to be, the more noisily or vigorously they demand it.

Given the situation, it's certainly possible that Bascom reacted to Cochise's denials with bluster, which Ward accurately conveyed to Cochise or which Cochise observed in Bascom's demeanor, tone of voice, and even his body language. (To an Apache, someone who placed his arms akimbo was intentionally delivering an insult, and it's not hard to imagine Bascom standing there, perhaps striking a pose, hands on his hips or thumbs in his gun belt.) A more experienced officer, like Captain Ewell, who had been in these kinds of encounters before and who had already won his spurs and therefore had little or nothing to prove (to himself or his troops), would have taken a more diplomatic approach, as indeed he had done in the past. Even if he had not believed Cochise's story about the Coyoteros, Ewell would have appeared to believe it in order to avoid insulting Cochise and to let him save face and make restitution. Force would have been a last resort, and bluster not a resort at all. But in Bascom's tent there was John Ward and, nearby, watching and listening, was Sergeant Robinson. Bascom understood that the way he comported himself would become part of the frontier army's story. He would have been a fool not to have known that this was a moment in which his reputation could be made—or damaged, if not ruined. Of course, he has been vilified as a fool by comments of his contemporaries. But Bascom was certainly intelligent enough to understand that he was squarely in the middle of a moment that would be important to his career. He could not have known, however, that he was also in the middle of a history-making moment. In fact, he would never know that.

Given the strangeness of the situation and the fact that Bascom was on his own for the first time, it's hardly surprising that he would have done things by the book, just as he had been taught to do at West Point. He had the security of his orders. He was "authorized and instructed" to use force if Cochise did not cooperate. Cochise was not cooperating and therefore he and his people there would become prisoners. It was a simple equation. No one knows whose idea it was to take Cochise and his family hostage. It's possible that Bascom and Morrison discussed that option, although Morrison gives the impression of lassitude in his handling of this whole affair, so most likely Bascom alone decided on this course of action. In either case, Bascom would have viewed it as just a first step in the application of force. He was making an arrest. And if things escalated, Bascom was ready for that too.

It's also useful to remember that this was 1861. Cochise's reputation as a fearsome wartime leader was yet to be forged. At this time, he was chief of one local group and had rival chiefs in the same area. He was recognized as a man of talents, but he did not have the reputation as a kind of mythic figure that the next ten years of warfare, and finally peace, would bring him. He was known to be a raider and a leader of raiders, but raiders were nothing more than bandits to the white settlers. So while his demeanor and presence were impressive, to Bascom he was just another Apache thief. Once Bascom got over the strangeness of the encounter, he would have realized he had Cochise outgunned and outmaneuvered. He held all the cards.

But Bascom had made another tactical mistake besides using Ward. He had given prior orders for the troops to surround the tent once the meeting got under way. Cochise's family outside would most certainly have been alarmed by the soldiers who were approaching the tent, rifles in hand. They would have been even more alarmed if the soldiers had fixed their bayonets, a distinct possibility in view of what happened later. There are no reports to substantiate this idea, but it's inconceivable that one of the Chiricahua outside did not say something to alert Cochise and his brother. A simple word would have been enough to put Cochise and Coyuntura on their guard.* The interpreter Ward would not have understood since he knew no Apache and was interpreting in Spanish. Chiricahuas were naturally suspicious and wary, largely because of their history of constant warfare and their own duplicitous tactics in raiding and war. They had not survived in this country amidst human and natural adversaries by being gullible or trusting; they were well versed in

---

* Sergeant Robinson's report suggests that the other Apaches were taken to a different tent, so it's possible they did not notice Bascom's posting of the guards.

the tactics of surprise and ambush. Certainly Cochise and his family did not come into camp expecting trouble. But their antennae were extremely sensitive. And when they detected something, they acted upon it quickly, without rumination.

Which is exactly what they did. Sergeant Robinson, who was standing close by the tent, recalled, "Finally it was decided that the sub-chief [Coyuntura] should go and find the boy and that Cochise must remain as a hostage. This ended the talk. As quickly as lightning both drew forth concealed knives, cut open the sides of the tent and darted out, Cochise to the front. The sub-chief darted through the rear, tripped and fell and was captured by a sentinel."[9]

Outside, the other Apaches tried to scatter, but the soldiers restrained all but one, who followed after Cochise, running and dodging past the startled Robinson and toward a hillside nearby. Another of Cochise's nephews also tried to run, but a soldier bayoneted him and pinned him to the ground. Strangely, the wound did not prove dangerous, but it was effective in preventing escape. Cochise's actions and the attempted escape of his relatives would have thrown the soldiers into some confusion as they scuffled with the Indians. Those not engaged in subduing Cochise's family would not have known whether they were supposed to shoot Cochise and the other warrior. They necessarily would have waited for Bascom's orders. Cochise and his companion therefore had a little time to put some distance between themselves and the soldiers. No doubt they were also dodging from juniper to boulder and zigzagging up the side of the rugged hill. Bascom would have needed a few seconds to recover from the surprise and also to deal with the confusion outside the tent, as the soldiers tried to secure the other prisoners, including Coyuntura. But after the initial surprise and scuffle, he gave the order to fire at the two fleeing warriors—"Shoot them down!"

It was the first time Bascom heard shots fired in anger.

It's worth remembering that the troops were using single-shot muzzle loaders firing .58-caliber minié balls and that the firing mechanisms consisted of hammers striking copper caps that acted as the primers. A new cap had to be placed for each firing. That the troops were able to fire at all quickly suggests that, as discussions were taking place inside the tent, the soldiers' rifles were already loaded, though perhaps not primed. And troops would not have loaded their rifles without Bascom's orders. That one of the warriors was bayoneted also reinforces the idea that the troops were prepared for trouble. (The soldier could have wielded the bayonet by hand, but this seems less likely.)

If that's the case (and admittedly it's speculation) the question becomes, why did Bascom have his troops load their rifles? That seems simple enough. He wanted to be prepared to apply the force he was authorized and instructed to use. He could easily envision a situation in which Cochise defied him and escaped. (After all, that's what happened.) Bascom had learned secondhand in Utah that when you have an Indian in your grasp you had better hold on to him, because you might not ever see him again. And with his orders in mind, Bascom wanted to be ready for any and all contingencies. And what if the wily Cochise used the occasion for a surprise attack? Bascom's duty was to protect his troops as well as his career. Having troops with loaded weapons in a tense situation is dangerous in case of confusion; less so if the troops are well disciplined. Bascom by this time had a good understanding of his men, and he did what most young officers would have done—he anticipated the worst. Or so he thought.

Besides, in his view, this was nothing more than a police action. Bascom had arrested Cochise and his brother, and the two of them and their family had resisted. "Shot while attempting to escape" was a phrase he would have been familiar with.* There was no downside to being prepared to do just that, and a very large downside to being unprepared. Hence the loaded weapons. Besides, why would Cochise and his brother try to run away if

---

* The following year, Mangas Coloradas was "killed while attempting to escape," after coming in for a parley with the army in New Mexico.

they were innocent? Flight was always a strong indicator of guilt. If they were killed trying to escape from arrest, no one would care, much less be critical.

Observers estimated that some fifty shots were fired, which, if true, means that nearly each one of Bascom's troops got off at least one round. And given the time it takes to reload a muzzle loader, few of the troops would have been able to fire more than one shot before Cochise escaped over the hill. Ward was using a pistol that probably held six rounds but was inaccurate beyond a few dozen or so yards. He was the first to respond to Bascom's order, but his marksmanship was apparently not up to the challenge.

As the two warriors raced toward the summit, Cochise's companion was hit and killed, and Cochise was wounded in the leg, though not seriously. The distance from the camp to the top of the hill was about two hundred yards, well within the range of a minié ball. Hitting a moving and dodging target is not easy, and it's most likely that Cochise was hit only because of the volume of fire, rather than the somewhat suspect individual marksmanship of the troops. Sergeant Robinson reported that the Apache with Cochise had stopped and drawn his knife to attack a pursuing soldier, who thereupon shot and killed him from close range.

The oral tradition avers that Cochise was still carrying his coffee cup when he reached the safety of the summit. It's not known whether he kept it as a souvenir of what, from that point on, he would consider the innate treachery of the white soldiers.

Meanwhile, Bascom now had three warriors as hostages—Coyuntura and two nephews (one wounded)—along with Cochise's wife and children.

BASCOM ORDERED HIS MEN TO BREAK CAMP AND MOVE TO THE STAGE station, a much better defensive position than the exposed Siphon Canyon. While they were in the act of moving, Cochise reappeared on the hill and asked for the return of his family, but Bascom ordered the troops to fire on him again. With one Apache killed and another wounded, Bascom no doubt believed that the genie was out of the bottle and that he was better off trying to eliminate Cochise than having him running loose and organizing an attack. Once again, though, the troops missed their target. After shouting some imprecations, Cochise disappeared, and the troops moved to the stage station. There they organized their wagons on the perimeter, filled in the gaps with earthworks and sandbags, dug rifle pits and a trench. The station buildings themselves were far too small to accommodate all the men and animals. When they were finished, they had built a strong defensive position against which few, if any, Apaches would have ventured a direct assault. There were, after all, more than seventy men behind those barricades. They had plenty of food and ammunition. And Bascom, or his sergeants, would have made sure their water casks were full before they broke camp. But those supplies would not last forever, and once they were inside the defensive position at the stage station, the spring would be one thousand yards away. The ground between the station and the spring was open until the last few yards and would expose troops to fire from the surrounding hills. The spring itself was nestled in a narrow tree-lined defile that offered perfect cover for an ambush. Water would become a problem.

That night the troops could see signal fires on the hills. Cochise was summoning his warriors and other friendly bands. In the darkness those pinpricks of fire would have seemed eerie to the troops, as would the sound of Apache singing.

No doubt Bascom conferred with his sergeants and the three Butterfield employees who must have been appalled at what they witnessed that day. All their delicate relations with Cochise and his people had been ruined. Their own lives were now at risk, to say nothing of their livelihoods. They were safe enough for the time being, but what would happen when the soldiers left? And what about the inbound stagecoaches? Unquestionably, both Wallace and

Culver advised Bascom to try to repair the damage if at all possible. He could start by releasing the hostages.

But that was not an option for Bascom—not until the Ward boy was released and the livestock returned. He knew his duty, and he was going to do it. Besides, how would it look if he let the prisoners go and then Cochise and all his band disappeared into Mexico, taking Felix Ward with them and metaphorically thumbing their noses at the army and Bascom? The hostages must be kept. Anything else would inevitably lead to the failure of his first independent mission.

Along the same lines, Bascom must have considered the possibility that Cochise was telling the truth about the Coyoteros. Perhaps they had kidnapped Felix Ward. But even if that were true, if Bascom released the captives, Cochise would have no incentive to retrieve the boy. As long as Bascom had the hostages, Cochise would eventually have to produce the boy, regardless of who kidnapped him in the first place.

The next morning, the troops could see a number of Apaches drawn up south of the station. They were within rifle range, but Bascom did not order any fire. Then one of them approached closer, carrying a white flag. Cochise wanted to talk. Certainly he had reconnoitered the army's strong defensive position and realized he could not overrun it without taking an unacceptable number of casualties. He would need a different tack, starting with a parley.

Bascom agreed, and so, also under a white flag, he, Robinson, Ward, and another sergeant named Smith walked out a hundred yards or so and met Cochise and two of his warriors and a chief of another band, named Francisco, summoned the night before by the signal fires. History has been hard on Bascom and his judgment, but there can be little doubt about his courage, for he and the others went to the meeting unarmed.

The result of the parley was an impasse. Bascom demanded release of the Ward boy; Cochise denied having him. Cochise asked for the release of his family; Bascom responded he could have them when he produced the boy.

After a few minutes of watching the impasse, the three But-terfield employees—Wallace, Culver, and a man named Welch—emerged from the station and headed toward the parley. Evidently, they believed their relationship with Cochise was durable enough to allow room for their diplomacy. Certainly it was better than the acrimonious situation between Bascom and Cochise, although they must have believed that Cochise's request for a parley was a hopeful sign. Apparently they did not know that the Chiricahua often used a flag of truce as a ruse to lure the unsuspecting into a trap.

As the three men walked toward the group, Bascom ordered them to go back, but they paid no attention. Then Wallace noticed Juanita gesturing to them, indicating that she wanted to talk. She was off to the side by a small ravine. Wallace and the other two went toward her. Wallace was presumably relying on his rela-tionship, real or imagined, with the young woman and perhaps thinking she was offering to help. When they got there, Juanita grabbed Wallace and held him while Chiricahua warriors sprang from their hiding places in the ravine and tussled with the other two men. Culver and Welch fought back and managed to escape and run back toward the station. Wallace was not so fortunate. Lured by love or ego, he was now a captive.

When Bascom and the others saw what was happening to Wal-lace, they too broke for the station, at which point concealed Apaches opened fire, while Cochise and his party ducked for cover.

As he was running back to the station, Culver was shot in the back, but he managed to make it to the station with the help of some soldiers. Welch, however, was shot and killed. Some accounts say the soldiers mistook Welch for an attacking Apache and shot him as he climbed the corral wall, but this seems unlikely since the troops would have had a fair view of the action in front of them. They were not behind the high walls of the corral but instead deployed around the station in their trenches and behind their sandbags.

Meanwhile, Bascom's party was sprinting toward the station. Sergeant Smith was wounded, though not dangerously, and the others managed to reach their lines unscathed, as the troops opened fire on the Apaches in the ravines. Bascom estimated the number of Apaches confronting him at five hundred—no doubt much too high a figure, but an understandable miscalculation under the circumstances. The Apaches must have been raising a fearful racket. By this time, Mangas Coloradas had arrived with his warriors. The as-yet-unknown warrior known as the Yawner was there too. He would come to be known as Geronimo.

It seems reasonable to suppose that Cochise fully intended to take Bascom and his men hostage, assuming Bascom still refused to release his captives. The warriors hidden in the ravines indicated the probability of foul play. Bascom, Ward, and the two sergeants would have been ideal hostages. The fact that they were meeting under a flag of truce would not have troubled Cochise's conscience. After Bascom's treatment of him and his family, Cochise would have considered capturing the soldiers nothing less than simple justice—and even better tactics. Besides flags of truce were a white man's invention, along with the rules governing them. Those rules meant nothing to the Chiricahua. By causing the disturbance, Wallace, Culver, and Welch almost certainly saved Bascom and the others from capture.

That night, more signal fires blazed in the mountains, and the troops could hear the Apaches' war dance. Some said they could also hear the sounds of women wailing, perhaps mourning their dead. In the general firing after the failed parley, several Apaches were thought to have been killed. But there was no way to know for sure. Besides, none of the troops had any experience with the Apaches and could not tell a keening song from a war song.

The next day was Wednesday, and the troops were running low on water. Robinson volunteered to take a squad and some animals to the spring. It was a dangerous mission given the exposed nature of the trail there and the number of places for ambush. But for some reason, the Apaches did not molest the soldiers, and they were able to water their mules and fill their casks.

Later that day, Cochise appeared on the crest of the hill opposite the stage station. He was in full view. Bascom and the troops must have been aghast at what they saw. Cochise was leading Wallace, who had a rope around his neck and his hands tied behind him. Wallace was a pitiful and pitiable sight, no doubt reflecting ruefully on the results of romantic miscalculations and other misjudgments concerning his relationship with Cochise. Cochise offered to trade Wallace for his family and said he would throw in sixteen government mules he had captured in an earlier raid. But Bascom was not going to give up his trump card, and he refused, once again demanding the return of the Ward boy.

This situation was difficult for Bascom—though decidedly not as difficult as for Wallace. On the one hand, the day before, Bascom had ordered Wallace and the others not to emerge from the station, even though Bascom had no authority over the Butterfield people. Wallace had ignored the order. That rankled, and Bascom probably thought that Wallace should not complain about suffering the consequences of his foolhardiness. On the other hand, it must have occurred to Bascom that Wallace's actions might very well have inadvertently saved Bascom and his party. Surely he owed it to the man to try to rescue him. Then, too, there was the natural human instinct to want to go to the aid of a man in such dire straits. But Bascom most likely kept coming back to the idea that his refusals would eventually produce Felix Ward, and he no doubt assumed that when that happened, Wallace would become part of the trade too. In fact, Bascom would insist on it. Until then, Wallace would have to take his chances. No doubt he would be uncomfortable in the meantime, but it would come right in the end. Bascom doubtless reasoned that Wallace would be safe enough since he was a valuable hostage.

Bascom also clearly understood that he had gotten himself into a bit of a bind. If he believed there were five hundred Apaches out there, he must also have calculated that the hostages he held were insurance against an assault. He did not understand that Apaches were unlikely to charge a strong defensive position manned by troops with long-range weapons; that was the white man's inexplicable idea of fighting, not the Apaches'. Still, the thought of possible assault reinforced Bascom's intention to keep a firm grip on his prisoners. If he gave them up to rescue Wallace, he might place his whole command in even more serious jeopardy. There would be nothing to restrain the Apaches then, and according to his calculations he was outnumbered seven to one.

Given the information Bascom had, and given what he knew and didn't know about fighting Apaches, it's hard to see how he could have handled the Wallace situation differently. He clearly had time to think about his options with regard to Wallace and must have expected Cochise to use the stagecoach driver as a hostage, assuming he didn't kill Wallace immediately. If he had wanted to do that, his warriors would have opened fire on Wallace, Culver, and Welch when they were at short range, instead of trying to capture them. It was obvious on reflection that the Apaches were after hostages to trade. Perhaps Bascom might have offered a one-for-one trade, but Cochise would certainly have rejected that since it would have cost him his hostage without achieving the release of his whole family.

There are some stories that a sergeant named Bernard advised Bascom to make a deal but that the young officer was too headstrong to listen. This is part of the unlikely lore surrounding the incident. In the first place, Bernard was not even there at that point and would arrive with the reinforcements. In the second place, the story has the distinct odor of the classic noncommissioned officer's dismissive opinion of a young officer. To NCOs, the army operated only because of the sergeants, and if it were not for the ignorant officers, things would always go smoothly. There were many useful and professional noncoms in the frontier army, but there was also a fair contingent of men who were putting in their time and bemoaning the fact that officers were placed above them. (The disgruntled German émigré Private Theodore Ewert was another example of this kind of class resentment.) In this case, one such was a man called Oberly, who would go on to future glory as a park policeman in Brooklyn, New York. Years later, he was interviewed by a reporter for the *New York World*. He claimed he was at Apache Pass, he claimed he was a color sergeant (an honorary regimental assignment in the U.S. Army, but not an official company rank), and he claimed that Bascom was a West Point "cadet." He also said that the Apaches had been entirely peaceful until disturbed by Bascom's blundering and that Bascom was generally drunk during the incident. (None of the other reports hints at any of this.) Oberly's motive appears to have been a lingering ill will and the desire to call attention to himself; his reconstruction of the events was therefore suspect, to say the least. And certainly his claim that the Chiricahua had been entirely peaceful was absurd.

In the afternoon, the westbound stage arrived at the station. The driver and guard must have been astonished when they pulled up to a military defensive position, earthworks and wagons and trenches and sandbags forming a perimeter within which were mules and soldiers' tents. The coachmen had no notion that there had been trouble with the Apaches, although they would have been alarmed when they had to stop to remove barriers the Apaches had placed across the road in the pass—some hay bales and rocks. The Apaches had planned to attack the stage, hence the barricades. But the stage was earlier than expected and, since the Apaches were distracted by another opportunity, the coach made it through to the station.

The distraction came in the form of an eastbound wagon train that was just then camping in a comfortable spot alongside the Butterfield road, well inside the western entrance to the pass. Having climbed up the pass from the Sulphur Springs Valley below, they had been in view for most of the day. And Cochise had his eye on some plunder, and, more important just then, a few more hostages.

Surely, some of the most courageous men in the Southwest were Mexican teamsters, who plied their thankless jobs hauling supplies through a country infested with their bitterest enemies. After centuries of raids and counterraids, outright warfare, and only short periods of occasional peace, Mexicans along the border must have known to a man that they had no chance to survive if they were captured by Apaches. Not only would they not survive capture, but their deaths would come only after hideous and prolonged torture. Even in periods of relative peace, they would have known that agreements with one group meant nothing to another group and that therefore they were never really safe. Their only hope of safety in their travels was being alert, since raiders generally would not attack a train that was well guarded. Normally, twelve well-armed and alert men would be sufficient to discourage an Apache attack—during relative peacetime, that is. But in Apache Pass just then events were in transition from the usual raiding to open warfare. And in that case the normal practices, as everyone understood them, were forgotten.

There were five wagons in the eastbound train operated by three Americans and nine Mexicans. They were headed for Pinos Altos and then to Las Cruces with wagons full of corn in sacks. The wagons were drawn by mules.

Apparently, the teamsters were not alarmed and not too suspicious. They must not have heard any firing the day before, even though they had been moving slowly across the Sulphur Springs Valley. Perhaps there was an acoustic shadow blocking the sound of the fighting. In any event, the twelve teamsters were not aware that trouble lay ahead. The worst they would have anticipated would have been the need to pay off some Apaches with gifts of corn. They had done that before and no doubt budgeted for that likelihood.

The train was about two miles west of the stage station when Cochise's warriors attacked. Perhaps they sent emissaries with signs of friendship in order to reassure the teamsters. But then the warriors sprang from their hiding places behind the rocks and trees beside the road and surrounded the startled teamsters.

The Mexican teamsters were tied to the wheels of the wagon to be tortured. The Apaches' favorite form of torture was to hang a victim head down over a slow fire so that his brains gradually roasted. (It may be remembered that this was how Cochise had tortured to death James Tevis's two companions—and it was the fate that awaited Tevis had he not been set free by a friendly Apache.) Alternatively, they sometimes tied a victim spread-eagled and built a fire on his abdomen. In this instance, they chose the head-down method and, after emptying the wagons of the corn and cutting the mules from their traces, they kindled the fires under the Mexicans' heads while the horrified three Americans watched and listened to the screams of the victims. The Apaches then set fire to the wagons and left the charred remains of the Mexicans still attached to the wheels.

Cochise now had three more American hostages to trade. Returning to his camp with the three terrified teamsters, Cochise ordered Wallace to write a note to Bascom. It said, in effect, that Cochise now had four American prisoners to exchange and that if Bascom treated his prisoners well, Cochise would do the same. They could then get down to the business of exchange. The note was tied to a bush where it was assumed the troops would see it.

There is some question about whether Bascom only saw the note days later or whether he saw it that night. In his report, he implies that he did receive it that night. But the fact that Cochise had upped the ante would not have changed Bascom's ideas about the hostages. All the factors still lined up in the same way. If Cochise really did have three new and anonymous hostages—and there was no reason to take him at his word—it changed nothing. Bascom was still surrounded, still potentially cut off from water. His primary defenses were the strength of his dug-in position, his firepower—and the hostages. The question of when and if Bascom ever got Wallace's note is therefore more or less irrelevant, because it would not have changed his strategy anyway. All it proved was that Wallace was still alive, and that, in itself, would have reinforced Bascom's belief that his strategy was correct. According to this reasoning, Cochise would not harm his prisoners, however many there were, because he needed them for a trade. For Bascom, therefore, keeping a tight grip on his own hostages was in fact a way of protecting Cochise's prisoners, protecting his surrounded position, and, ultimately, rescuing Felix Ward. What's more, Cochise's cautiousness was indicated by his failure so far to attack the troops getting water each day. Clearly, Cochise was restraining his warriors because of his fear for the hostages. All of that made perfect sense to Bascom. Bascom was trying to think like his opponent, just as he had been taught to do at West Point. He was assuming Cochise's options were limited as long as Bascom held the hostages. But that assumption, eminently reasonable to a white officer, was wrong.

Cochise was not finished gathering hostages. He was watching the western entrance of the pass for the arrival of the eastbound stage. En route from Tucson, the stage arrived at the pass in the still-dark early-morning hours of Thursday. Here again the Butterfield people had no reason to anticipate trouble, so they were stunned when they reached the vicinity of the charred Mexican wagons and a volley erupted from the ravines along the road. One mule was killed and another wounded, while the driver, King Lyons, was wounded. The conductor, William Buckley, jumped down and cut the dead mule from the traces, then helped Lyons get inside the coach. One of the passengers was 2nd Lieutenant John Rogers Cooke of the Eighth Infantry and son of Philip St. George Cooke of Mormon Battalion fame. (Cooke, with his company of infantry, had established Fort Breckinridge in May 1860. He was shortly thereafter joined by the two companies of dragoons under Moore and Lord, with the more senior Moore assuming command.) Undoubtedly, Cooke helped Buckley at least by firing some pistol shots toward the muzzle flashes of the Apaches. Also on board was A. B. Culver, the brother of Charles Culver, the wounded stage station agent. Certainly he also added some fire to support Buckley as he tried to disentangle the mules. Somehow Buckley got things organized and started the remaining mules toward the station, still under fire. He urged the frightened mules as fast as possible, and even though the Apaches had torn down a small stone bridge over a slight arroyo, Buckley was able to career across and make it to the station.

Like Bascom, John Rogers Cooke was a second lieutenant, although he had studied engineering at Harvard, not West Point. His commission dated from June 1855. He owed his commission to the influence of his father, but he was a competent soldier and would go on to become a general in the Confederate army, much to the disgust of his father, who remained loyal to the Union. Cooke's sister married J. E. B. Stuart, West Point '54 and Confederate cavalry officer. Cooke, therefore, was already something of army royalty, and it would have been surprising if, when he arrived, Bascom had not deferred to him to some degree. After all, not only was Cooke the son of a well-known cavalry colonel, he was senior to Bascom. Indeed, from this point on, Bascom was no longer technically in command, although the two young officers must have worked out a division of labor. It would also have been surprising if Bascom had not appreciated Cooke's advice and experience. The friendly face of a colleague would have been very welcome just then.

In the morning, the troops were not attacked when they took their animals to water. These were confusing signals to Bascom. Why would the Apaches attack a stagecoach in the dark and yet leave the watering party unmolested? Still more puzzling was the absence of any sign of the Apaches. They seemed to have left. But how could that be? Bascom still had the hostages. If the Apaches had left without Cochise's family, Bascom's whole strategy would turn out to be wrong. No, he reasoned. They were still around somewhere. And, of course, he was right about that.

The Apaches had left the pass but only temporarily. Cochise had moved the women and children south, into the Chiricahua Mountains, to be away from the fighting and any army patrols that might be sent to scour the hills and mountains in and around the pass. Then he and his warriors made plans to attack the soldiers on the following day. The plan would involve a two-pronged approach, with one group of warriors surprising the watering party. The object there was to lure a strong relief party from behind the barricades and so weaken the defenses. That would allow a second party of warriors to charge the outpost and rescue the hostages without taking too many casualties. It was a good plan, especially because it was totally out of character for an Apache to make a direct assault on a defensive position. Cochise probably assumed that the surprise element of such desperate tactics would work to his advantage. Ironically, Bascom did not know much about fighting Apaches and so would not have been surprised by a frontal assault. He had actually organized his defensive perimeter with that very possibility—even that expectation—in mind. In this case, his inexperience and classical military training would combine to work in his favor. (Standard military theory posited that an attacker needed a three-to-one advantage to take a prepared defensive position. Bascom assumed he was outnumbered by more than twice that number.)

While the Apaches were planning, Bascom and the others were deciding that they needed help. They needed a doctor to look after the wounded, and they needed reinforcements, especially cavalry who could scout the area to determine what the Apaches were up to. The stagecoaches would also need mounted escorts. A. B. Culver volunteered to make the dash for Tucson, and Bascom assembled a small squad of soldiers to go with him part of the way but then to veer off for Fort Buchanan to summon the assistant surgeon and some reinforcements. Culver was to contact the Butterfield agent in Tucson, who was then to send word to the dragoons at Fort Breckinridge, asking them to come and come quickly.

The intrepid squad left in the darkness, their mules' shoes muffled. They had no way of knowing that the Apaches had headed south with their families, and the ride to the western mouth of the

TERRY MORT

pass must have been a very long one, every boulder and arroyo offering a possible ambush. They walked their mounts to avoid making too much noise and to preserve them for the long trip ahead, and that slow pace added to the soldiers' tension.

A fundamental difficulty in writing an accurate history of men in war is the knowledge of what actually happened—and didn't happen. That knowledge can sometimes devalue or ignore the fortitude of men who were there at the time, in the moment, and who had no idea of would happen next—although they had a very good idea of what *could* happen. The handful of men riding for help had seen Wallace with a rope around his neck, and they knew of the attacks on the stagecoaches along this very road. It didn't take much imagination to wonder if they might be next. And yet they went anyway.

They made it through without incident, though, much to their intense relief and no little surprise. It took twenty-four hours to make the trip. The soldiers arrived at Fort Buchanan and alerted Assistant Surgeon Irwin, who assembled a squad of some fifteen men and set out the following morning in a severe snowstorm. At the same time, Culver arrived in Tucson, having made the 120-mile trip in twenty-four hours by changing mounts at the Butterfield stage stops at the Dragoon Springs and Cienega Stations. In Tucson, Culver reported to Agent William S. Oury* who dispatched a rider to Fort Breckinridge, asking the commanding officer there, Lieutenant Isaiah Moore, to come with all speed and telling Moore that Oury would meet him at Ewell Springs at the base of Apache Pass.

---

* William S. Oury was the brother of filibuster Granville Oury. William seems to have had a lucky streak, for he was sent as a messenger to Sam Houston just before the Alamo was attacked by Santa Anna. He then fought in the Battle of San Jacinto, in which Santa Anna's army was annihilated and Santa Anna taken prisoner. Oury then went to California as a Forty-Niner and finally ended up in Tucson as a Butterfield employee. He also led the infamous expedition to Camp Grant that resulted in the massacre of Apache women and children.

Chapter Twelve

RETRIBUTION

Wrath, sing goddess, of Peleus's son Achilles.
                                    —Homer, the *Iliad*

*. . . so we killed our prisoners, disbanded, and went into
hiding in the mountains.*
                                    —Geronimo[1]

IT WAS SNOWING IN APACHE PASS TOO. THE SOLDIERS CONSIDERED
that an advantage because even Apaches could not travel through
snow without leaving tracks or traces. The formidable Sergeant
Robinson led a squad of soldiers to the spring to look for signs
of the Apaches, but the pristine snow revealed no traces of
human movement. Robinson climbed to the top of the nearest
hill and signaled the all clear to Bascom, who then sent most
of the mules to the spring, even though in the past the mules
had been sent in shifts. Eventually there were fifty-six mules
gathered by the spring, guarded by a squad of soldiers under
Robinson's command.

At that point, the first prong of the Apache attack came in the form of an estimated (by Robinson) two hundred Apaches, who appeared from over the surrounding hills in a position to cut the troops off from the station. The troops were steady, though, and fired volleys that wounded or killed several Apaches. As Robinson remembered: "They were in war dress—or, in other words, naked and painted, with the usual covering around the loins, and singing their war song. At the gait they were coming, it seemed as if they intended to sweep everything before them, both men and animals. Our party consisted of about twenty reliable soldiers, four or five of them underneath at the spring looking after the herd, the remainder near me. We opened fire at once and had a good show at them for some minutes, which had the effect of changing their course to the left, so as to leave the way to the station open."[2] Given the weather, it seems odd that the Apaches were "naked." Maybe Robinson was mistaken, although Apaches did like to strip down for battle, perhaps because they had learned that a wound from a bullet that carried fabric with it often became dangerously infected. Naked or otherwise, they made an imposing demonstration. And that was the object of the exercise—that and to capture the mules. These homely and useful animals seemed to exercise an irresistible attraction for Apaches.

Sergeant Robinson was wounded in the fighting at the spring. The Apaches "opened a plunging fire on us from the [opposite] ridge. . . . I was hit in the right leg," he recalled. "[T]he ball entering on the outer side of my right leg near the knee . . . passed downwards and out above the ankle on the inner side. I could only move a few paces, and sat down under a little cactus bush and reloaded my piece. . . . I was in an exposed position and received some attention from them. The greatcoat I wore testified to that fact which contained many holes."[3]

The unfortunate King Lyons, who had been wounded during the attack on the eastbound stage, was killed at the spring. He had been there to look after the fourteen mules owned by the Butterfield Company.*

Hearing the firing, Lieutenant John Rogers Cooke, as the senior officer on the spot, judged the extent of the danger to the watering party, assembled a relief squad, and rushed to the action, leaving Bascom in charge of the station defenses. The Apaches at the spring swooped down and drove off the entire herd of mules, while the soldiers under Cooke's command fought their way to the troops at the spring. Cooke's departure was the signal Cochise was waiting for. It appeared to him that the diversionary attack at the spring had achieved its object. At that point, Cochise began a direct assault on the station, designed to overwhelm the depleted defenders and rescue the hostages. But his ruse at the spring had not worked after all. Bascom had sufficient troops in a strong defensive position to discourage Cochise's plan. After an initial probe, and after receiving some well-directed fire from the soldiers, Cochise and his warriors retreated out of range. And that was the end of the battle.

Though he didn't know it yet, Bascom had won his first fight, according to the rules he lived by—he had repulsed an attack and retained possession of the field. He estimated that between five and twenty Chiricahua had been killed. (The Apaches later admitted to three killed.) His own losses were negligible—Robinson and Smith wounded. There were two Butterfield employees killed and one wounded, but these were not Bascom's responsibility, officially, at any rate. All things considered, Bascom could tell himself he had done well in his first combat action. True, he had lost nearly all his mules, but they were only so much property and in time could be replaced. No doubt he hoped his commanding officer would see it that way too. The army did not like to lose property, but it liked losing battles and soldiers even less. Then, too, when the dragoons

---

* One version of the story suggests that there was another man named Lyons there and that he was the one killed at the spring. This remains something of a mystery.

arrived, they might be able to recover the animals. Of course, there was the problem of Wallace and the three other Americans whom Cochise claimed to have. Well, the Apaches had tried their hand at attack; now they would necessarily revert to a strategy of prisoner exchange, so those four, if there were four, would ultimately not become casualties. That only made sense, didn't it?

Assuming your enemy thinks more or less the same way you do can often lead to an unpleasant surprise. And that is especially true when the enemy is from an entirely different culture with different values and modes of living. Certainly Bascom had every reason to assume Cochise would return to negotiation over the hostages. Any reasonable person would have thought the same. Perhaps Cochise might try another attack or two, but he and his warriors had shown they had no stomach for direct assault against a well-prepared defensive position. (For which, by the way, Bascom could thank his West Point training.) Ultimately, Cochise would have to relent and return to the bargaining table. And that, no doubt, would come sooner rather than later, assuming Bascom's messengers had gotten through and the relief columns were en route.

But Cochise did not see things that way. Thwarted and angry, he returned to his camp and tortured his four American hostages to death, mutilating their bodies so much that Wallace could only be identified by his gold teeth. Cochise then transferred the tattered and shattered remains to a place along the Butterfield road not far from the burned wagons and charred bodies of the Mexican teamsters.

Perhaps the torture was done by the widows of the warriors killed in the battle. The numerous lance wounds in the bodies suggested that possibility. "When a brave warrior is killed, the men go out for about three Mexicans," explained an Apache. "They bring them back for the women to kill in revenge. The women ride at them on horseback, armed with spears."[4] It's even possible that this happened without Cochise's knowledge, although his command over his local group was firm—especially in a combat situation—and it seems unlikely that the women or the warriors would destroy valuable assets without permission.

No, it seems most likely that Cochise approved of the torture.

The question that puzzles anyone who thinks about this affair is—why? Why would Cochise destroy his primary assets in this stalemate with the Americans?

The most obvious answer is uncontrollable rage. When he returned to his camp, frustrated by the unsuccessful assault on the station, he may have come upon the woebegone prisoners tied and huddled, and, releasing his furious temper, attacked the prisoners with his lance. Seeing this, other warriors may have joined in, so that for a few minutes the Apaches simply went berserk. They did not care about the loss of these assets; they simply saw before them the wretched and miserable representatives of the white race, the ones who had brought their detestable civilization to these mountains, the ones responsible for the ineluctable change that the Chiricahuas viewed with fear and hatred. Worse, these men were contemptible as they cringed under the threat of torture and then cried out when the lancing began, not stoically accepting pain the way a Chiricahua was expected to do, but weeping and pleading and screaming and in so doing enraging the Apaches even further. This was the wrath of Cochise, unreasoning and volcanic. These hostages were symbols of everything the Chiricahuas loathed; they were the harbingers of the Chiricahuas' demise. And that is why Cochise had the bodies taken to a place where they would be found by the white soldiers. They were four bloody symbols and messages of his now implacable hatred, not only for the men who held his family hostage, but for the encroaching and spreading stain that was the white culture. They were a message of resistance.

We will never know, of course, but it's even reasonable to surmise that Cochise himself killed all four men, not wanting to share this release with anyone, not even his comrades.

*Poor fool, no longer speak to me of ransom, nor argue
     it.*
*In the time before Patroklos came to the day of his
     destiny*
*Then it was the way of my heart's choice to be
     sparing*
*Of the Trojans, and many I took alive and disposed of
     them.*
*Now there is not one who can escape death, if the gods
     send*
Him against my hands in front of Ilion, not one
*Of all the Trojans and beyond others the children of
     Priam.*
So, friend, you die also.[5]

                                        —Homer, the *Iliad*

The analogy of Cochise and Coyuntura to Achilles and
Patroklos may seem a bit of a stretch at first. But in fact there
are surprising parallels between the Chiricahua culture and
that of the Homeric Greeks as depicted in the *Iliad*. Both linked
raiding for plunder and hostages (especially women) as a source
of honor. Both made raids for cattle and sheep. Both were warrior
cultures that celebrated the individual hero, and both trans-
mitted their culture through an oral tradition of storytelling.
Both were decentralized societies composed of small groups
that came together in times of war. Both had priests and seers
who prophesied the future. Both had mountain-dwelling gods
who participated directly in the lives and careers of the mortals.
And while there is less torture among the Greeks, when Achilles
killed Hector he dragged his body behind his chariot, and, in
an odd parallel, there is a story that Cochise actually dragged
Wallace behind his horse. That story may not be true, but it
does appear at least plausible, given Wallace's ragged final condition. And both societies placed great emphasis on relationships

between warriors. Achilles sulks beside his ships until his best friend, Patroklos, is killed; only then does his unquenchable rage overtake him and send him looking for revenge. Cochise's brother was more than a sibling—he was a confidant, adviser, and protector, literally a brother in arms. At the time Cochise may have killed his prisoners, Coyuntura was still alive, but Cochise certainly understood that his well loved brother was in great danger, as events would prove. And finally, in a historical oddity, the Chiricahuas under Cochise's leadership would go on to fight a war that lasted just over a decade, essentially the same length of time it took the Greeks to destroy Troy.

While these parallels between two societies may be interesting, it is fair to ask if they are at all relevant. To this extent, they are—the narrative of Cochise's wrath is still being discussed because we recognize in it a classic story of a warrior who is driven by desire for revenge and who leads his people in an epic and bloody conflict. The story resonates because we recognize its mythic elements, whether we make the direct connection or not. "The word used to describe . . . wrath is *menis*," writes historian Caroline Alexander, "which is also the first word in the Iliad: 'Wrath, sing goddess, of Peleus's son Achilles.' *Menis* can be summarized as 'enduring anger, justified by a desire for rightful vengeance, said especially of gods, of dead heroes, but also of humans . . . especially of Achilles in the Iliad.'"[6] Today, George Bascom is largely forgotten, but Cochise and his story are well remembered, not just because of the story's dramatic elements, but also because of Cochise's close resemblance to the archetype of the epic hero.

There is still another variation on the archetype of the hero, a variation that fits well with Cochise's subsequent actions, which is the resistance hero, the guerrilla chief who befuddles a large and powerful nation of oppressors. History is littered with these characters, some more deserving of respect than others. There are those who consider these characters romantic, as indeed some of them were.

Cochise's torturing of his hostages is also emblematic of a very recognizable psychological condition. Consider this excerpt from a study of combat trauma in Vietnam. The soldier is talking about his reaction to the death of a comrade: "I just went crazy. I pulled him [a Vietcong] out of the paddy and carved him up with my knife. When I had done with him he looked like a rag doll that a dog had been playing with. I lost all my mercy."[7]

While that sort of psychological condition is deplorable, it is by no means hard to understand or recognize.

Of course, Bascom would have scoffed at all such psychological or mythic comparisons, as would most of the others in the army, and all of the white settlers in the territory. To them, Cochise was nothing more than a thief and murderer. But they were in the moment. And in that particular moment, to Bascom and his men, Cochise was simply a dangerous leader of savage warriors who were trying their best to kill them. The mythic narrative had yet to be constructed because the war was just beginning.

Bascom had won his first fight, but at the moment he was not sure of that. The great uncertainty was the relief columns. Were they coming? He had no way of knowing.

But they were.

Bascom has been criticized for not sending out patrols to discover the prevailing mood of the Apaches. But, here again, geography played a role. The mountains surrounding the stage-station defenses were rugged and difficult. Bascom had lost most of his mules, and an infantry patrol would have been a useless and dangerous exercise. Because of the terrain and the innumerable hiding places available, Bascom would have had to send out multiple patrols, which would have weakened his defensive position—his primary asset, along with the hostages. Besides, multiple small patrols would have been easy targets for Apache ambush. Bascom could not in good conscience have reduced his defenses and at the same time placed many small patrols in great hazard. What was needed for patrolling was cavalry, and Bascom had summoned the horse soldiers. Until they arrived, his best option was maintaining his defensive position. If the Apaches were still in the neighborhood, they would make their presence known. If they had disappeared, acknowledging defeat and leaving the field and prisoners, well, so much the better. At this point, Bascom no doubt felt that the recovery of Felix Ward was secondary and not worth risking his command. At least he had his prisoners to show for the patrol.

Assistant Surgeon Irwin and his relief force arrived on Sunday, one week from the day Bascom had come to Apache Pass. Irwin's commission dated from 1856, which meant that Bascom was now third in the chain of seniority.* On his way across the grasslands between Dragoon Springs and Apache Pass, Irwin had run across three Apaches who were traveling north, driving a small herd of cattle they had stolen in Mexico. These three were probably Coyoteros, although there is some thought that they might have been Chiricahuas. The fact that they were traveling north in this district could support either theory. In any event, Irwin was able to capture the three, a sure indication that these Apaches had no idea of what was going on in the pass. That section of country is flat, and in the clear desert air, the Apaches would have seen the soldiers approaching with plenty of time to escape. But they didn't try to run, most likely because they knew they were over the border and in U.S. territory; they had not bothered Americans and had no reason to be afraid of troops, whom they probably saw coming and going through the pass on many occasions. What's more, it was commonly understood by the Apaches that they were free to do their worst in Mexico, as far as the United States was

---

* As an army surgeon Irwin was a staff officer, which meant he would not have official seniority over line officers. But Irwin was known as a "fighting doctor," and his considerable frontier experience would have offset any chain of command technicalities.

concerned. They therefore did not flee when they saw Irwin and his men approaching. Consequently, it was easy for Irwin to take them as prisoners, and he took them through the pass to Bascom's fortified stage station.

The army now had six warriors, as well as Cochise's wife and children as bargaining chips. Unfortunately for Bascom and the other officers, there was no one to bargain with, for, inexplicably, the Chiricahua had disappeared. Mangas Coloradas and Francisco had returned to New Mexico, and Cochise's warriors had gone south into the Chiricahua Mountains to rejoin their families.

How could this be? What about the Chiricahua dedication to immediate family and the extended family? What about the iron bond between brothers? Would Cochise actually leave his family in the hands of the army? Why not return to negotiations in order to release them? True, he had murdered the four hostages, but Bascom did not know that yet. In the back of his mind, Cochise must also have figured that there were other hostages to be had, unwary travelers. The stagecoaches could be stopped until the impasse was resolved, but other travelers used the pass and the flat desert roads on both sides of it. Or perhaps he could lure some soldiers from their defensive position with another flag-of-truce ruse. He was not out of options quite yet.

Consequently, it is inconceivable that he did leave. The other bands could certainly be excused because it was obvious that a military solution for the Apaches was out of the question. There were too many troops and they were too well dug in. And Cochise must have surmised that the Americans had sent for help. As a result, there was no reason to have such a large body of warriors congregating, consuming rations and simply watching impotently. What's more, a group that size used a campsite that would be easier to locate if and when the army decided to send out patrols. They might as well disperse.

But Cochise must have stayed, perhaps with a small group of warriors. He would have been in the hills, waiting and watching for a chance to free his people, feeling that stealth or trickery might succeed where assault had failed. Not to remain, not to try to rescue them would have been a violation of the entire Chiricahua belief system and culture, not to mention normal human emotion. It is impossible to believe that he blithely turned his back on his family and disappeared into the mountains to the south.

Things got worse for Cochise a few days later when Lieutenant Isaiah Moore arrived with seventy dragoons. A graduate of West Point, class of '51, Moore had received his commission on February 1853. He was now the senior officer present. The Butterfield agent, William Oury, was with Moore.

During the next two days, Moore and Bascom led the mounted troops on scouts through the surrounding hills, looking for Apaches. They didn't find any but that meant nothing. When Apaches didn't want to be found, they weren't. And assuming Cochise had stayed in the vicinity, he and a small group of warriors would have had no trouble following the progress of the army's large scouting party and eluding them.

On Monday, February 18, Irwin and Oury and a squad of troops were scouting to the west of the station, and they came upon the remains of the four American hostages. It was Oury who identified Wallace by his gold teeth. Sickened by the mutilated bodies, the soldiers buried the four men then and there. The location was only a few hundred yards from the burned-out Mexican wagon train.

Now it was the Americans' turn to be outraged, and on the following day the troops marched their captives to the site. They were going to hang the six warriors from the trees above the graves of the hostages. The soldiers must have felt some sort of grim desire for symmetrical retribution, or for symbolism. Why bring them to this very spot otherwise? It was the senior officer present, Lieutenant Moore, who authorized the hangings. Some reports say that Bascom objected, but Moore overruled him and assumed full responsibility. Whether Bascom was hoping to keep his hostages for a still possible trade with Cochise or whether he objected on humanitarian grounds is impossible to say. Most likely it was the former, but perhaps it was a bit of both. It hardly needs saying, though, that Bascom's instincts, honed by his West Point training, would have had him defer to the judgments of his senior officer. It was also his legal and moral responsibility. The discredited modern defense of "I was just following orders" was not discredited then. Irwin added the weight of his seniority, saying that no matter what the others did, he intended to hang his three captives. They, of course, had nothing to do with the murders of the four white men; they had been in Mexico on a raid. But the officers were in no mood to discriminate; as far as Irwin was concerned, they were all Apaches and, by definition, all worthy of the noose.

Irwin's harshness may be puzzling. After all, he had not been involved in any real action so far—not at the pass, that is. Of course, the sight of the mutilated four hostages must have disturbed him deeply, as it did all the officers. But both Moore and Irwin were in favor of the hanging, while Bascom was hesitant. One possible explanation is that both Moore and Irwin had been stationed in Arizona for several years. Irwin had been at Fort Buchanan since December of 1857 and before that he was at Fort Union in New Mexico and Fort Defiance. He had been in the Southwest since January of 1856, while Bascom was still in his second year at West Point. Irwin and Moore (who served with Ewell at Buchanan until being transferred to Breckinridge) had had more than enough time to absorb the realities of warfare against the Apaches, which included their elusiveness, their cruelty, their thievery, their alternation between peace requests and raids, their decentralized social structure that made it impossible to arrange comprehensive treaties, their constant commuting across the border to Mexican sanctuaries where the army could not follow—in short, all of the frustrations of fighting guerrilla war with limited resources. They would also have been quite familiar with the complaints of the white settlers as represented by their old comrade Sylvester Mowry. Most likely, they came to agree with his views on the subject of Apaches. And they had put up with several years of primitive living conditions in ramshackle forts, all the while regretting the lack of opportunity for advancement. They had been doing a thankless job and had developed some very hard edges along the way. Now they had six prisoners, and it hardly mattered that these six had nothing to do with torturing Wallace and the others. They were Apaches, and as far as these officers were concerned, the world would be better off without them.

Through the interpreter Antonio, an Apache-speaking scout who arrived with Moore, Bascom explained to the prisoners what was about to happen. They asked to be shot instead, and at least one cried out for mercy. Another said he didn't care; he was happy because he had killed two Mexicans that month. They asked for some whiskey, but that request was also denied.[8]

The soldiers looped ropes over the boughs of four oak trees, and, according to Robinson's account, the Apaches were "hoisted so high by the infantry that even the wolves could not touch them."[9] Robinson's use of the term "hoisted" implies strongly that the Apaches actually strangled to death. Their necks were not broken by a fall as is usually the case in a hanging. It would not be at all surprising if this was the very result the soldiers were looking for. After all, if they simply wanted to kill the six, they could have just shot them and been done with it. This rather more elaborate execution with its grisly strangulation looks very much like revenge, especially given the carefully selected setting. The troops were saying that they too could send messages in the form of corpses.

There was some discussion about what to do with Cochise's wife and children, but apparently the soldiers had had enough of capital punishment that day, and they decided that, once they returned to Fort Buchanan, they would release them. Perhaps they felt Cochise's wife would make a good messenger. (One story, spread by the less-than-reliable Oberly, says that the soldiers played a card game, seven-up, to decide the question, but this seems a little too melo-dramatic. Besides, army policy was generally not to harm women and children, and the after-action reports would not have looked so good if they had executed them too.)*

It seems possible that somewhere in the nearby surrounding hills Cochise was watching, unable to do anything but stand by and let an indelible image burn in his memory.

On the other hand, perhaps not. Years later, Cochise told General O. O. Howard: "The worst place of all is Apache Pass. There six Indians, one my brother, were murdered. Their bodies were hung up and kept there until they were skeletons."[10] That, too, seems incredible, because the Chiricahuas, despite their dread of death and ghosts, or maybe because of it, had very strict burial customs. Once someone died, his relatives were responsible for preparing the body for burial. No one else wanted that job, and only relatives would do it. As part of the process, all traces of his property were either buried with him or burned. In the case of a warrior, his favorite horse, saddle, and weapons would be buried with him, often in some crevice or cave that could then be sealed and hidden. Nothing was to be left to remind his relatives of his death, and his name was never to be mentioned. How Cochise could have left his brother's body hanging until it was a "skeleton" must remain a puzzlement that contradicts the notion that he had stayed in the area, watching. (Ravens and buzzards would have made short work of those bodies, even if the wolves could not have reached them. It is impossible to imagine that Cochise could have watched that without doing something.)

---

* Here again it's important to remember the distinction between the regular army and the regiments of volunteers, such as Chivington's Colorado Volunteers, who committed the atrocities at Sand Creek. Of course, women and children were sometimes killed during regular army attacks on villages; Custer's action at Washita is an example. But there is an obvious difference between the violence and confusion of an attack and cold-blooded execution.

But even if Cochise had not witnessed the executions, and even if he had not remained in the area, his wife would have informed him once she made her way to his camp. She was an eyewitness and probably counted herself fortunate not to be hanging next to Coyuntura. Why did Cochise not return for the bodies as soon as his wife told him of the hangings?

Also, the place of execution was a good two miles from the stage station and the squad of soldiers who had been left there as guards. Nothing would have prevented Cochise and his followers from a nighttime visit to retrieve the bodies—at least those of his family. Of the several mysteries associated with this story, Cochise's failure to retrieve his brother's body—and those of his nephews—is the most puzzling.

It is at least possible that Cochise had been wounded in the final assault on the stage station and incapacitated. In that case, his warriors would have carried him from the field. A year or so later, when Mangas Coloradas was wounded in another battle with the army in that very same Apache Pass, his warriors carried him off to Janos, Mexico, where they delivered him to a terrified Mexican doctor with the choice of either healing him or dying. That explanation makes the most sense, except there is no record of Cochise being seriously wounded. He certainly never mentioned it afterward, although he was forthcoming in his discussions about his subsequent actions—after the Bascom incident.

So the mystery of the bodies remains.

In any event, as far as the Chiricahua were concerned, the spirits of Coyuntura and the others had gone to the happy place beneath the ground where life was lived exactly as it had been in the upper world. In fact, it was better there, because unlike the upper world, where the Chiricahua way of life was being increasingly threatened, "in the place beneath," things would go on as they always had.

After hanging the six prisoners, Bascom and Moore led their troops back to their respective forts, where each wrote a report of the action. Bascom was commended for his handling of the situation. Whether his commander fully approved or was simply wishing to avoid controversy that might derail his own request for leave is another unanswerable question. It's useful, though, to remember that in 1861 the army's campaigns against hostile tribes were assessed to a large extent by casualty counts—Indians killed, captured, or surrendered. This was especially true in campaigns against the utterly nomadic Apaches. The Apaches rarely had any property or farmland to attack and destroy, unlike, for example, the Navajos, who had cornfields and orchards and herds of sheep and cattle. (Navajos were elusive raiders too, but their economy consisted of agriculture and herding as well as raiding.) Even the Chiricahua shelters were just woven-reed wickiups, easily abandoned without a second thought, and easily replaced in another campground. The women could build one in a matter of hours. In the warmer dry months, they might not bother with wickiups at all and would live quite comfortably beneath an open-air ramada. A campaign of scorched-earth devastation, such as the one Colonel Kit Carson led against the Navajos in 1863, was therefore impossible to conduct against the Apaches. Nor did the Apaches maintain and cherish huge herds of horses, like the Comanches—herds that could be captured and destroyed, so that the Comanches' wealth and means to hunt could be simultaneously devastated, as the 1874 campaign of Ranald Mackenzie in Texas demonstrated. Nor did the Apaches go into snowbound winter camps like the Northern Plains Indians, whose stores of food and shelter could be attacked and burned, leaving the Indians destitute and starving. (Both Custer and Miles adopted this strategy, Custer in the 1860s, Miles in the 1870s.) In the milder Southwest, the Apaches could hunt year-round—and raid to collect cattle. Destroying their cached food supplies was therefore a waste of time, or, at the worst, merely an inconvenience to the enterprising raiders. Then there was the Apaches' tenacious attachment to mountain living, so that difficult geography made finding them and fighting them all the more frustrating.

Success against Apaches could therefore only be judged by numbers killed or captured. And it hardly mattered how those casualties occurred. The army believed, or hoped, that once they had killed enough of them, the rest would surrender and agree to a reservation—or, even better, just go away to Mexico and stay there. And so while Bascom had not been able to recover the Ward boy, the army could well believe he had something to show for his patrol—Bascom's estimated five to twenty Apaches killed in the fighting to go with the six left hanging. At least that was a plausible enough interpretation of the events, from the army's point of view. And that sort of score would go down well with the civilian population too.

Some writers note that Bascom was subsequently promoted to first lieutenant and then captain, implying that the army warmly approved of his action. But his promotion had nothing to do with the action in Apache Pass and everything to do with the outbreak of the Civil War. Professional officers were suddenly at a premium, and even the most junior subalterns found themselves promoted, not by seniority as in peacetime, but by necessity.

There is no doubt that Bascom made serious mistakes in Apache Pass, and that all of them were, if not predictable, certainly unsurprising. Bascom was a representative of his culture, the white civilization, and the culture of the army. He had been a serving officer for nearly three years. (And it's worth remembering that the army was accustomed to placing great responsibility on junior officers.) Before Apache Pass, he had had little contact with Indians (except the Goshutes) and no contact at all with the Apaches. As a result, when he encountered the strange and imposing Cochise, Bascom most likely became uneasy and fell back on what he knew—giving orders and demanding that they be obeyed. Further, there was precedence for taking hostages: Ewell had done something very similar with successful results. (So had Cochise.) In other words, the idea of hostage taking did not originate with Bascom.* Then, in the chaos of the escape, Bascom ordered his troops to open fire. Given who he was and what he knew—along with his specific orders from Morrison—it's not surprising that he acted as he did. Given his instructions, he must have felt that not firing on the fugitives would have brought more criticism than otherwise. He wanted to make a name for himself, no doubt, but even more important, he wanted to avoid failure and subsequent censure. He had grown to maturity in a culture at West Point that punished even the smallest indiscretion or variation from the rules or from orders. Assigning blame, when things did not go according to plan, always seemed to be the army's first priority.

Of course, in hindsight, his order to the troops to fire was a mistake. (It's interesting to wonder about the history of the Southwest had Bascom's troops been better shots.) But from that point on, Bascom's actions do not really deserve the opprobrium he has received over the years. He made an effective defense of his position and did not take many casualties. (All of the killed were civilians and not under Bascom's command.) Later, when it came to the crucial decision of what to do about the captives, he had little choice but to defer to the three more senior officers, all of whom were in favor of executing the six. Regardless of what he thought personally, it was ultimately not Bascom's decision to make. That was the responsibility of the senior officer present, Lieutenant Moore—a responsibility that Moore directly accepted. Had Bascom objected even more strenuously than he did, his seniors would have overruled him, noted his unwelcome reluctance, and executed the prisoners anyway.

---

* Nor did it end with him. In 1868, none other than George Custer took three Cheyenne chiefs hostage in order to secure the release of two white women captives.

Chapter Thirteen

Aftermath

*When the bombardment of Fort Sumter in April 1861
finally plunged the nation into Civil War, the frontier
army suddenly ceased to protect the frontier.*
—Robert Utley[1]

IN A VERY REAL SENSE, THE TRAGEDY OF SLAVERY REACHED INTO THE
Southwest and changed forever a culture and a people who had
never seen an African, although they understood and practiced
slavery themselves. Had there been no southern slavery, there
would never have been a Gadsden Purchase, and most of the Chiricahua homeland would have remained in Mexico. Some northern
abolitionists even asserted that there never would have been a war
with Mexico, a war they believed was fought to acquire territory
and extend the institution of slavery.

The subsequent Civil War played a cruel trick on the hostile
tribes, for when the western troops abandoned their forts and
went east, the tribes came to believe the old way of life might be
continued forever. And that same war gave the Apaches a mistaken
sense of confidence that did them no good when the war ended, and

283

the white people turned to the question of resettling the Southwest. Had the Apaches and Navajos and Comanches and all the others read the eastern newspaper reports detailing the bloodbaths between vast armies of the whites, they would have recognized their coming doom, "the iron hand of destiny," in Sherman's words. But that level of catastrophe was beyond the imagination of the tribes and probably beyond the imagination of any human, in the circumstances.

Cochise always claimed that Bascom's actions ignited the war with the Chiricahuas. But the resulting fire would have been containable in the Southwest had it not been for the Civil War. One month after the affair in Apache Pass, Texas seceded from the Union, March 4, 1861. The following month, the rebellious South Carolinians fired on Fort Sumter, and the war was well and truly on.

Texas had long cast covetous glances toward New Mexico. Texans had originally claimed their borders extended to and included the rich Rio Grande Valley all the way to Santa Fe. With the potential of a Texan thrust into New Mexico, the army decided it needed all its resources to protect the Rio Grande Valley, which was far more densely populated and valuable in terms of agricultural production than southern Arizona. Then there were the mines at Pinos Altos. The federals also needed to block the Confederate designs on western expansion, for it was clear to anyone who thought about it that the Confederates would ultimately want to march to the Pacific, to the ports and gold mines of California, as well as north to the mines of Colorado. And so, in July of 1861, the troops at Buchanan and Breckinridge were ordered to destroy both forts and move to New Mexico to meet the threat from Confederate Texas. Bascom's unit as well as Moore's and Lord's dragoons went to Fort Craig in the Rio Grande Valley, 120 miles south of Albuquerque. (John Rogers Cooke, on the other hand, resigned his commission to join the Confederacy, one of 313 regular army officers who did so.)[2] The army's move understandably horrified the settlers of Arizona, who would now be utterly exposed to the attacks of the fully aroused and vengeful Apaches. Indeed, the settlers knew very well what was coming, for the Apaches had already begun to escalate the ferocity and number of their attacks throughout the territory.

As a feeble countermeasure, the settlers organized a small force of rangers, including James Tevis, to provide some protection against Apache attacks. These attacks were so widespread and vicious that many, if not most, of the ranchers and farmers in southern Arizona left everything and fled the territory. One such party of evacuees was typical. Ranchers from the Sonoita Creek, Tubac, and Tucson area formed a party of some fifteen wagons, twenty-four men, sixteen women, seven children, and a large herd of cattle, sheep, horses, and goats.[3] Traveling east and hurrying to catch up to the troops who were headed for New Mexico, they were attacked by Cochise's warriors. The Chiricahuas ran off the herds of animals and fired on the train, which, in classic fashion, circled the wagons as the whites fought for their lives. Women loaded rifles while the men fired at the attackers. A number of white men were killed and the wagon train was forced to retreat as they watched the Apaches depart with a herd estimated at thirteen hundred head of livestock.

Ranches along the Santa Cruz Valley were raided, the settlers killed, and the ranch houses wrecked.* Stage stations were attacked and destroyed, teamsters ambushed, and either killed or, if captured, tortured to death over fires. One such stage-station manager was the unlucky Anthony Elder, who had been the manager at Apache Pass but transferred because of a run-in with Cochise. Elder did not survive his second encounter. He and eight others were killed at the Stein's Peak station near today's border of New

---

* John Ward somehow escaped attack, probably because his ranch was so impoverished. He died in 1867. His son, Felix, was raised by the Coyoteros who captured him. As an adult, he was called Mickey Free, and he served as a scout for the army in the later Apache wars.

Mexico and Arizona. Two of the nine were unfortunate enough to be captured.

Sylvester Mowry, holding out at his mine, wrote to the secretary of war in August 1861, just a few weeks after the local forts were evacuated, "Every farm and rancho is abandoned, the people have taken refuge in Tucson, Tubac or followed the troops. The loss of property is immense. I am holding my place at great expense. In fact, it is a garrison. . . . I am constantly prepared for a fight." (Mowry's southern sympathies would soon cost him ownership of his mine when a column of volunteer Union troops arrived from California on their way to New Mexico.) In fact, not all ranches were abandoned; the indomitable Pete Kitchen held out at his fortresslike ranch in the Santa Cruz Valley, although he was attacked and lost a herd of some four hundred cattle. But Mowry's letter was not much of an exaggeration. He went on to say that the "Arizona Apaches. . . . openly boast that they have driven the Americans, soldiers and all, out of the country."[4]

Certainly Cochise and his fellow chiefs believed they were responsible for the mass exodus of white settlers. The sight of the army heading east followed by frightened families in wagon trains, ripe for attack, gave him grim pleasure. He was not behind every raid or attack, nor were the Chiricahuas the only tribe up in arms. But they were very aggressive. Here was the opportunity for Cochise to avenge the deaths of his family and at the same time to wipe out the hateful stain of the mines and miners, not only Mowry's but also Pinos Altos—and simultaneously enrich the band with the spoils of war. The Chiricahuas' emboldened tactics—the fact that they uncharacteristically attacked well-guarded wagon trains—indicate that the distinction between raiding and warfare no longer applied. This was war for the sake of war, for the sake of revenge, but plunder was a welcome residual benefit.

To make matters worse for Arizona, with the Civil War looming, Congress decided the Butterfield stage line was not tenable anymore. For one thing, it ran through Texas and so could easily be shut down by Confederate interests. For another, it passed through New Mexico and Arizona, where the hostile tribes were most active; in the summer of 1860 alone, ten drivers had been killed by Comanches and Apaches.[5] But the mail connection with California was still vitally important, so Congress voted to move the line north to the central route, abandoning John Butterfield's truly astonishing but impractical achievement after a mere three years. Congress decided to revoke the contract in March, a month after the Bascom affair, the month Texas seceded, and a month before the Civil War broke out. It was clear that the choice of the southern route had been a mistake, made for political rather than practical reasons. Now that so many southern states had seceded or were on the verge of secession, the southern party no longer controlled the debate about mail routes, and what was left of Congress easily made the decision to move north.

The decision had everything to do with the old squabbles between North and South and virtually nothing to do with the practical feasibility of the southern route. But the fact was, Butterfield was losing money. The length of the route coupled with the remote stations made it very expensive to supply. Indian raids in Texas, New Mexico and Arizona led to the loss of much livestock, not easily replaced. Even if the Civil War had been averted, Congress would never have renewed the contract for the southern route. Butterfield could not have continued without increased subsidies from Congress, but Congress would never have authorized higher subsidies when shorter and less expensive routes were available.

The Bascom affair and subsequent war with the Apaches had no direct impact on Congress's decision to move the Overland Mail route. It's unlikely that most members of Congress even heard about problems with the Apaches by the time they got around to voting on the mail contract. But Cochise, mistakenly, made that connection. The decision to abandon the line undoubtedly reinforced his opinion that he and his people were driving the detested whites out of the country. As far as the Chiricahuas were concerned, the removal of the line represented a clear military victory for them.

Closing the southern route of the Butterfield Overland Mail had an impact on the local economy in Arizona. Ranchers and farmers who supplied food for both the animals and men of the stage line lost a small but useful market. People who provided services, such as teamsters, farriers, blacksmiths, harness makers and repairers, and even stockmen who were called upon to replace worn-out horses and mules, all lost business as a result of the closure. Station managers and hostlers lost their jobs. Towns like Tucson lost the business from passengers passing through. Even the whiskey peddlers were discomfited.

More important for the local economy, ranchers, farmers, and merchants also lost the business from the now empty and burnt-out forts. And so southern Arizona was hit by two disasters simultaneously—increased Apache attacks and significantly reduced markets. Both disasters were directly related to the loss of the army because of the outbreak of the Civil War. Even those settlers who were intrepid enough to stay wondered if they could survive economically, to say nothing of surviving actually. Many—in fact, most—decided they could not.

Those few Arizona settlers who stayed realized that southern Arizona was now isolated from the outside world. With Unionist California to the west and Confederate Texas to the east, Arizonans needed to ally themselves with someone. Many of the locals, like Mowry, were sympathetic to the southern cause, and they held a convention in Mesilla to discuss the issue. As a result, Arizona declared for the Confederacy in March 1861, though it had no legal status as a territory or state. Indeed, there was no "Arizona"; it was just a commonly used name for a region of the New Mexico Territory. Once the army evacuated the two forts, the locals no doubt hoped the Confederate government would send troops to replace the departed federals.

The Confederates wasted little time in marching on New Mexico. A column of Texans under Colonel John R. Baylor arrived in Mesilla on July 25, 1861, and brushed aside the federals, who made a feeble attempt at defense before retreating precipitately. On August 1, Baylor proclaimed the "Confederate Territory of Arizona." This new territory included New Mexico and Arizona more or less south of the Gila River and extending all the way to California. (On February 14, 1862, the Confederate Congress proclaimed that the Territory of Arizona was now part of the southern Confederacy. In Tucson, Granville Oury, former filibuster and brother of William Oury, former Butterfield agent, was elected territorial delegate to the Confederate Congress.) The Chiricahuas were now part of the third sovereign nation in the last fifteen years, a fact that they would have considered humorously irrelevant, had they known about it.

Of course, it was one thing for the Confederates to proclaim a new territory and another to acquire and keep it by force of arms. Standing in their way was the newly reinforced federal garrison at Fort Craig, a hundred or so miles up the Rio Grande. That fort was under the command of Colonel Edward R. S. Canby—the same Canby who had led one of the columns during the campaign against the Navajos at Fort Defiance. Part of Canby's command were Kit Carson and his First New Mexico Volunteer Regiment, Moore and Lord's dragoons, and the several companies of the Seventh Infantry.

In a microcosm of the larger Civil War, Canby's comrade in the Navajo campaign, Maj. Henry H. Sibley, had resigned his commission and joined the Confederacy. He was appointed brigadier general, and in December 1861 he took command of the Texas forces and started making plans for a thrust northward along the Rio Grande.

The two would clash in the Battle of Valverde, which took place in the neighborhood of Fort Craig. Unfortunately, Lieutenant Moore, the officer who authorized and took responsibility for the hangings in Apache Pass, would not live to participate in the coming battle. His West Point records simply say that he "died on January 16, 1862." Sergeant Robinson reports that when he and Moore were returning from a routine patrol, Moore suddenly pulled out his pistol and shot himself in the head. Robinson also says that Moore had been "despondent" of late, and while it's tempting to wonder if Moore was bothered by guilt over the affair in Apache Pass, that seems unlikely. More likely, he was simply worn out from the hardship of frontier service.

As Civil War conflicts go, the February 20 and 21 battle at Valverde was not very large in terms of numbers engaged— three thousand for the Union and twenty-six hundred or so for the Rebels. The Rebel forces were mostly all cavalry. The Confederates claimed victory, because they retained possession of the field after charging and routing the Union troops and forcing them to retreat to Fort Craig. The Confederates were able to continue their campaign to the north, where their objective was the capture of the federal territorial capital at Santa Fe. From there they intended to thrust into the gold fields of Colorado. The federals, however, still occupied Fort Craig—a position that could block the Confederate supply line to Texas. Strategically, then, Valverde was not such a clear-cut federal defeat as the Confederates supposed. As it turned out, the Confederate campaign to Colorado would be blocked by a federal victory at Glorieta Pass—a disaster for Sibley, who lost most of his supplies and was forced to retreat to Texas.

Though the battle at Valverde was relatively small, it was nonetheless fierce. Bascom was in command of his old Company C of the Seventh Infantry. He had been promoted to captain and assigned to the Sixteenth Infantry, but he had not been able to join his new outfit by the time the Rebels arrived. He found himself in the thick of the action: ". . . C and F companies suffered most of the regiment's casualties in this battle because these were the two companies involved in repelling the bloody late afternoon Confederate assault on the left of the Union line," writes John C. McManus.[6] They may have repelled an initial charge, but not a second one. A Texas cavalryman described the action along the river: ". . . in this charge we carried everything before us, routing the enemy; we drove them to the river where they 'took water' on short notice."[7]

The federal troops retreated back to Fort Craig, and Canby requested a truce to collect the dead and wounded. The Confederates agreed, satisfied with their gains for the day. Reports of casualties varied according to the source. But Union killed exceeded one hundred out of the three thousand engaged, while wounded exceeded one hundred and fifty. The Confederates lost somewhat fewer men, but not by much. There were five Union officers killed in action. The mortuary detail found one officer's body on a sandbar in the middle of the Rio Grande, a victim of the Texas cavalry's final charge on the Union left.[8] The Texans had deprived Cochise of the chance for personal revenge against George Bascom.

Most likely, Bascom died fighting as his troops retreated. There is no way to substantiate that except we do know he was a brave officer. Moreover, the army later named a fort after him, a desolate outpost in eastern New Mexico near Tucumcari. Had Bascom not comported himself well during the battle, the army would hardly have honored him in this way. The fort was built to counteract Apache and Comanche attacks in the area. Bascom's name would therefore continue to be associated with the Indian wars, if only for a few brief years.

With the closing of the Overland Mail, Apache Pass and Apache Springs returned to their previous owners—another source of satisfaction to Cochise and his people. This would be temporary, though. The following year, a column of Union troops from California would come through on their way to New Mexico. They would fight a battle against Cochise and Mangas Coloradas and defeat the Apaches, primarily through the use of mountain howitzers firing explosive shells—a weapon that demoralized the Chiricahuas, who might otherwise have overwhelmed lead units of the column. The Californians under the stern command of James Carleton recognized the strategic value of the pass, and decided to build and garrison a fort there, Fort Bowie. For the remainder of the Apache wars, Fort Bowie would be a key installation. As mentioned, the initial fort was a typical set of wretched hovels, but over the next few decades it would grow into a respectable-looking installation.

There followed ten-plus years of war between the white settlers and the army on one side and the Chiricahuas on the other. It was guerrilla war, with all that that entails. Cochise made skillful use of the border, retreating into Mexico when it suited him and returning to Arizona when he felt it was tactically sound.

Finally, in 1872, General O. O. Howard, a devout Christian who had lost an arm in the Civil War, bravely went into the Dragoon Mountains with only a small escort to find Cochise and arrange peace terms. The timing was good, for Cochise had grown weary of the constant tension of war—although, of course, he was in part responsible for it—for it had settled into a series of attacks and reprisals on both sides. That he still harbored hatred for Bascom and the army was clear; he specifically mentioned the incident during his talks with Howard.

After reasonably cordial exchanges of views on the war and the possibilities of peace, lasting over a period of days, Cochise finally said to Howard, "Give me Apache Pass for my people and I will protect the road to Tucson. I will see that the Indians do no harm."[9] Howard agreed and thereby put an end to ten years of open warfare that had started so many years before with a confrontation in the same Apache Pass that Cochise now claimed. In concluding the agreement, Cochise said, "[H]ereafter the white men and the Indian are to drink the same water, eat of the same bread, and be at peace."[10]

When Howard went off to alert the troops at Fort Bowie that there was to be a truce followed by a lasting peace, Cochise demanded that Howard's aide, Lieutenant Joseph Sladen, remain in camp as a guarantee that Howard would come back. If Cochise smiled at the irony of the arrangement, no one noticed, especially Sladen, who was initially and understandably nervous but grew less so during his several days as a hostage.

Cochise's people were to be guaranteed the Chiricahuas Mountains and, of course, Apache Pass along with the Dragoon Mountains to the west. They would be given regular rations distributed by a white agent, Tom Jeffords, whom Cochise had known and come to trust. In return, they would cease attacking white settlements and traffic.

Cochise kept his word until his death two years later. After that, all hell broke loose again when the government decided the Chiricahuas must move from the Apache Pass reservation. It would be another dozen years before peace was finally established with the Chiricahuas, and that was achieved only by their surrender and deportation to a prisoner-of-war camp in Florida, where they languished for several years before being moved to reservations in Alabama and Oklahoma. Finally, in 1913, some small groups moved to New Mexico and merged with the Mescaleros, while the rest stayed in Oklahoma. In total, there were fewer than three hundred remaining. And while they steadfastly held on to their religion, their warrior culture had ceased to be.

What are we to make of this story, this Bascom affair, as it has come to be known? Did it start a war with the Chiricahuas in general and Cochise's Chokonens in particular? Was it responsible for ten years and more of terror on the border? Certainly it sparked the wrath of Cochise. And that undoubtedly intensified the brutality of his attacks, in which he now dropped the former distinction between raids and war. Now the object was not only plunder but blood, vengeance. Had the army not hanged his brother and nephews, the distinction between raiding and war might have been maintained—no small point in the Chiricahuas' thinking. The death of a warrior, and especially the death of a brother, required blood atonement. We cannot understand why Cochise left his brother and nephews dangling from an oak branch, food for scavengers, but we can understand his fury and enduring hatred of the army in particular and the whites in general. His moral standing, of course, is more than a little shaky, given the fact that he tortured his captives to death before the army hanged the prisoners. And, in fact, it's more than likely that his torturing caused the death of his brother and the others by outraging the soldiers, who might otherwise have been content to keep them as prisoners. It's not hard to believe that that thought occurred to Cochise in moments of quiet reflection. He could and famously did blame the army for the ten years of violence that resulted. But had he not killed and mutilated his hostages—and left them as a message—the outcome might have been, almost certainly would have been, different. To what extent, therefore, did he revisit his wrathful decision? Did he wonder now and then whether his violent declaration of war stemmed as much from a sense of regret, even guilt, as from outrage? Did he acknowledge to himself that he was also at least partially responsible? The truth is, he made the most important mistake. Not to consider that proposition oversimplifies the incident and reduces it to a formulaic melodrama in which the Apaches played the role of victims and the army, the blundering oppressors. Moreover, to assume he cared nothing about these questions is to line up with those who considered the Apaches not fully human, little more than savage animals. In fact, to assume Cochise felt no sense of guilt and regret is more than a bit patronizing.

Regardless of whether he had private moments of doubt or regret, he remained implacable as a leader, for reasons both cultural and personal. And given his implacability, there was no formula for satisfaction; Cochise and his warriors would kill whenever they could and as many whites as they could. There was no endgame, no way to satisfy Cochise. More than ten years would have to pass before he grew tired of evading the armies of Mexico and the United States, once the Civil War was over. Finally, he grew weary of fighting.

While Cochise's anger was the engine behind the war with the whites, it seems obvious that conflict would have inevitably broken out between Cochise's band and the white civilization that was infesting the territory, even if there never had been a George Bascom. The Chiricahuas would have continued raiding; it was who they were. They would have run off mining-company stock, and attacked isolated ranchers and their families and teamsters carrying freight. And, inevitably, some warriors on a raid would have been killed, and that would have sparked the same spiral of retaliation that resulted from the Bascom affair. Perhaps Cochise would not have been so personally involved and committed, but as war leader of his band, he would have been responsible for seeking reprisals nonetheless.

Many well-meaning whites believed that the Chiricahuas could be talked into giving up their old ways and taking up the Bible and the plow. But that would have been impossible. To give up their religion, to give up their attachment to the mountains where their gods lived and looked after them, to give up their culture of raiding, the very means by which a boy became a man, and to dig in the earth like women? Never. If they did all those things they would cease to be Chiricahua, with no new identity to replace the old. In fact, the only way General O. O. Howard was ultimately able to make peace with Cochise was his guarantee of a reservation in the Chiricahua and Dragoon Mountains and the corresponding agreement not to hinder the Chiricahua raids into Mexico. In return, Cochise agreed to stop attacking Americans. That was his only concession. Of his culture and way of life and even his well-loved mountains, he surrendered nothing. What's more, he and his people could live on the (promised) rations distributed by the government while still enjoying forays into Mexico, the place where boys became men through a timeless rite of passage, and men gained prestige and wealth.

Chapter Fourteen

EPILOGUE

Show me a hero and I will write you a tragedy.
— F. Scott Fitzgerald

IN THE CONTEXT OF THE COUNTLESS ENCOUNTERS BETWEEN THE army and the settlers on one side and the Indians on the other, the Bascom affair was hardly a major battle. There were casualties on both sides, true, but compared to the rivers of blood shed in the Civil War—and in the total settlement of the West—the incident in Apache Pass was insignificant, militarily. Little more than a police action.

But the story still resonates today, while hundreds of similar incidents are forgotten. Why?

In the first place, it is historically important, because Cochise made it so. His perception of the event became the accepted view. In his eyes, the incident started a war between the Chiricahuas and the white settlers of Arizona and New Mexico. It was a turning point. But from the white settlers' and the army's perspectives, the Civil War and the closing of the forts allowed the Apaches, who had been raiding regularly anyway, to step up their attacks and level of ferocity. Therefore, while Cochise regarded the incident as a watershed in his relations with the whites, not many others did—until years later when Cochise told his story.* There is no small irony in the fact that we know about Bascom today primarily because Cochise made the story important. Officers who knew Cochise later, like Howard, Bourke, and Sladen, essentially accepted Cochise's version. And by that time, Moore and Bascom had both been dead for over a decade.** Their view of the story was lost.

The meeting in the tent was significant for Bascom too, although in a different way. When he faced Cochise, Bascom was looking into the face of an ancient way of life that had hardly changed in centuries, only adapting other cultures' modern weapons and little else. Like so many young officers on foreign assignments, he was confronting the "other." All Bascom's assumptions about the virtues of his civilization were contradicted by the man standing before him, a man who looked profoundly different, as well as menacing, primarily because of that differentness. Bascom suddenly understood that he was a stranger in a strange land. His uneasiness is not only understandable but also typical of countless other officers who traveled into foreign lands on missions they only partly understood and who encountered alien people whose very strangeness challenged their identities and values. Out of his element and faced with the unknown, Bascom fell back on the known, on army procedures and his orders. It would have taken an exceptional officer to feel and do otherwise, and Bascom was not exceptional. He was no Wordsworthian "Happy Warrior," who, "when confronted with some awful moment to which heaven had joined great issues, good or bad, was happy as a Lover, and attired with sudden brightness like a Man inspired." No, he was just a youthful soldier who had

---

* In his 1872 journal, *Making Peace with Cochise*, Captain Sladen sympathetically recounts Cochise's version of the Bascom affair. Bourke does as well in his memoirs, although some of the details are different.

** All that's left of Fort Bascom today is a plaque in the New Mexico desert.

struggled with mathematics and finished next to last in his class. He was ordinary and therefore, recognizable. Few have known a Wordsworthian Lord Nelson. But everyone knows a Bascom. In that sense, he suggests the universal.

The events in Apache Pass can also be regarded, without too much hyperbole, as a human tragedy, both in the events themselves and in their aftermath. In fact, the story of Cochise in Apache Pass is a microcosm of the larger tragedy of the Chiricahuas.

In classical, Aristotelian tragedy, the plot involves a change in the hero's condition—from good to bad and often to catastrophic. "Its action should be single and complete, presenting a reversal of fortune involving persons of renowned and superior attainments," wrote Aristotle.[1] The reversal stems from an error that the hero makes. "The change of fortune which [the hero] undergoes is not due to any moral defect or flaw but a mistake of some kind."[2] In other words, the action that follows is the result of character, not providence or destiny or some outside agent. The hero has free will. And yet there is the sense that his mistake was predictable, a function of his character. He is, therefore, responsible for what transpires, although his action often unleashes a response that seems out of proportion to his mistake.

Tragedy also has a clear structure—a beginning, middle, and end. That is what Aristotle meant when he said, "[T]he action should be single and complete." It is self-contained and aesthetically sound as a result. There are no loose ends. The object of watching the hero's struggles is to arouse fear and pity in the audience and so provide a cleansing of emotions, a catharsis. The members of the audience watch as the hero lurches inexorably on, and because they already know the outcome (since Greek tragedy was based on known stories and myths), their fear and pity are intensified as the hero moves blindly on to an inevitable and disastrous result.

In the Bascom incident, the two major characters both made mistakes—a series of them, in fact. But Bascom is not the tragic hero of this drama. He suffered no reversal of fortune. And, as mentioned, he was hardly a "person of renowned and superior attainments." His death in combat the following year was unrelated to the events in Apache Pass, and so while we may pity a young officer who died doing his duty, we cannot see him as a tragic hero, in the classical sense.

Cochise, on the other hand, fits the mold. He *was* a "person of renowned and superior attainments," a recognizable heroic archetype, and he made the worst mistake of all and suffered for it. His brother and his nephews were killed and his people endured more than a decade of war—not because of Bascom, but because of Cochise. His mistake was torturing and murdering the four hostages and then leaving their mangled remains where the army was sure to find them. It is impossible to believe that the four were killed without his knowledge, and it seems at least likely that he was directly involved in it. After all, he had done those things before and would do so again. But Cochise might well have gotten away with the crimes if he had simply hidden the bodies or left them in an obscure ravine. His intentional display was an act of defiance, a kind of hubris, and the direct cause of the execution of the six Apaches. That, along with the horrifying spectacle of the nine charred Mexicans, still hanging from the burned wagon wheels, doomed his brother, his nephews, and the three other Apache prisoners. (This is not to suggest that the six Apaches received justice, but simply to connect cause to effect.) It was a loss, a reversal of fortune, that Cochise never got over emotionally.

Cochise's mistakes stemmed directly from his character. Rage and cruel violence were never far from the surface. The murder of the four hostages and the subsequent years of war were the natural and escapable result of his violent and implacable nature. Neither the killing of the four Americans nor the burning of the Mexicans can be justified by Bascom's hostage taking, though Cochise may have considered the killing of his escaping companion justification enough, along with his own slight wound. But there was violence and revenge in Cochise's heart long before Bascom arrived on the scene. Ravaged Mexican villages attested to that.

The Bascom affair has Aristotle's tragic structure too—a beginning, middle, and end. It starts with the buildup to and the confrontation in the tent. Then follows the siege at the stage station, and finally, the discovery of the hostages' bodies and subsequent execution of the Apaches. That classical structure, a self-contained story, makes it interesting and satisfying. The protagonists certainly could not see any sense to the events as they were unfolding. Quite the contrary. As with most combat situations, the protagonists' primary emotions were confusion and uncertainty. And afterward there were many different versions of events, which suggests that the participants did not perceive coherence in anything that happened. But in retrospect we see that the incident actually has a discernible plot, which other, mostly forgotten historical events, do not. And that may be one reason why those other events have been forgotten. Historical events with clear plots approach the level of art—retrospectively, of course—and have greater impact as a result.

In sum, in both its characters and its plot, the Bascom incident contains the key elements of tragedy.*

Two warriors, so different in every way and products of their vastly different cultures, are joined together in history. The one, young and dedicated to his profession, would die in less than a year, sodden and disheveled on a sandbar in a river far from home, killed by his own kind. The other, angry, grieving, and violent, would fight on

---

* Custer's Last Stand has many of these same elements and is, of course, the most famous story of the Indian wars.

for more than a decade. But he would finally make peace, a peace that he could almost believe was a victory for his people. Cochise would honor that peace for two more years and then, dying from disease, not wounds, be buried in some secret place in his beloved mountains. He would be spared the knowledge that his people and their warrior culture would soon start fighting the Americans again and, in defiance of all efforts to change their way of life, would ultimately succumb to an expanding civilization that could not tolerate the Chiricahuas' bloody intransigence. Like Cochise's own story, the demise of the Chiricahua people has about it tragic inevitability. To survive as themselves, to maintain their identity, they would have to continue raiding and warfare; to survive physically in the evolving new world, they would have to change utterly; to change utterly, they would cease to be themselves. And surely this wider story of the Chiricahuas, sinners who were sinned against, also meets Aristotle's first criterion for tragedy—a reversal of fortune, from good to bad, and, in the case of the Chiricahuas, from good, as they defined and understood it, to nothingness.

But in 1861, all of that was in the distant and unknowable future. Now, as his war was just beginning, it was a time for Cochise to savor his position. Camped in Apache Pass, a place suddenly free of the despised white men, with the stars bright in the thin atmosphere, Cochise must have thought, "Well, yes, Ussen has decreed that this is our land. Many of the whites have fled the territory; more will go. Soon we will be rid of them forever. We will see to that." Though his heart was no doubt heavy from the loss of his brother and nephews, and though part of that heaviness must have been from knowledge of his own role in their loss, he had the consolation of victory, however illusory—and the confidence that there would be future victories that would secure this country for the Chiricahua forever.

On the other hand, maybe in moments of quiet reflection he understood that there would be no permanent victory, that this was all very temporary. Well, perhaps it was, but was not life itself temporary? Apache Pass proved that, not that proof was necessary. Yes, life was temporary. Who knew that better than a warrior? Who knew that better than he did?

> *A generation of men is like a generation of leaves; the wind scatters some leaves upon the ground, while others the burgeoning wood brings forth—and the season of spring comes on. So of men one generation springs forth and another ceases.*
>
> —Homer, the *Iliad*

ENDNOTES

Chapter One
1. Wagoner, *Early Arizona*, page 185
2. Emory, *Report on the United States and Mexican Boundary Survey*
3. Sweeney, *Cochise*, page 125
4. Cremony, *Life among the Apaches*, page 191
5. Ball, *Indeh*, page 141
6. Sladen, *Making Peace with Cochise*, page 64

Chapter Two
1. Eisenhower, *So Far From God*, page 286
2. Ibid, page 288
3. Norris et. al., *William H. Emory, Soldier Scientist*, page 13
4. Ibid., page 297
5. Eisenhower, *So Far From God*, page 75
6. Grant, *Memoirs*, page 912
7. Eisenhower, *So Far From God*, page xxiii
8. Ibid., page 369
9. Cremony, *Life among the Apaches*, page 117
10. Utley, *Frontiersmen in Blue*, page 158
11. Eisenhower, *So Far From God*, page xxii
12. Ibid., page 357
13. Ibid., page 369
14. Ibid., page 109
15. Waugh, *The Class of 1846*, page 80
16. Bourke, *On the Border with Crook*, page 127
17. Ibid, page 134
18. Ball, *Indeh*, page 136

Chapter Three
1. Opler, *An Apache Life-Way*, page 183
2. Utley, A *Clash of Cultures*, page 9
3. Opler, *An Apache Life-Way*, page 183
4. Bourke, *On the Border with Crook*, page 125

5. Josephy, *The Indian Heritage of America*, page 167
6. Opler, *An Apache Life-Way*, page 351
7. Eisenhower, *So Far from God*, page 375
8. Krauze, *Mexico: Biography of Power*, page 155
9. Bailey, *Indian Slave Trade in the Southwest*, page 9, passim
10. Bourke, *On the Border with Crook*, page 117
11. Bailey, *Indian Slave Trade in the Southwest*, page 75
12. Ibid., page 173
13. Ibid, page 174
14. Ibid., page 108
15. Norris et. al., *William H. Emory, Soldier-Scientist*, page 52
16. Sweeney, *Cochise*, page 37
17. Thrapp, *The Conquest of Apacheria*, page 9
18. Ball, *Indeh*, page 10
19. Sweeney, *Cochise*, page 57

Chapter Four
1. Norris et al, William H. Emory, *Soldier-Scientist*, page 77
2. Utley, *Frontiersmen in Blue*, page 99
3. Dary, *Red Blood and Black Ink*, page 107
4. Ibid, page 126
5. Woodworth, *Manifest Destinies*, page 322
6. Bourke, *On the Border with Crook*, page 1
7. Smith, *The View from Officers' Row*, page 120
8. Bourke, *On the Border with Crook*, page 119
9. Ball, *Indeh*, page 99
10. Thrapp, *The Conquest of Apacheria*, page 15
11. Cremony, *Life among the Apaches*, page 287
12. Ball, *Indeh*, page 58
13. Ibid., page 19
14. Ibid., page 129
15. Ibid., page 19
16. Dary, *Red Blood and Black Ink*, page 113
17. Mowry, *Arizona and Sonora*, page 234
18. Smith, *The View from Officers' Row*, page 110
19. Cremony, *Life among the Apaches*, page 178
20. Smith, *The View from Officer's Row*, page 16
21. Dickens, "The Noble Savage," article in *Household Words*, 1853
22. Cremony, *Life among the Apaches*, page 94
23. Smith, *The View from Officers' Row*, page 2
24. Mowry, *Arizona and Sonora*, page 68

Chapter Five
1. Victor Davis Hanson, *The Father of Us All*, page 137
2. Norris et.al., *William H. Emory, Soldier-Scientist*, page 157
3. Morrison, *The Best School in the World*, page 142
4. Ibid., page 142
5. B. H. Liddell Hart, *Sherman*, page 9
6. Morrison, *The Best School in the World*, page 105

7.   Morrison "Educating Civil War Generals." Quoted in Kobrick: "No Army Inspired: The Failure of Nationalism at Antebellum West Point."
8.   B. H. Liddell Hart, *Sherman*, page 10
9.   Eisenhower, *So Far from God*, page 357
10. Waugh, *The Class of 1846*, page 128
11. Kobrick, "No Army Inspired: The Failure of Nationalism at Antebellum West Point," passim
12. Morrison, *The Best School in the World*, page 85
13. Ibid., page 120
14. Waugh, *The Class of 1846*, page 135
15. Morrison, *The Best School in the World*, page 96
16. Waugh, *The Class of 1846*, page 64
17. Kobrick, "No Army Inspired: The Failure of Nationalism at Antebellum West Point," page 14
18. Morrison, *The Best School in the World*, page 159
19. Grant, *Memoirs and Selected Letters*, page 878
20. Morrison, *The Best School in the World*, page 52
21. Waugh, *The Class of 1846*, pages 7, 8
22. Morrison, *The Best School in the World*, page 70
23. Waugh, *The Class of 1846*, page 60).
24. Ibid., page 20
25. McPherson, *Battle Cry of Freedom*, page 149
26. Morrison, *The Best School in the World*, page 131
27. Waugh, *The Class of 1846*, page 13
28. Kobrick, "No Army Inspired: The Failure of Nationalism at Antebellum West Point," page 11
29. Waugh, *The Class of 1846*, page 38

Chapter Six
1.   Opler, *An Apache Life-Way*, page 72
2.   Cremony, *Life among the Apaches*, page 320
3.   Ball, *Indeh*, page 32
4.   Emory, "Report on the United States and Mexican Boundary Survey," quoted in Norris et. al., page 166
5.   Bock, *Sonoita Plain*, page 39
6.   Ball, *Indeh*, page 57
7.   Opler, *An Apache Life-Way*, page 224
8.   Bourke, *An Apache Campaign in the Sierra Madre*, page 103
9.   Opler, *An Apache Life-Way*, page 446
10. Utley, *Frontiersmen in Blue*, page 235
11. Bourke, *An Apache Campaign in the Sierra Madre*, page 92
12. Bourke, *On the Border with Crook*, page 125
13. Scott, *The Mark of the Warrior*, page 70
14. Cremony, *Life among the Apaches*, pages 86, 87
15. Bourke quoted in Smith, *The View from Officers' Row*, page 157
16. Ibid., page 178
17. Basso, *Western Apache Raiding and Warfare*, passim
18. Bourke, *Apache Medicine Men*, page 56

19. Opler, *An Apache Life-Way*, page 139
20. Junger, *War*, epigraph
21. Sladen, *Making Peace with Cochise*, page 99
22. Ibid., page 101
23. Bourke, *An Apache Campaign in the Sierra Madre*, page 33
24. Fuller *The Conduct of War*, page 38
25. Basso, *Western Apache Raiding and Warfare*, page 264
26. Ibid., page 265
27. Roberts, *Once They Moved Like the Wind*, page 222
28. Opler, *An Apache Life-Way*, page 168
29. Ibid., page 59
30. Ibid., page 465
31. Ibid. page 336
32. Bourke, *An Apache Campaign in the Sierra Madre*, page 26
33. Ibid., page 18
34. Basso, *Wisdom Sits in Places*, page 62
35. Ibid, page 84
36. Bourke, *An Apache Campaign in the Sierra Madre*, page 91
37. Basso, *Western Apache Raiding and Warfare*, page 259
38. Ibid., page 272
39. Hughes, *The Hemlock Cup*, page 28
40. Opler, *An Apache Life-Way*, page 205
41. Ball, *Indeh*, page 62
42. Basso, *Western Apache Raiding and Warfare*, page 272
43. Opler, *An Apache Life-Way*, page 202
44. Basso, page 274
45. Opler, *An Apache Life-Way*, page 200
46. Ibid., page 230
47. Opler, *Myths and Tales of the Chiricahua Apache Indians*, page 83
48. Ball, *Indeh*, passim
49. Ball, *Indeh*, page xvii
50. Jacoby, *Bloodlust*, page 130

Chapter Seven
1. Smith, *The View from Officers' Row*, page 6
2. Jackson, *Custer's Gold*, page 30
3. Nat'l Park Service Historic Structure Report
4. Utley, *Frontiersmen in Blue*, page 40
5. Utley, *Frontiersmen in Blue*, page 41
6. Ibid., page 41
7. Brooks, *The Mountain Meadow Massacre*, page 59
8. Ibid., page 146
9. Remini, *Joseph Smith*, page 6
10. Ibid., page 35
11. Ibid., page 175
12. Twain, *Roughing It*, page 127
13. Moorman, *Camp Floyd*, page 15
14. Twain, *Roughing It*, page 118

15. Stegner, *The Gathering of Zion*, page 284
16. Twain, *Roughing It*, page 104
17. *New Orleans Courier*, April 3, 1857 quoted in Moorman, Camp Floyd, page 12
18. Stegner, *The Gathering of Zion*, page 276
19. Brooks, *The Mountain Meadows Massacre*, page 13
20. Ibid., page 25
21. Moody, *Stagecoach West*, page 149
22. Ibid., page 149
23. Stegner, *The Gathering of Zion*, page 275
24. Brooks, *The Mountain Meadows Massacre*, page 30
25. Ibid., page 24
26. Ibid., page 34
27. Ibid., page 39
28. Ibid., page 60
29. Ibid., page 128

Chapter Eight
1. Ormsby, *The Butterfield Overland Mail*, page 141
2. Moody, *Stagecoach West*, page 150
3. Ibid., page 139
4. Ibid., page 168
5. Boonslick Historical Society Quarterly, June 1997
6. Moody, *Stagecoach West*, page 160
7. 177 Woodworth, *Manifest Destinies*, page 73
8. 178 Moody, *Stagecoach West*, page 146
9. 179 Frank A. Root: *The Overland Stage to California*, quoted in Moody, *Stagecoach West*, page 159
10. Demas Barnes, quoted in Moody, *Stagecoach West*, page 244
11. Twain, *Roughing It*, page 44
12. Moody, *Stagecoach West*, page 12
13. Twain, *Roughing It*, page 23
14. Ibid., page 54
15. Ibid., page 89
16. Moorman, *Camp Floyd*, page 100
17. Twain, *Roughing It*, page 149
18. Moorman, *Camp Floyd*, page 75
19. Ibid., page 75
20. University of Utah on-line
21. Moorman, *Camp Floyd*, page 125
22. Ibid., page 58
23. Ibid., page 58
24. Ibid., page 58
25. Ebenezer Crouch, quoted in Moorman, *Camp Floyd*, page 76
26. Charles Bailey, Diary, quoted in Moorman, *Camp Floyd*, page 77
27. Ibid., page 67
28. Ibid., page 215
29. Ibid., page 226
30. Ibid., page 234

31. Ibid., page 255
32. Brooks, *The Mountain Meadows Massacre*, page 182
33. Utley, *Frontiersmen in Blue*, page 21
34. Sladen, *Making Peace with Cochise*, page 37
35. Moorman, *Camp Floyd*, 167
36. Twain, *Roughing It*, 147
37. Moorman, *Camp Floyd*, page 274
38. Utley, *Frontiersmen in Blue*, page 22
39. Smith, *The View from Officers' Row*, page 182
40. Moorman, *Camp Floyd*, page 274
41. Moorman, *Camp Floyd*, page 271
42. Utley, *Frontiersmen in Blue*, page 171

Chapter Nine
1. Sweeney, *Cochise*, page 129
2. Ormsby, *The Butterfield Overland Mail*, page 85
3. *Chicago Tribune*, quoted in Moody, *Stagecoach West*, page 97
4. Ormsby, *The Butterfield Overland Mail*, page 94
5. Ormsby, *The Butterfield Overland Mail*, page 52
6. Ibid., page 130
7. Ibid., page 94
8. Tevis, *Arizona in the 50's*, page 55
9. Sweeney, *Cochise*, page 119
10. Ibid., page 138
11. Tevis, *Arizona in the 50's*, page 106
12. Sweeney, *Cochise*, page 140
13. Ibid., page 140
14. Bourke, *An Apache Campaign in the Sierra Madre*, page 4
15. Smith, *The View from Officers' Row*, page 92
16. Bourke, *On the Border with Crook*, page 445
17. Sweeney, *Cochise*, page 125
18. Wagoner, *Early Arizona*, page 418
19. Sweeney, *Cochise*, page 127
20. Ibid., page 127
21. Wagoner, *Early Arizona*, page 415
22. Sweeney, *Cochise*, page 422, note 1
23. Ball, *Indeh*, page 25
24. Sweeney, *Cochise*, page 133
25. Ibid., page 134
26. Ibid., page 141

Chapter Ten
1. Waugh, *The Class of 1846*, page 288
2. Tevis, *Arizona in the 50's*, page 42
3. Waugh, *The Class of 1846*, page 511
4. Ibid., page 135
5. Wagoner, *Early Arizona*, page 410
6. Utley, *Frontiersmen in Blue*, page 42
7. Bourke, *On the Border with Crook*, page 104

8.   Wagoner, *Early Arizona*, page 400
9.   Utley, *Frontiersmen in Blue*, page 41
10. Wagoner, *Early Arizona*, page 413
11. Utley, *A Clash of Cultures*, page 32
12. Utley, *Frontiersmen in Blue*, page 38
13. Sweeney, *Cochise*, page 146
14. Ibid., page 164
15. Foote, *The Civil War*, Vol. 2, page 479
16. Sweeney, *Cochise*, page 152

Chapter Eleven
1.   Utley, *Frontiersmen in Blue*, page 249
2.   Tevis, *Arizona in the 50's*, page 106
3.   Sladen, *Making Peace with Cochise*, page 64
4.   Bourke, *On the Border with Crook*, page 434
5.   Ibid., page 1
6.   Sladen, *Making Peace with Cochise*, page 63
7.   Opler, *An Apache Life-Way*, page 456
8.   Smith, *The View from Officers' Row*, page 100
9.   Robinson report: "Apache Affairs in 1861"

Chapter Twelve
1.   Sweeney, *Cochise*, page 158
2.   Robinson, Apache Affairs in 1861
3.   Ibid.
4.   Opler, *An Apache Life-Way*, page 351
5.   The *Iliad*, quoted in Alexander, *The War That Killed Achilles*, page 168
6.   Ibid., page 159
7.   Ibid., page 169
8.   Sweeney, *Cochise*, page 163
9.   Robinson in *Sports Afield*
10. Sweeney, *Cochise*, page 167

Chapter Thirteen
1.   Utley, *Frontiersmen in Blue*, page 212
2.   Ibid. page 212
3.   Sweeney, *Cochise*, page 183
4.   Ibid., page 190
5.   Moody, *Stagecoach West*, page 201
6.   McManus: *American Courage, American Carnage*
7.   Wagoner, *Early Arizona*, page 449
8.   Taylor, *Bloody Valverde*
9.   Sladen, *Making Peace with Cochise*, page 65
10. Sweeney, *Cochise*, page 363

Chapter Fourteen
1.   Aristotle, *Poetics*
2.   Ibid.

BIBLIOGRAPHY

Books (Editions listed are those used for reference in the text):
Alexander, Caroline, *The War that Killed Achilles*, Viking, 2009
Aristotle, *Poetics*
Bailey, L.R., *Indian Slave Trade in the Southwest*, Tower Publications, 1966
Ball, Eve: *Indeh*, University of Oklahoma Press, 1988
Basso, Keith, *Western Apache Raiding and Warfare*, The University of Arizona Press, 1971
Wisdom Sits in Places, University of New Mexico Press, 1996
Bock, Carl E. and Jane H., *Sonoita Plain*, The University of Arizona Press, 2005
Bourke, John Gregory, *On the Border with Crook*, University of Nebraska Press, 1971
An Apache Campaign in the Sierra Madre, University of Nebraska Press, 1987
Apache Medicine Men, Dover, 1993
Brooks, Juanita, *The Mountain Meadows Massacre*, University of Oklahoma, 1962
Cremony, John C., *Life among the Apaches*, University of Nebraska Press, 1983
Dary, David, *Red Blood and Black Ink*, Alfred A. Knopf, 1998
Eisenhower, John S.D., *So Far from God*, University of Oklahoma Press, 1989
Foote, Shelby, *The Civil War: A Narrative*, Random House, 1963
Fuller, J.F.C., *The Conduct of War*, DaCapo, 1992
Grant, U. S., *Memoirs and Selected Letters*, The Library of America, 1990
Hanson, Victor Davis, *The Father of Us All*, Bloomsbury Press, 2010
Hughes, Bettany, *The Hemlock Cup*, Alfred A. Knopf, 2010
Jackson, Donald, *Custer's Gold*, University of Nebraska Press, 1972
Jacoby, Russell, *Bloodlust*, Free Press, 2011
Josephy, Alvin M. Jr., *The Indian Heritage of America*, 1968
Junger, Sebastian, *War*, Hachette, 2010
Krauze, Enrique, *Mexico: Biography of Power*, Harper Perennial, 1998
Liddell Hart, B.H., *Sherman*, DaCapo, 1993

McManus, John C., *American Courage, American Carnage*, Forge Books, 2009
McPherson, James M., *Battle Cry of Freedom*, Oxford University Press, 2003
Moody, Ralph, *Stagecoach West*, University of Nebraska Press, 1998
Moorman, Donald R., *Camp Floyd and the Mormons*, The University of Utah Press, 1992
Morrison, *The Best School in the World*, The Kent State University Press, 1986
Mowry, Sylvester, *Arizona and Sonora*, Bibliolife, 2009
Opler, Morris Edward, *An Apache Life-Way*, University of Nebraska Press, 1996
Myths and Tales of the Chiricahua Apache Indians, University of Nebraska Press, 1994
Ormsby, Waterman, *The Butterfield Overland Mail*, The Huntington Library, 1942
Norris, Milligan, Faulk, *William H. Emory, Soldier-Scientist*, The University of Arizona Press, 1998
Remini, Robert V., *Joseph Smith*, Viking, 2002
Roberts, David, *Once They Moved Like the Wind*, Simon and Schuster, 1993
Sladen, Joseph Alton, *Making Peace with Cochise*, Edited by Edwin R. Sweeney, The University of Oklahoma Press, 1997
Taylor, John, *Bloody Valverde*, University of New Mexico Press, 1999
Terrell, John Upton, *Apache Chronicle*, Apollo, 1974
Tevis, James H., *Arizona in the 50's*, Brocking J Books, 2007
Thrapp, Dan, *The Conquest of Apacheria*, The University of Oklahoma Press, 1975
Twain, Mark, *Roughing It*, Oxford University Press, 1996
Woodworth, Steven E. *Manifest Destinies*, Vintage, 2010
Smith, Sherry L., *The View from Officers' Row*, The University of Arizona Press, 1990
Stegner, Wallace, *The Gathering of Zion*, University of Nebraska Press, 1992
Sweeney, Edwin R., *Cochise*, The University of Oklahoma Press, 1991
Utley, Robert M., *A Clash of Cultures*, National Park Service, 1977
Frontiersmen in Blue, University of Nebraska Press, 1981
The Indian Frontier, University of New Mexico Press, 1984
Wagoner, Jay J., *Early Arizona*, The University of Arizona Press, 1975
Waugh, John C., *The Class of 1846*, Ballantine Books, 1994

Articles and Reports:
Army Medical Bulletin Number 51
Bascom, Lieutenant George N. "Report to D.H. Manny, Asst. Adjt. General, Santa Fe, NM"
Bell, Bob Boze, "Cut the Tent, Unleash the War," True West Magazine, Jan. 11, 2011
Biographical Register of the Officers and Graduates of the United States Military Academy at West Point, N.Y., 1802 to 1891
Boonslick Historical Society Quarterly, June 1997
Dickens, Charles, "The Nobel Savage," Household Words, 1853
Journal of Arizona History, Vol. 42, No. 3, "Eyewitness to the Bascom Affair" by Douglas C. McChristian and Larry L. Ludwig

Kobrick, Jacob, "No Army Inspired: The Failure of Nationalism at Antebellum West Point," Concept, Vol. 27, 2004

New York Times, January 17, 1860 "The Army at Camp Floyd"

New York Times, November 29, 1885 "The Whites Advised to Attack and Slaughter Them"

New York World, c. 1890, "Officer Oberly of Brooklyn Tells What he Knows About It"

Report to the Secretary of War, 1860: Colonel Fauntleroy to General Scott, Aug. 26, 1860

Robinson, Major D. USA, Ret. "Apache Affairs in 1861"

Robinson, Daniel, "The Affair at Apache Pass," Sports Afield, August, 1896

ACKNOWLEDGEMENTS

A PROJECT OF THIS KIND NATURALLY RELIES ON THE ASSISTANCE and cooperation of a number of people. Special thanks go to Larry Ludwig and staff at Fort Bowie who provided invaluable documents and insights as well as a personal tour of the key sites in Apache Pass. Also, thanks to the staff of the U.S. Army Heritage and Education Center in Carlisle, PA, and at the Library of the USMA, West Point, both of whom provided important original documents. Agent Don Fehr of Trident Media placed this project with Pegasus Publishing—an ideal fit given the enthusiasm and assistance of publisher Claiborne Hancock and his colleagues, Pat Sims and Maria Fernandez. Thanks also to Colin Harrison who recommended me to Trident Media and who, on an earlier project, sharpened my perceptions of the evils of repetition. Also, thanks go to Al Hart, former agent, now retired, who was a steadfast supporter for over a decade, and last but not least to the Staff of the Arizona Historical Society in Tucson who provided cheerful assistance in collecting the photographs.

INDEX

INDEX

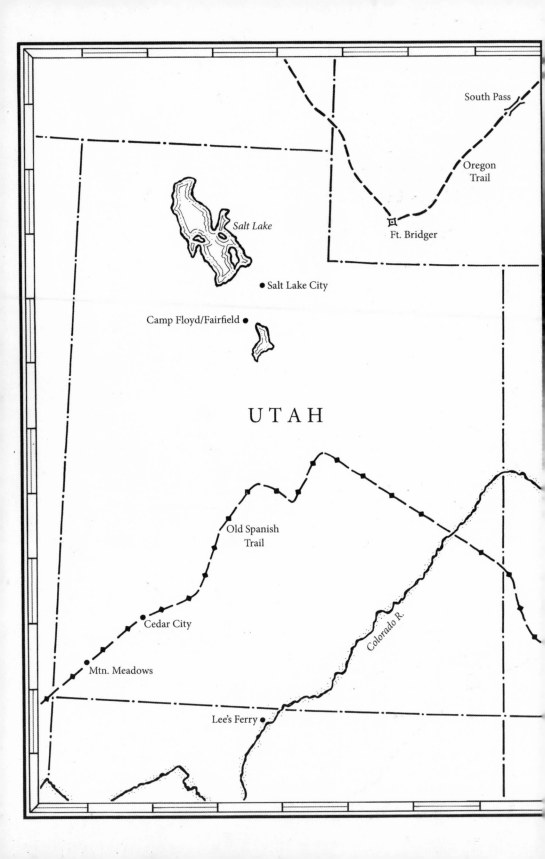